Welcome to the *EVERYTHING*® series!

These handy, accessible books give you all you need to tackle a difficult project, gain a new hobby, comprehend a fascinating topic, prepare for an exam, or even brush up on something you learned back in school but have since forgotten.

You can read an *EVERYTHING*® book from cover-to-cover or just pick out the information you want from our four useful boxes: e-facts, e-ssentials, e-alerts, and e-questions. We literally give you everything you need to know on the subject, but throw in a lot of fun stuff along the way, too.

We now have well over 100 *EVERYTHING*® books in print, spanning such wide-ranging topics as weddings, pregnancy, wine, learning guitar, one-pot cooking, managing people, and so much more. When you're done reading them all, you can finally say you know *EVERYTHING*®!

FACTS
Important sound bytes of information

ESSENTIALS
Quick handy tips

ALERT
Urgent warnings

QUESTIONS?
Solutions to common problems

THE EVERYTHING® Series

Dear Reader,

Have you ever stopped to consider how many projects you take on in the course of a given year? Perhaps you made improvements to your kitchen, or planted a backyard garden. You may be in the throes of planning your daughter's wedding or your parent's fiftieth anniversary party. The office manager may have put you in charge of finding the new office location or you may be in the midst of installing a new computerized inventory system for your store. From home improvements to massive corporate IT undertakings, all projects take planning and proper execution to insure success.

This book is designed to take you on a tour of the many aspects of project management. It is not intended to put you on a career course in the project management field, but simply to help guide you through your own life projects. Communications and leadership skills, assessing risk, monitoring your progress, and making back-up plans are all covered in layman's terms with examples from backyard to business projects.

Whether you are list and detail oriented, as I am, or prefer a broad approach with minimal paperwork, you can easily absorb all the fundamentals of managing a project from inception to completion.

The book itself was a long and challenging project, with many milestones passed as I wrote. The real success of this book, however, is now in your hands, as you use it to guide you into your upcoming projects. Good luck!

Sincerely,

Rich Mintzer

THE
EVERYTHING®
PROJECT MANAGEMENT BOOK

Tackle any project with confidence
and get it done on time

Rich Mintzer

Adams Media Corporation
Avon, Massachusetts

EDITORIAL
Publishing Director: Gary M. Krebs
Managing Editor: Kate McBride
Copy Chief: Laura MacLaughlin
Acquisitions Editor: Bethany Brown
Development Editor: Christel Shea

PRODUCTION
Production Director: Susan Beale
Production Manager: Michelle Roy Kelly
Series Designer: Daria Perreault
Layout and Graphics: Arlene Apone,
Paul Beatrice, Brooke Camfield,
Colleen Cunningham, Daria Perreault,
Frank Rivera

An Everything® Series Book.
Everything® is a registered trademark of Adams Media Corporation.

Published by Adams Media Corporation
57 Littlefield Street, Avon, MA 02322. U.S.A.
www.adamsmedia.com

ISBN: 1-58062-583-5
Printed in the United States of America.

J I H G F E D C B A

Library of Congress Cataloging-in-Publication Data
Mintzer, Richard.
The everything project management book:
tackle any project with confidence and get it done on time /
by Rich Mintzer
p.   cm.
Includes index.
ISBN 1-58062-583-5
1. Project management.   I. Title.
HD69.P75 M56   2002
658.4–dc21   2001055209

This publication is designed to provide accurate and authoritative information with regard to the subject matter covered. It is sold with the understanding that the publisher is not engaged in rendering legal, accounting, or other professional advice. If legal advice or other expert assistance is required, the services of a competent professional person should be sought.

—From a *Declaration of Principles* jointly adopted by a Committee of the
American Bar Association and a Committee of Publishers and Associations

Illustrations by Barry Littmann.

*This book is available at quantity discounts for bulk purchases.
For information, call 1-800-872-5627.*

Visit the entire Everything® series at everything.com

Contents

Acknowledgments

A project unto itself, this book was the culmination of hard work and a lot of excellent sources. Thank you to Pam Liflander for getting me started on this project, and to Leah Bloom and Bethany Brown for their assistance at the home base, Adams Media. Roger Reece, alias Buford P. Fuddwhacker, of Fuddwhacker Consulting; Nat Giventer at AIG; and Wally Bock, consultant, speaker, and author of *Net Income* and *Banking in the Digital Age,* provided valuable insights. Wendi Hahn, May Gardner, June Tanenblatt, and especially Sway Ciaramello, a New York–based Project Manager and Technology Consultant, provided additional help and resources. And finally, special appreciation goes to Elizabeth Schoch for her support and assistance, and to my wife Carol, who is always supportive during book projects.

Introduction

Like a well-written story, a successful project has a beginning, middle, and end. It all starts with the so-called idea phase, when someone or several people decide to begin a project—whether it's planning a wedding reception, moving to a new office, building a patio, or creating and implementing a new inventory system for your company. The middle phase of a project is that lengthy stretch beginning with lists, plans, strategies, and blue prints and ending with the final result of the plan. Hopefully, that end result is a completed project that all team members can take pride in having accomplished. It is also something that can be reviewed to determine what was done right and what was done wrong.

Projects are essentially "plans that need to get accomplished in a set timeframe and within a set budget." Project managers are, therefore, the leaders in charge of getting these projects accomplished. Picking up eight rowdy ten-year-olds, getting them into your station wagon, and driving them to and from soccer practice without your head exploding is a project. Pulling together 200 local volunteers, setting aside a specific day, and cleaning up the neighborhood is a project. Setting up and staffing a new branch office for your company in another part of the country is a project. Building a working volcano for your daughter's science fair is also a project.

What each of these examples has in common is the planning, scheduling, budgeting, problem-solving, and time constraints that go into it. Those are the common denominators. There is also a set goal to each and every project. It is the goal that sets the project on course.

A project is separate from your daily routine or an ongoing process that does not have a defined end result. It is that special "something" that needs to be accomplished in hopes of fixing, improving, expanding, or selling something. It can be providing a service or the act of creating something original.

How can good project management skills help you? These skills can guide you in learning the best approach to accomplishing your project goals within the time frame and budget allotted . . . and without additional stress or unnecessary risk-taking. How often have we seen the old black and white film clips of early airplanes falling apart upon take off or going in circles and never leaving the ground? The good project manager gets the plane in the air safely, without spending excessive time or money.

I remember watching the *Ed Sullivan Show* on television as a child. Ed would sprinkle novelty acts between singers, comics, and other popular performers. One such novelty act was the infamous plate juggler. This performer would set up nearly a dozen poles and then set plates in motion spinning high atop each pole. The quintessential project manager, his task was to keep each plate spinning until the end of his allotted time. Somehow he did it. The modern project manager often feels as though he or she has those plates spinning high overhead. The best project managers don't let them fall. However, like the performer on Ed Sullivan, your skills will require some practice—okay, a lot of practice—but the more you understand about the many components of project management, the more plates you'll be able to keep spinning or the more complex projects you'll be able to comfortably undertake.

Get the Software You Need

It's important to note, early on, that the computer is a tremendous asset to managing projects. Software programs, discussed later in the book, can help organize and facilitate even the most complex projects and make project management that much easier. Technology and the modern corporate project manager go hand in hand (literally) as their laptop and cell phone are rarely far from their grasp.

A search of the Internet for Project Management will provide numerous programs, MBA courses, and adult learning seminars on the subject. The complexities of high-level project management are outlined in many top business primers. While all of this is vital to the modern day career project manager, and may help the rest of us as we familiarize ourselves with the projects we will be undertaking (by personal choice or as assigned), software is not the key element to successful project management. Software and technology cannot replace learning, planning, proper execution, people skills, decision making, and hard work. As the old saying goes, "If it came in a box, everyone would have one." To paraphrase, "If it came in the software program, everyone would be a marvelous project manager."

Before Technology As We Know It Today

Prior to the days of high-tech project management tools, there were successful projects. The Wright Brothers did get that plane to fly, Lindbergh landed safely after crossing the ocean, and despite the Depression, the Empire State Building rose to great heights. Let's not forget a little project known as the Egyptian Pyramids, which were built with no Gantt Charts, no flowcharts, and *probably* no online brainstorming sessions. Yet somehow this marvelous feat of engineering was completed using ramps made of mud brick and rubble to lift large stone blocks. A series of inner walls were constructed by teams of workers, each wall of decreasing height, creating a sort of step pyramid which was then filled in with packing blocks and covered with casting blocks to create the outer structure. You'd better believe there was some level of project management. Ancient structures around the world and inventions throughout the centuries are the result of completed projects, all managed in some manner and most fraught with setbacks and rethinking along the way. Even unsuccessful projects have had positive outcomes. After all, Columbus didn't set out to discover America, did he?

Projects and You

Everyone is involved in projects at many levels, from school projects to personal projects to business projects. At some point everyone also becomes a project manager. You probably don't realize how many projects you have embarked on and how many you have completed over the years.

Did you schedule and lead a scout troop on a hike? Perhaps you were asked to organize the company picnic? At one time or another, everyone finds himself either a leader or team member of some project. You might be one of two people, or one of hundreds involved, depending on the size of the project. There is no set time limit for a "project;" it need not take x number of days or weeks to qualify. Projects may be one day long or occupy an entire year. Likewise, there is no budget requirement that defines a "project." A science project may be completed for $5 and a new warehouse may be built for $2 million. Projects vary greatly—even writing this book is a project.

In this book we'll look at all aspects of project management in a reader-friendly, noncorporate manner. We'll start by addressing the question of what a project is and where it comes from, then look at some of the bigger issues a project manager faces, such as whether or not the project is feasible or should even be started. We will look at the significant areas of project management including team selection, leadership styles, resources, scheduling, planning, project monitoring, conflict resolution, and completing and evaluating your end results. Along the way, we'll touch upon numerous examples of projects at a wide range of levels, from corporate to organizational and fund-raising drives, to building your home patio or furnishing the room for your new baby. At all levels, from big business to small business to personal endeavors, projects include similar attributes. Learning the basics of project management will help you on many levels.

Meanwhile, look for projects all around you. You'll probably be able to write down about five you've that been involved in, if you sit back and think about it for a while. As you read through the book, think back on those projects that you've taken part in. Did the people involved adhere to the advice offered? Did they go wrong for one of several reasons mentioned in the book? What you learn in these pages will help you stay on track with your future projects. Good luck!

CHAPTER 1

What Is Project Management?

People are faced with numerous projects throughout the course of life. If you can manage projects to successful results, then you will be able to meet your current goals and embark on new ones. Although you may not want to manage projects professionally, knowing what it takes to complete a project will help you handle various areas of your life. You will learn how to manage people, risk, and resources, and monitor the ongoing results. You will also hone your organizational and overall "people" skills—key tools for successful project management!

So, You Have a Project

To manage a project, you first need to understand what constitutes a project. After all, if you're in charge you should have a firm grasp of what you are in charge of. Let's take a look at some of the key components of a project:

- *A project needs a specific goal.* You don't just get together, do some work, and see what happens.
- *A project has a time frame.* Projects have a beginning and an end, they do not continue endlessly.
- *A project has a final outcome or result.* For better or for worse, each project produces results.
- *A project has a budget and requires resources.* Resources may include skilled individuals, reference materials, special equipment, information systems, or other tools of the trade.
- *A project requires a plan of action defining what needs to be done, when, and by whom.* Plans, procedures, schedules, software programs, and various systems for tracking the work that is being done may all be necessary to keep your project on course.
- *Projects can be evaluated on their own.* Apart from other tasks and chores you may perform at your job or in your daily routine, a project stands on its own to be evaluated by one person (which could be you if you are doing a personal project), or by many people (if your project is put before the shareholders or the public at large). Political campaigns are, in essence, projects that are put before many people, the voters.

As a project manager, you need to put all of the pieces together. Call it a puzzle, a battle plan, or liken it to putting together a ball club (a project for a general manager and team owner)—you are the person who is responsible for the end result. It is up to you, as project manager, to ultimately see that the project is completed on time, comes in under budget, and achieves the anticipated results.

Good project managers are able to look at the big picture. They know what needs to be done and can determine how to successfully attain the desired results in a timely, cost-efficient fashion. They can also determine the shortcomings—or potential shortcomings—that must be dealt with to keep a project on track. A project manager may also determine that a project is simply impossible to complete. Although Rome was not built in a day, someone probably hired a project manager to attempt it!

QUESTIONS?

What is a project?
A project is a plan, proposal, or scheme that requires a concerted effort within a specified amount of time. It involves a task that is undertaken by a group of people, such as updating software and training employees in its use; or one person, such as learning a language.

Successful professional project managers can make a great deal of money by pulling together all of the pieces of the project puzzle for large-scale, often complicated, undertakings. Even if you're not planning on a career in project management, these skills will be helpful in many aspects of business and in your personal life.

Where Do Projects Come From?

You may select projects or have them selected for you. Personal projects are usually done at your own discretion, allowing you to select the projects you undertake. This might include planning a vacation or remodeling your home. A business project may also be self-initiated. For example, if you own your own business or you simply decide your workload is slow, you can take the next two weeks to rearrange your office for maximum efficiency.

A project at work, however, is often the result of your boss or supervisor selecting you to head up a specific assignment. In some instances, you may have made a suggestion about how to run the company more efficiently. For example, maybe you proposed a better way to handle sales strategies or a better computer set up. The boss may let you "run with it" and you find yourself on the verge of a project. In other instances, the company simply needed someone to handle a task and, as they say in the game of tag, "You're it."

Another type of project arises out of a common need. This could be a community need or a project to meet the growing needs of a particular group. Organizations, associations, and various charitable groups are constantly engaged in planning and carrying out projects that benefit others. A severe storm might elicit the need for a community effort to clean up and restore a neighborhood. You might volunteer your time and abilities to oversee a fund-raising project initiated by your daughter's school.

There are also projects that "fall in your lap." Your daughter is getting married, and you're the only one who can plan the wedding. Your boss assigned Fred Flintstone to plan the upcoming company picnic, but Fred suddenly quit the company and ran off with Wilma to Rock Vegas. Guess who's in charge now? With any luck at all, you will fall into a project early on and not after the previous project manager has put in a lot of work that needs to be reassessed and often redone.

No matter how the project comes to you, you will still need to have a specific end result in sight. That clear goal is what you will work toward. You will also need to plan and set a schedule, stay within your budget, and utilize your resources—whether the project consists of your two children helping you build patio or a team of twenty-five so-called experts helping you develop a formula that prevents wrinkles. The size, cost, and manpower will vary, but the basics of assessing the project requirements, setting the wheels in motion, and having the resources to get to your desired conclusion on time are still the same.

The Sponsor and the Stakeholders

The way in which you came to be project leader will affect some of the variables. A self-generated project makes you the sponsor of the project. The impetus for the project came from you. At work, however, the sponsor of the project is ultimately responsible for the end result. This could be your immediate superior, the company president, owner, or perhaps a top executive. He or she will often be responsible for the financial backing (through the company) and may select key team members as well as experts and advisors. The sponsor or individual(s) requesting the project may very often set the time frame as well. An organization or a group may sponsor a project (such as an annual fund drive for a charity) meaning that they set the budget and time frame. You then act as project manager.

ALERT

The more adaptable you are to working under various systems, the more valuable you can become as a project manager. Recognize the needs of the sponsor of the project and become familiar with the parameters that are in place. Some project managers work well within any type of constraints while others need more flexibility.

Beyond the sponsor (or those who requested the project be done) are stakeholders who will also have an interest, personal or financial, in the end result. The more stakeholders involved, the more you need to appease a variety of people. If you've made your home office more efficient through remodeling, you are the primary stakeholder. The other stakeholders are your clients, who will benefit from your increased ability to complete work more quickly. In corporate or small business settings, stakeholders may include the following:

- Upper management
- Stockholders
- Executives
- Managers
- Clients
- Customers

Any party interested in or affected by the outcome of the project is a stakeholder. This will also include project members who are responsible for the work they contribute to the project. Stakeholders may contribute ideas on a regular basis, be involved in a hands-on manner, or not be involved in the actual work of the project at all. Stakeholders may be the community at large. Everyone in the city who will be using the new bridge is not necessarily working on it, but they all will benefit from the ease with which they will be able to drive to work once the bridge is completed. You'll read more about the stakeholders later in the book.

Let's Talk Project Management

Okay, so now we have a general idea of what constitutes a project and how it might come to land in your hands. But what exactly is project management and why is the term so popular today?

The producer of a television show has a project: twenty-six episodes in one season to be taped within an allotted budget and time frame. The producer is therefore responsible for pulling together the cast and crew; arranging for a sound studio, sets, other locations; selecting theme music; and identifying all of the elements that go into making the program a reality. From finding the writers to watching his or her name roll by on the closing credits, the producer is managing the project. No matter what the size of the project (called the scope, in project terminology), all of the pieces need to be put together. All of the players need to be in place, on the same page, and progress must be accounted for. As project manager, you are the ringleader of the circus, the captain of the ship, or the leader of the band . . . but just until the project is over. Remember, projects are specific, not open-ended or ongoing like your daily job. An open-ended work situation is not a project.

Project management means organizing, running, and bringing a project to its conclusion. It includes the following:

- Defining the goal of the project
- Determining the results you expect to be accomplished
- Working within a budget
- Setting up a schedule
- Selecting your team, and establishing individual roles
- Making sure the tools and technology are in place
- Monitoring ongoing progress
- Maintaining team morale
- Dealing with problems that arise

- Keeping stakeholders abreast of your progress
- Bringing the project to completion
- Assessing what went right and what went wrong

Take a look at this example:

Project: Boost company morale and spirit by creating and
             managing a company softball team
Time frame: March 15th through July 31st

- *Defining the goal of the project:* Put together company softball team to help bolster company morale and "team spirit."
- *Determining the results you expect to be accomplished:* Have fun and develop camaraderie with your coworkers.
- *Working within a budget:* Don't exceed the cost budgeted for t-shirts printed with the team name; balls, bats, and other equipment; refreshments; trophies; and other expenses.
- *Setting up a schedule:* Include one week for team tryouts, three weeks for practice, and fifteen weeks for a season against other local company teams (work in conjunction with other teams to arrange playing schedule).
- *Selecting your team:* Choose fifteen players plus coaches and perhaps a scorekeeper. To do this you'll assess each person's ability to bring something to the team.
- *Establishing the roles of each individual:* Determine who will play each position, who'll bring refreshments, who'll keep the bats in their car trunk, etc.
- *Making sure the tools and technology are in place:* Make sure you have enough bats, balls, equipment, etc.
- *Monitoring ongoing progress:* Keep track of who's hitting well, who's not, who might be better at a different position, etc.
- *Maintaining team morale:* "Okay we lost, but we'll do better next time. Let's go out for a team dinner."
- *Dealing with problems that arise:* "Frank can't pitch this weekend, he's in bed with the flu."

- *Keeping stakeholders abreast of your progress:* "Okay boss, you can brag about us now, we've won three in a row!"
- *Bringing the project to completion:* The season is over, the team won ten games and lost nine. Everyone is feeling good and has that "company spirit." Mission accomplished!
- *Assessing what went right and what went wrong:* Players enjoyed themselves but games ran late on certain evenings, making some people tired the next day. Next season games should start a half-hour earlier.

A rough example indeed, but you get the idea. As project manager, or in this case team manager, you know what is expected of you. When you move from little league to the major leagues, the stakes get higher and there are a lot more stakeholders. At every level, however, the basic concerns and responsibilities of the project manager remain the same.

Project Management Today

Although projects can be found dating back hundreds and thousands of years, "project management" has become a buzzword in the modern business world. Improved technology has allowed and enabled a vast increase in the number of projects to be completed in the workplace. Projects that would have once taken months to complete now take weeks, and new projects follow on their heels. The latest software makes tracking multiple projects easier, and training courses in project management demonstrate new tricks of the trade. The booming economy of the late 1990s made it feasible, from an economic standpoint, for companies to engage in more new endeavors than ever before. New products, new locations, and enhanced services were all the byproducts of the increase in projects.

While a recession could mean a drop-off in big business projects, there will always be a need to complete projects successfully. If nothing else, project management can teach you how to see the "big picture" and organize all the smaller components of any significant task you undertake.

You Are Already a Project Manager!

You've probably managed many projects before and aren't even aware of it. Use the following worksheet to list a project that you've undertaken at work, at home, or elsewhere, such as a community project. Next to the project you've listed, write down what your goal was when you started and when the project was supposed to be completed. Then think about how the project turned out. Who else was involved? Did your plans come to fruition? What obstacles did you overcome? Did you have to switch gears along the way and try a different approach? As you proceed through the book, you'll see other charts, graphs, or lists that may help you.

FACTS

The Internet and modern telecommunications have spurred the project management train along its path. More people have access to software and training courses through distance learning. More highly trained individuals mean that project managers need to be that much more on top of their task to manage these new experts.

A good project manager knows not only how to manage projects, but also how many projects he or she can manage at one time. For example, if you're planning your daughter's wedding and building the new back patio, you may not be in the best position to chair the annual school book sale. After all, you don't want 2,000 schoolbooks accidentally delivered at your daughter's wedding, do you? You also don't want to run yourself into the ground. Projects add a level of stress to your life, so three projects may add three times as much stress. In business, you might not be in a position to turn projects down. However, everyone reaches a saturation point and you must discuss with your superiors the potential pitfalls of taking on too many projects at one time. Know your limitations. Taking on too many projects at one time can lead to poor management of one or all of your projects. It can also lead to stress and great confusion!

PROJECT:

Goal: ....

Approx. start date/planned completion date: ....

Budget: ....

Resources (what did you need to buy?): ....

....

....

....

Human resources (who else was involved?): ....

....

....

....

Any conflicts along the way? ....

....

....

....

Did you need to change or alter your plans? ....

....

....

....

Did you complete your project on time? ....

....

....

....

On a scale of 1 to 10, with 10 being the best, how would you rate the final outcome of the project?

....

If you feel it could have been more successful, identify how things fell short.

....

....

....

Is the Big Picture Big Enough?

As noted previously, projects can begin in many ways. You might trip over a carton while entering your garage and decide that it's time for a major garage sale to clean up all the junk in there. Poof! You have a project: organize and hold a garage sale. Your boss might come into your office complaining that vacuum sales are down and that you need to create a better product that knocks out the competition before the end of the fiscal quarter. Poof! You have a project: get a team together and create the ultimate vacuum cleaner! The president of the PTA calls your house. At first you let the call go on the answering machine, pretending you aren't home. Then, out of guilt, you pick up. Before you know it, you are in charge of selecting the computer system for the new computer lab opening when the new school year begins. Poof! You have a project: evaluate and select a computer system that is user-friendly for grade school students and within the budget for the school.

ESSENTIALS

Seasons and holidays often inspire projects. For example, many retail businesses choose January or February to do their inventories, when things are relatively quiet. In your personal life, you may use the summer break from school to plan your family's vacation or hold an annual garage sale.

The first question should be whether the project is feasible. That is, can the project be done or is it impossible? Is the big picture big enough? If the electronic wiring of the school isn't ready for modern technology and the cost of rewiring the school is $4,000, the project won't work on a $3,000 budget. There are other initial concerns to consider before you commit yourself to a project. For example:

- Do you need the approval of someone else (including legal or community approval) before you embark on and complete a project? A documentary about the Grand Canyon will not happen if the filmmakers do not attain a shooting permit. Likewise, you may need the go-ahead from senior executives before you decide to reallocate the parking spaces in the company parking lot. Zoning permits, construction licenses, and numerous external factors need to be considered before embarking on a project.

- Are the resources available? A company softball team may be hard to form in a company with only six people. Before you organize the team, you need to determine if you can get the manpower, the funds, the tools, the equipment, and other important elements while staying within the budget. Often you can use ingenuity, but sometimes the odds are stacked against you. A construction project will not work if the only cranes in town are all in use the week that you are looking to rent one. This isn't to say you can't be ingenious and have a crane imported from another area, or have the project altered so you'll need the crane a week later, when one is available. However, if this will not work because of your budget, you may be in trouble. It's always worth looking at the big picture and determining if there are any major issues before proceeding.

Do a Feasibility Study

While it's impossible to predict obstacles that will arise once the project is under way, it's a good idea to take some time to make an overall assessment of the needs of the project and how they correlate to the budget and time frame before you decide to start. A feasibility study takes into account the variables of the project, including budget, resources and time constraints, and determines the likelihood that it can be done. Take a long, hard look at a feasibility study and don't continue with the project if you determine that it simply can't be done.

Evaluate the Cost

Another factor that will influence your decision to begin your project is whether or not you feel that the project will be cost-effective. Will the benefits you hope to gain be worth the price you will pay to get there? This is more than just a financial question. After all, if you are taking time away from your kids' homework so they can help you complete the family project of building a patio, aren't you doing more harm than good?

Isn't their education and doing well in school more valuable? Likewise, if you own a small business and you have everyone involved in a new promotional campaign at the cost of providing efficient service to your current customers, do you stand to lose more than you may potentially gain? Bringing in new customers is good, but not at the cost of losing long-time, valued customers. There are always trade-offs.

Weigh the Positives and Negatives

A positive outcome to a project is the desired result. This could come in the form of more customers, more business, less turnover, less stress, higher morale, or perhaps even more rewarding results such as homes for the homeless, toys for underprivileged children, or a cleaner environment. Personal goals might mean a more comfortable living environment or a higher value to your home should you plan to sell it. Projects can have numerous desired outcomes, some are personal, while others are career-based or business-oriented.

ESSENTIALS
Sometimes a project's benefits are not measured in dollars. Your health, stress level, and the needs of your family may be at the root of your decision to move forward with a project. A simple list of pros and cons might be your "cost-analysis" when deciding whether to take that family vacation.

Cost-benefit analysis is the "formal" method used by many companies to determine the value of the project. The individuals or the company sponsoring a project use detailed methods to determine all the factors involved to calculate whether or not the benefits outweigh the costs (financial, manpower, time, etc.). While a company has to evaluate this process (usually, this has been done before the project lands in your lap), you need to do your own version of cost-analysis on your projects.

In a small business, you'll need to determine whether the project will be more costly than it's worth. Adding a new computerized system to an office may cause a slow-down or even bring the current workload to a standstill. If, however, you are running a small retail business that relies on selling goods and you are doing well (and have a successful method of keeping inventory), you may not need to lay out the money or take the time to train your staff to run the new computer. Don't embark on a project because everyone else is forging ahead into the high-tech world.

Keep in mind that cost-analysis is not a black and white concept. You need not say yea or nay, but can throw in a "maybe if we . . ." response. More often than not, the stakeholders can reach a compromise. A two-level bridge may become a one-level bridge because the local government has neither the funds nor the resources to build two levels. The compromise to build a one-level bridge makes the project cost-effective. It can be done in a shorter time frame, for a lower budget, and will require less manpower. Likewise, you may decide to get a smaller, less expensive computer system for the store and only train three people to use it. You may decide that leaving your business for two weeks during the summer might not be a good idea, so your two-week vacation in August might become a one-week vacation.

Compromise is good. It is often a necessity when getting a project off the ground. As project manager you may or may not have a say in reaching this compromise. The decision to open one branch office instead of two, for example, may have been made before you were ever asked to manage the project.

Evaluate Your Strengths

Another reason a project may not be feasible for you as project manager is because it is not something you have time to complete, or feel you have the background to accomplish. We all have strengths and weaknesses. Generally you will not select, or are not selected for, projects that would not be appropriate for you to handle. While research and a degree of learning may be factored into the overall equation, the reality is that if you know absolutely nothing about golf, you may not be the person to set up and run the company golf tournament. Knowing about something, however, doesn't mean you need to be an expert. Many Major League baseball managers and coaches were not always good ball players. The same holds true in other areas as well.

Determine Your Availability

If you can only allot twenty hours a week to a project and your own business is currently requiring you to put in fifty hours a week, you may not be able to effectively take on the additional workload. Many people attempt to overextend themselves and end up not only jeopardizing the project, but wasting the valuable time and energy of others. If the project can't fit into your schedule, don't agree to manage it. If the boss says it's your responsibility, like it or not, then you'll have to juggle or find a way to delegate your other responsibilities.

Has It Ever Been Done?

So, you're studying the cost-analysis breakdown. The benefits outweigh the negatives, but only barely. You're staring at your screen, thinking, maybe, just maybe, someone's had to do something like this before.

One of the most significant factors in determining whether or not to embark on a project is whether or not it's been done before. While Charles Lindbergh in his plane, Benjamin Franklin with his kite, and Magellan in his ship were certainly thinking quite the opposite, you may be hoping there is a template or at least some documentation of similar projects that have already been completed. While you won't become famous, you might stand a better chance of success if you can model your project after a previous endeavor and put your special signature or touch on it. After all, the wheel has been invented, so you need not start working on it from scratch!

One of the most important reasons for keeping accurate documentation of a project as you proceed is so that the next project team can have something to look at to see how it was done previously—for better or for worse. Evaluating previous projects is very important at any level of project management. Even making plans for a trip or planning a Sweet Sixteen party means calling and asking questions of others who have been to the same place or planned a similar party. If you're planning a convention, a conference, or a seminar for your company or your organization, surely you will want to look at the previous conferences and seminars. Historical information is useful, so find out where prior events were held, what resources were used, who was on the planning team, and whether or not the project stayed within budget.

> Sometimes businesses start on a project hoping they will generate the funding later. This can be very risky, as many dot-com companies have found out. The first phase of the project should be to create a marketing plan to gain the funding necessary to proceed.

When analyzing previous projects, you need to analyze all the elements involved with an open mind. You also need to consider the time, place, budget, and resources of that project in comparison to your project. If, for example, the last team was clearly understaffed and everyone had to put in significant amounts of overtime to complete the project, then you will know from the start that you'll need a bigger team—which might require more money in your budget. On the other hand, if it took a team of five people a year to complete a project in 1991, a decade later you may find that it could take five people half that amount of time. Thanks to the Internet, more efficient computer systems, and a host of technological developments, teams and projects tend to progress more efficiently. Conversely, if someone planned a wedding for $25,000 in 1988, that same wedding today might cost $45,000. Account for a variety of factors when looking at previous projects. Obviously the project most recent and most similar to yours will be the most informative.

Here are some other considerations:

Budget. Of course, costs are higher today than they were several years ago. Make sure the budget accounts for the rising costs and higher rates charged by experts in the field. Also look at whether the previous project came in under or over budget. See where the last team cut corners and determine whether or not you can cut those same corners if necessary.

Personnel. All factors being equal (comparable budget based on today's figures, a reasonable time frame, and so on), you may need to account for changes in personnel. Marvin, the expert who did all the work five years ago, left your business. Does anyone know how to work with a blowtorch as well as Marvin? Do you have the same level of expertise available to you that the previous team had, or will you be out looking for Marvin?

Leadership and management. Just because the last chief executive said "no problem" to holding the annual new client luncheon in his backyard doesn't mean the new chief executive wants you anywhere near his property. A new regime means new rules to follow.

External factors. The previous project manager imported materials for the project from a foreign country. Because of internal political strife, the country has stopped all exportation of the materials you need. You can't control rules, laws, jurisdictions, and other factors. If you're planning an outdoor event, external factors can be as basic as the weather. No matter how similar all of the available resources may be, some things are going to be out of your hands. Try to be aware of as many of these factors as possible and see if you can work around them.

Contingency plans. Did the previous project managers have backup plans or strategies? Sometimes these are not included in the documentation if they were not implemented.

Turnover problems and conflicts. You may not be able to foresee who will leave halfway through a project or what problems or conflicts are likely to arise. However, if you see a trend that developed during the previous project you may be forewarned as to where the problem areas lie. If some of the same individuals are involved, you'll know ahead of time which people did not work well together. This can range from competitive sales reps to sibling rivalry among your kids. You'll be able to pay closer attention to issues where potential conflicts lie as identified by evaluating the documentation of previous projects.

When evaluating a previous project, you should also look at the subsequent results. Did retail sales increase significantly after the company took its business onto the Internet? How long did it take for the benefits to appear? Will that same time frame work for your project, or do you need faster results to stay competitive?

Treasurers usually have last year's budget handy when making up the current annual budget. Accountants have the previous tax return nearby when working on the current return. You too can benefit from having the documentation of previous projects handy, whether they are yours, your predecessor's, or ones you've researched that have similar key characteristics. Remember, no two projects will be exactly the same as long as human beings are involved. Try to use a close match to guide you.

So, It's Never Been Done

There are those instances when you're doing something new and innovative. Perhaps you are teaming up to create a brand new game to market for the upcoming holiday season. Do you complete the project and roll out 10,000 boxes with the game ready to play? Perhaps you roll out ten games and hand them to friends and family members to play.

ESSENTIALS

Some projects will prove beneficial when you complete them. A new patio, for example, will be a place for relaxing by your pool. But the patio will also serve a long-term goal: when you sell your house, its value will be higher because of the addition. Keep in mind that goals need not be reached immediately for a project to be deemed successful.

Projects that involve a new product or a new way of carrying out a certain task most often require that you factor in a "test run" or a "pilot phase." When the television networks are interested in a new series, before taking the time and allocating the expense to produce a full season, they order a pilot episode or perhaps a run of six episodes during the summer months. When you buy a new car, you take a test drive. It's the same with new, innovative projects.

To do a successful test run, or pilot, you'll need to set your schedule to account for completion of a prototype, or a sampling. It's not uncommon to see small sample packages of a new food product being handed out. This way the project can get feedback from consumers as to whether they like the taste or not. Film scripts have several rewrites before anyone picks up a camera to start shooting. Then, as the film is being shot, scenes are looked at carefully and reshot if the director and producer don't like what they see. If you're lucky, in a project to develop a new product, you'll have a budget that allows you to conduct focus groups.

FACTS

Like snowflakes, no two projects are exactly alike. No matter how similar the objectives, resources, personnel, budget, time frame, and results, it's impossible for two projects to be identical. There are always surprises along the path from your original objective and starting point to your conclusion. More experienced program managers will identify the differences between projects and adapt accordingly.

It's also important that everyone working on the project understands that this is a test—it's only a test. This doesn't mean that 100 percent effort is not required, but that there will be changes implemented after you receive feedback on the pilot or sampling. Team members need to understand that there will be some trial and error, and they should not be discouraged if the initial prototype needs major revisions.

While installing a new computer system in your store, you might select a new software program. Before loading a wealth of information into the system, you might start training a small group of users. This way you'll see if you are utilizing the program most efficiently before you proceed.

Pilots and test runs serve to:

- Save money, since you need not start all over with a project if you run into a snag
- Solve problems at a preliminary level
- Bring an early halt to projects that simply will not reach their desired goal. How many products have hit the shelves only to be major bombs? And some of these did go through focus groups!
- Prevent a stressful and potentially disastrous result when you roll out the final project.

Have a Contingency Plan

In a perfect world, we would only choose to take on projects that were easy to manage, would come in under budget, and could be finished prior to their desired due date. From the perfect vacation to the 500 percent increase in sales—whatever the project, personal or business, it would go exactly as planned.

That was fun, now let's return to reality. Every project is fraught with potential pitfalls. As project manager you need to play devil's advocate and ask all the "what ifs." While you don't want to paint too bleak a picture, you do need to be prepared to address what can go wrong before taking on the project. This will have you thinking of scenarios for which you may need a contingency plan before you even begin.

In the 2000 baseball season, the St. Louis Cardinals team's project goal was to win its division title. When the star first baseman, Mark McGwire, went down with injuries, the team was not simply going to sit by and wait until he returned. It had scouted other first basemen in advance, knowing that McGwire had a history of injuries. The team immediately traded for a veteran first baseman (Will Clark) to fill in the position in case McGwire did not make it back during the season. As it turned out, McGwire did not return as a starter, and the Cardinals did win the division because they were ready with a contingency plan. You should also have a contingency plan ready in case any of your key personnel suddenly jump ship or can't complete the project for any reason.

You should also be prepared in case there is an unforeseen change in the schedule. Leave yourself enough flexibility that you can adjust your schedule. Are you ready with some morale boosters should there be dissention in the ranks? And what if money is running out faster than you anticipated or the cost of something has suddenly changed? You might be planning to stay at your favorite hotel in San Francisco, only to learn that the rates have gone up or a convention has been booked for the week you planned to travel. Do you have the extra money or can you find another hotel to your liking? If you have some leeway in your budget you'll be okay. If you have a second choice of hotels you'll also be okay.

ESSENTIALS

Conduct focus groups throughout your product development. Determine what your clients like or don't like about similar products on the market. Bring in samples of your prototype to get feedback on whether your product has improved and meets your clients' new demands.

It's always in your best interest to think about what you will do in case you need to shift gears. If you're heading up a project to publish a small company directory, have an illustrated cover as a backup in case the photos for the cover cost more than you anticipate. If it's cold and rainy on the day of your daughter's outdoor wedding, have a plan to set up the festivities indoors. In the real world, contingency planning is in the back of every project manager's mind. The more complex the project, the more contingencies shift to the front of the project manager's mind.

Along with pitfalls to the overall project, other situations can arise that may shake up your best intentions. For example, you may find that:

- *Everyone does not have the same understanding of the project.* All members of the project need to have a clear picture of both the goal and their roles.
- *People are at different stages of the project.* Make sure everyone is keeping up. If not, find out why not. Is the schedule unrealistic? Is someone goofing off? Is there a misunderstanding?

- *There's a mutiny growing.* Is morale sinking faster than the Titanic? Make sure everybody is happy. Try not to overwork people and remember to praise a job well done (as discussed later in this book). You also need to determine, and make sure involved parties understand, the consequences if people simply do not hold up their end of the agreement to complete their part of the project.
- *There's a lack of communication.* Three people should not be handing you the same completed task. Make sure everyone is communicating with one another.
- *Team members are finding that your instructions are unclear.* Write everything down, review it, and ask for questions. Make sure, from the outset, that everyone has a firm grasp of the project and their particular roles in it.
- *The sponsor has thrown you a curveball.* It's not uncommon that midway through a project, the sponsor decides to make a change that alters the project. Somehow, you're going to have to grin and deal with it accordingly. This may mean reallocating funding, changing your schedule, or reassigning a team member.
- *There's a lack of flexibility.* You may find that your schedule has left you no room for error or to accommodate changes that arise during the project. From the beginning, it's important that you factor in some degree of flexibility. If the sponsor has set up the parameters and it's out of your hands—it simply must get done!—then you may need to micro-manage those areas or individuals that are not keeping up with the schedule.

It's important to look at a project from a realistic perspective. Things *will* go wrong. Even at a wedding, something will go wrong. The only flexibility you can build into such a personal project is an understanding that something will happen: You can be ready to laugh at it, do your best to fix it, or simply let it go. Most projects are not life or death, so the ability to go with the flow and do what you can do make things better is often your best ally. Be realistic, not idealistic, as a project manager.

Don't Just Wing It!

The project: To get fifteen minutes of comedy material together for your stand-up comedy act audition in six months. How do you get started? Do you hire a writer to work with? Do you practice long and hard? Do you watch the style of other great comics? Do you hone your skills before hitting the comedy clubs? You may do all of these, and if you're well organized, you'll set a schedule, allocate how much money you plan to invest in your new career, and look at the resources you will need to become the next successful comic.

The best stand up comics look like they are standing before an audience, improvising effortlessly. It just rolls off their tongues . . . or so it seems. A good comedy act takes lots of practice, and lots of trial and error. Comics review tapes of themselves and work very hard to get the right material. They then become so well skilled at delivering it that it often sounds as though they're "just winging it."

QUESTIONS?

Do I need documentation?
Projects can be formal or informal, and there are parameters including a budget, time frame, and specification of resources. Whether casual or contracted, most projects proceed best when plans and parameters are documented in some manner. This can be anything from a handwritten, one-page list to a contract drawn up by lawyers; it depends on the nature of the project.

Anyone who believes he or she can go into a project and just "wing it" is fooling himself. Ninety-nine percent of the time this approach does not work. Often, the team is so eager to get off and running that the members jump into the project before they've done their homework. Every project needs to be properly planned. Lack of adequate planning is the single biggest cause of project failure.

When a writer tries to write a screenplay, he or she is best served by writing a comprehensive outline, or treatment, first. Screenwriters often say that if they've done their research and created a good outline, the script almost writes itself as everything falls into place. The same holds true for a project. The better the preparation, the better the end results.

Preparation may mean detailed planning or simply a rough draft, depending on the nature of the project. It's important, however, that you put together your plan, that you have something in writing, and that all areas are covered in some manner. Even improvisational comedy troupes practice for many hours, honing their comedic skills.

Before we go into more detail about the many areas of project management, let's close this chapter by saying that as a project manager, you need the following:

- A clear understanding of the project's goal
- The ability to plan
- Solid communication skills
- The ability to be flexible and adaptable when necessary
- The ability to evaluate others, yourself, and the overall project
- Determination to complete, in a timely fashion, what you've started

Above all else, a good project manager must be a good listener and a good juggler, make sound (not snap) decisions, stay organized, know when to call in expertise, and keep his head even when others are losing theirs! In other words, never let 'em see you sweat.

CHAPTER 2

Setting the Wheels in Motion

Every project serves a purpose and has an aim or objective. If the project accomplishes its goal within set parameters (such as the budget), it is deemed successful. One of your first tasks as project manager is to determine how you will achieve that project's goal in accordance with the parameters set forth by the project sponsor. It is important that you carefully assess the project and have (in writing) the terms, such as when the project, or parts thereof, are due to be completed and what the budget constraints are.

Clear Vision

It's extremely important that everyone involved in the project has the same clear vision. Everyone should be able to clearly communicate the same goal or objective of the project. If the objective is vague or if anyone has a misconception of where the project is headed, encourage them to speak up before the wheels start rolling.

Contracts, project requests, charters, and statements of work are all written documents that include the details of a specific project in writing. Any such document serves as an important way of ensuring that everyone has the same understanding of the overall conditions of the project. Documents also serve as the primary resource if everyone has forgotten part of the original plan, or if the team needs to verify anything.

SSENTIALS

Before you agree to proceed as project manager, consult with experts and team members (or potential team members) to get a firm idea of how long each task will take. If you're planning a wedding, for example, you'll need to know how long the ceremony will run before you schedule the start of the wedding reception.

Is Everybody Happy?

It's important to know who is sponsoring the project and who all the stakeholders are when you agree to do a project. You want to appease the sponsor and meet the needs of the stakeholders, some of whom will be on your project team.

For example, if you're running a carnival to raise money for your daughter's school, one goal is meeting the expectations of the school's vice principal who put you in charge. You'll also need to please the principal, the members of the PTA (who raised the funds for the carnival), and the local school board (which may have specific rules and regulations). Ultimately, of course, the parents and children who are your customers will judge your success. Needless to say, the more stakeholders there are who may benefit from a project, the harder it is to please everyone.

It's important to take note at the onset of all potential opposition to your project. Are you dealing with two people picketing your store or an entire town blocking your construction crew? Address the level of opposition; if it's significant, you'll have to determine in advance how it will be handled. If opposition is too strong, you will have to alter your entire plan. Keep the following points in mind:

- Look around carefully for people or groups who oppose the project
- Try to address their concerns and educate opponents of the benefits your project will have on them
- Try to reach a compromise if necessary
- Alter, or even cancel, your project in extreme cases where opposition is too great

Old Ways Versus New Ways

While you evaluate a project, prior to starting the wheels in motion, you will want to think about your methods of carrying out and managing activities. Do you have ironclad methods or are you open to change?

When planning a major conference, one person always says, "That's the way we've always done it, so we should do it that way again." Another person says, "Let's be open to new ideas. New people may provide us with better ways to accomplish some of our objectives." Who's right?

FACTS

Sticking with tried-and-true methods is less risky and offers a proven track record, but the methods may be somewhat outdated and limit your creativity. Trying new methods poses greater risk because these methods are often unproven, but they often allow for more creativity and can save you time and money.

They are both right. Tried and true methods that work should not be discarded. They have proven to be effective and there is a low level of risk involved—they are not likely to cause the project to go off track. But, new ideas open up the potential for positive growth. Examining new methods means matching them against tried and true methods of the past. Do they achieve the same and more, or do they achieve less? It's hard to measure quality, but sometimes you can improve upon a job well done.

Also, new ideas may invigorate the people involved, and generate renewed enthusiasm. If a team is pulled together to work on a project, and they know that it will be the same routine as the last project, they are less enthusiastic than if there are some new elements of the project. Likewise, new team members can provide creative new ideas.

It's important to learn from the past while considering the potential advantages of new methods. Projects need to utilize the hard work and results of past successes as well as take advantage of advances in technology and education. Someone who is not open to change is limiting his or her potential for a highly successful project. Conversely, someone who refuses to acknowledge the previous methods may be so steeped in new methodology that he or she forfeits what can be learned from past history and experience for the sake of technology. To find the right balance, a project manager needs to be open to both sets of ideas, old and new.

Competition

Among the many factors to consider as you size up and assess the project is whether or not your time frame or resources are impacted by competition. You may not be the first person with the innovative idea to sell baklava over the Internet. Therefore, your project to get your new site, *www.ultimatebaklava.com,* launched by March 1st may require altering your time frame to beat your competitor, who is working on a project to launch *www.bestbaklava.com.*

QUESTIONS?

What are deliverables?
Deliverables is a common buzzword that refers to "the defined end products, results, or services produced during the project." A project goal can also be a deliverable.

If you learn that your competition is also working on a project to offer competitive products or services, you will have the added pressure of beating them to the punch. You may need to find ways to cut corners and create shortcuts to beat the competition, or at least have your product ready to go at the same time as your competitor.

Friendly competition to create a better product or develop the first of a particular item can be positive for a team that steps up to the challenge. Nonetheless, winning a competition at the risk of an inferior product or service is not really a victory, as you have not achieved the true goal of the project: produce a quality item or service that meets a specific need or solves a problem.

Are You Ready to Roll?

Take a look at the following list of questions to see if you are ready to move forward into full-scale project planning:

- Have you established the goal of the project?
- Does everyone involved have a clear understanding of that goal?
- Have you identified all stakeholders (management, team members if any, customers, and anyone else the project stands to directly, or even indirectly, affect)?
- Will you be able to explain the objectives of the project to all the team members and stakeholders?
- Are you clear about what stakeholders are expecting from this project?
- Have you identified opposition, if any, to this project?
- Have you defined the scope of the project (the size of the project in terms of budget, resources needed, potential impact on business or the community)?
- Are all the initial parameters in writing?
- Have you established a time frame for all deliverables?

Before you forge ahead, solidify your team, and put the plans on the drawing board (or on your software program), there's one more important step: Establish the rules of the game. Let's take a closer look.

Rules of the Game

Projects need to have a hierarchy set up and a chain of command in place. You're planning the family camping trip and have put Timothy in charge of the tents, William in charge of food and cooking supplies, and Maxine in charge of locating and booking the campground. Now, if anyone comes up with a great idea for cooking on a hibachi, they'll know to run it by William.

Similarly, if you're launching a new Web site, the technical crew will need to report to the head of technology while the people writing the site may be working with the content manager or editor. There may be a manager to whom the sales team reports. In a larger project, there are a number of levels of command.

Rules and guidelines must also be established for team members, such as:

- Progress reports must be handed in every Friday.
- If you miss three practices, you're off the team.
- All requests for supplies must be put in writing.
- We'll only serve turkey sandwiches at team luncheons.

Spell out all the rules and guidelines as clearly as possible. But be careful: too many rules can spoil the project! Make sure your rules and regulations are really necessary for the good of the project, not simply because you love to watch people jump through hoops.

ALERT

All parameters and communication should be clearly spelled out. "I'll need it by the end of the day tomorrow" is better than "Hand it in as soon as you can." Likewise, "We're going away from August 16th to the 28th" is better than "Let's plan to go on vacation sometime in August."

Lines of communication must also be set up clearly. Not everyone needs to receive an e-mail each time someone has an idea. If the set designers have a new concept for the backdrop for the community production of *Death of a Salesman*, by all means share it with the producer, the director, and the people building the set. But the understudy for Willie Loman doesn't need to be deluged with talk of curtain measurements while he's trying to learn his role. Likewise, the head of sales need not be included in a technical e-mail discussion that does not concern him.

Make sure that you have a smooth-running project system. If everyone knows how to accomplish their tasks within a set framework and whom they need to speak to if they have problems or questions, you'll be starting off on the right foot. Also, as project manager, it's critical that you keep the lines of communications open between you and your team.

Do Your Homework

You'll hear constant talk about the project phases, starting with initiating the project and moving into the planning process. There are countless graphs, charts, diagrams, pyramids, flowcharts, and other manners of presenting the series of steps needed to effectively manage a project. Theories, methodology, and discussion of these steps are important only to the point at which you understand what the steps mean. Once that has occurred, it's time to stop talking, put down the graphs of the "big picture," roll up your sleeves, and get to work!

Yes, there are a tremendous number of aspects and elements that can be discussed regarding projects, and plenty of buzzwords and project-friendly phrases, but the bottom line is that at some point it will be time to get busy. This separates those who talk about projects and those who actually do them. If you're a doer, then start the project by doing your homework.

Research

Homework includes plenty of research. You need to gather information from as many applicable sources as possible. You will also need to verify that your sources are accurate, especially if you surf unfamiliar territory on the Web. In business, you will want to review the minutes of meetings leading up the formation of the project. You may also want to look at the following:

- Company reports
- Previous project reports
- Pertinent documents
- External reports, such as neighborhood studies, demographic studies, and consumer studies
- Books, articles, and Web sites that pertain to the nature of your project

You may even review personnel files to find people with expertise in certain areas. You'll also want to use the Internet or your local library to gather facts and figures that support the projected outcome of the project. You'll need to scope out anything that exists in the media that may be helpful. Anything that can lead to resources will also be of value. As you build your team, you'll be able to delegate tasks accordingly, and the team members will be able to seek out information on their own.

ESSENTIALS

Holding meetings with team members as you build the team will allow you to share and gain information. You will be able to describe the overall project and they may be able to demonstrate their knowledge of a specific area. Take good notes.

You cannot expect to lead a team effectively unless you know the project's scope, details, and place in the bigger picture (which could be the company or the world). You need to be able to answer questions and show that you have a firm grasp of what is being done and how it will commence effectively. You also need to network—it's very important. Talk with other team leaders (especially those who have led similar projects) and potential team members, as well as others who you feel can provide information. Gather benchmark data against which you can measure vendor quotes, resource prices, your projected project time frame, etc.

Any project needs some degree of research before it gets off the ground. Besides making the initial determination of whether a project is or is not feasible (see Chapter 1), you'll need to investigate ways to proceed and research all possible pros and cons of the process you select.

Before you build a new bathroom in your house, you'll need to read up on the latest in bathroom fixtures and get an idea of how the plumbing operates in your home. You may have to look at blueprints of the house and assess the land before you start work.

Without doing solid research, how will you know if you have the best team members or whether you have someone who can't perform the job? You can't hire someone to create a new data entry system for your business if you don't know whether they've done such a project before. Likewise, you don't want a computer software program that is wrong for your project. Every step of the way, you will have to do research or have others do research for you (and for the good of the project). If people are doing research on your behalf, make sure they know exactly what you are looking for so they don't waste your time (and theirs) searching for extraneous or unnecessary information.

Research and searching for information is also significant in that it will help you return to your stakeholders with valuable materials that may benefit them and even alter their projected results. You may have discovered a city ordinance that will force you to alter your plans slightly, or a new technology that will help you complete the project a week earlier than expected. Run your discoveries by your stakeholders. Often they will have information to share with you as well.

Action

One of the most common pitfalls of projects is failing to get them done on time without a mad rush to the finish line that often results in a less than satisfactory outcome. Many people who take on a project spend far too much time planning, plotting, and arranging and rearranging their schedule. After all that, they realize they've jumped into the "take action" phase too late. A good project manager knows the value of the initial planning process, but also knows when the time is right to stop planning and start doing. Planning is important, but even a marvelous plan that never gets off the ground, or gets off the ground way too late, is not worth the effort because the risk of failure increases.

Avoid diminishing returns by using your resources effectively. Just because a computer software program has 800 functions, it doesn't mean you'll need all 800 for your project. Focus on the project, not the mechanics! Once you have everything up and running, move on.

Your Attitude and People Skills

Learning the basic principles of project management is certainly important. Studying, fact finding, and learning as much as possible so that you are respected as a knowledgeable project leader is also extremely important.

Setting the Mood

There is, however, another aspect of leadership, and that's your attitude. How you approach the project and the project team is key to keeping everything on track. As is often the case, the crew takes its cue from the captain—that's you, their fearless leader. If you approach a project with confidence in your own abilities and your team's ability to complete the job on time and under budget, you'll be ahead of the game. At the beginning of any project, the leader must set the tone. A project leader who expresses an attitude of "We'll probably all die trying" doesn't exactly get the team off to flying start. A leader who tells his team, "This project will be a challenge, but I am sure that by working together we can get the job done!" sets a much more positive, "can-do" tone.

Get in touch with your feelings about doing this project. To effectively lead a project you must believe in it. This isn't to say you won't have some doubts or questions, but belief in what you do factors into a successful project. It's very hard to fake enthusiasm for a project that you do not believe will work. If your heart's not in it, your team members, friends, family, neighbors—whoever is involved—will get wind of your true feelings at some point.

It's not just a positive attitude and hard work, however, that make a successful leader. Leadership (discussed at greater length in later chapters) includes gaining the respect and trust of those working with you. Respect for you as a leader is directly related to your respectful treatment of the team. Give your team the respect it deserves by being a leader who not only talks to his or her team and explains what is necessary to be accomplished, but puts equal effort into listening.

"Man of the People"

Any project—whether it's a business deal or an anniversary party—requires people skills. You need to know how to:

- Give clear instructions and review key points carefully
- Respond to questions, inquiries, and criticism in a timely manner
- Be accessible
- Praise or reward a job well done
- Listen to new ideas
- Present positive alternatives
- Criticize ideas, not individuals
- Recognize that there are distinctly different personalities and accept those various personalities
- Have respect for cultural differences
- Separate personal feelings from the work of the project

SSENTIALS Good relationships are vital to your project's success. Just as a successful sports team needs to have a strong sense of camaraderie and follow solid leadership, a project team needs the same strong bond, whether it is made up of two people or 200.

The manner in which you approach the project and how you deal with whomever is involved either directly or indirectly is important.

Likewise, you'll also have to deal effectively with the stakeholders. But keep in mind that no matter how well you lead, you'll never please everyone. That's another aspect of leadership that you'll have to accept. A "people-pleaser" can actually jeopardize a project by trying to make everyone happy at the expense of doing a sound job.

Decisions and Assumptions

Based on the nature of the project, decision making will follow a certain procedure. A group or organization may have clear-cut methods by which decisions are made, and as project leader, all you can do is work within these set parameters. Other projects (and this is very common) will have some decisions made by those initiating the project, but will allow room for your decisions and those of team members whom you have authorized to make such decisions.

When making unilateral decisions, take a broad view, then narrow down your options to make the decision easier. If you're deciding which vendor to hire and looking at a list of twenty vendors, narrow it down to two or three that fit your needs. Then do your evaluating. If you need help in making a decision on which software programs to buy, ask someone who knows more than you about the various software programs. The best leaders always know when to make a unilateral decision and when to ask for help. There is also a tendency to err on the side of caution. It's usually in your best interest to try an approach that has fewer risks and unknowns. If you are trying something out of the ordinary (or riskier), have a backup plan. If video conferencing won't work, audio conferencing might. Be ready to make the decision to shift to plan B, the safer route, when necessary.

Knowing when to make a decision is very important for any project manager. There's a vast gray area between jumping the gun (when you make a decision without all the information) and being stalled at the gate, too afraid to decide anything. Decisions need to be made in a timely fashion and supported by sound research, information, planning, and logic. If you always stay one step ahead of the project in your planning and strategizing, you'll be better prepared to make quick decisions. Keep these tips in mind:

- Keep thinking of what comes next
- Expect, and plan for, the unexpected
- Have sound reasons for your decisions and get support or approval—even if you've been given the green light to act on your own
- Stand behind your decisions, but be prepared to compromise if necessary
- Make decisions within the rules and regulations of the company, organization, business, neighborhood, or larger body—even families have a series of unwritten rules
- Learn from decisions that didn't work in the past
- Document your decisions in writing or on your computer

It has been said that if you make an informed decision, most of the time it will be the right one. If it isn't, hopefully it will be easy to repair.

ESSENTIALS

If you are having trouble making a decision, try making a "decision tree." It is a graphic model that you create on paper to help you put your thoughts in one place. Use a main decision point as the stem, and add branches indicating decisions that are made from that central point. The branch continues on to show probable outcomes from the decision, allowing you to plan accordingly.

You may have heard the phrase, "When you assume, you make an ass out of you and me (ass u me)." Making assumptions can have the same result when managing a project. "We've tried it before and it hasn't worked" doesn't mean it won't work now. Just because your family never wanted to go to Washington, D.C. on prior family vacations, it doesn't mean they won't want to go this year. The kids are older and learning more about the government. Just because your boss never gave you the go-ahead to build a heliport on the roof, it doesn't mean she's going to shoot down your project again.

You should not assume for many reasons:

- Old policies may have been revised.
- New people, with different ideas or philosophies, may now be in charge.
- Antiquated systems may have been updated.
- There may be more money in the company, association treasury, or tucked under the mattress.
- Laws or ordinances may have changed.

Assumptions can lead to pleasant surprises or disasters. A business owner recalls his assumption that it would take two days for the new supplies to arrive because they had to come by way of local roads since the only nearby highway did not allow commercial traffic. As it turned out, the ordinance banning commercial traffic from the highway had been altered and commercial vehicles could travel on that roadway during peak traffic hours. Instead of the usual two days to get supplies, it only took one day. The project could suddenly move forward ahead of schedule because the project manager had made an incorrect assumption.

Defining Specific Objectives

Objectives lead to work—work designed to achieve the objectives. Therefore, the more clearly (and often succinctly) you can define an objective, the better chance the work will be done with the correct objective in mind. When laying out your objectives, or plan of action, keep in mind the following:

- Don't talk "tech," "lingo," "jargon," or "slang." Not everyone knows the terms, acronyms, code names, trendy nicknames, etc. Speak plain English (or the language of your team members).
- Be clear and realistic about deadlines. Nothing, as noted previously, can be done "yesterday." Set realistic deadlines and make sure everyone is clear what is due when.

- Don't be so specific and regimented that your team ends up operating like robots. Give them the leeway to be creative and innovative. Not only will they be more motivated, but some marvelous new ideas come from allowing a degree of flexibility.
- Don't be so loose that you have no parameters or direction to guide and focus your team. You don't want people thinking that any old way they accomplish the job is fine. You'll need to be accountable for the methods employed by, and money spent by, your team. Finding out that your team saved money by buying the new computer system from some guy in the back of a van may not be a good thing!

The better you communicate the objectives of the project, the more likely the project is to reach the desired conclusion. Miscommunication to, and misdirection of, team members are primary reasons for projects not reaching their goals.

Don't micromanage your team. It does nothing to boost morale, foster independence, or encourage growth. Regardless of your intent, micromanaging tells your team members that you don't have faith in their ability to do their work. The only times you may need to micromanage are when you are falling behind schedule or have a team member who is not doing his or her job properly.

Defining Key Resources

To complete almost any project, you will need resources, people power, and plenty of "stuff." Your "stuff" is whatever you need to complete the project, whether it's the goods to be sold or project tracking software, heavy machinery, or pens and paper. The resources are key to making the project come to life.

Committing to resources, financially and contractually, means looking closely at your budget and the needs of the project. The tighter the budget, the more important it is that you run a streamlined project, and the more efficiently you'll have to utilize your resources. Your overall project resources will include:

- *How many people you need for the project.* This is not necessarily the number of people who will be involved at any level, but the number of people you will need to get the project accomplished. In addition to identifying who you'll need to actually achieve your goal, you'll need to determine for how long, and at which stage, each person will be involved.
- *Materials, tools, and supplies.* Determine what supplies are necessary to complete each aspect of the project. What will team members need every step of the way? Don't get caught without resources midway through a project on a tight deadline.
- *Tracking materials and technology.* If the project doesn't directly involve technology, as creating a Web site or installing a security system would, you'll need to determine what technology is and isn't needed to create, organize, and monitor the project. Depending on the complexity of the project, you may already have the computer capabilities to track the project. If you're putting together a golf outing for your fraternal association, you may simply fill in the names and information on an Excel or Word program. A camping trip for the neighborhood scout group may not require any technology, just a notebook to write down names and a list of supplies.

ESSENTIALS

List all of the significant resources in advance—those that you simply must have to make the project a success. Keep one eye on your budget and the other on your resources. Also keep in mind—and this is very important—you will very likely require additional resources along the way.

You should also discuss resources with your team members. Make sure everyone has what they need and knows how to use it. A new computer is wasted on a team member who is not computer literate. Also, listen to team members and look at similar projects to get an idea of what resources were required in the past. Ask your neighbor what tools he used to build his patio before you start building yours. Then you can buy the same tools—or better yet, borrow his!

The Sum of the Parts

A successful project is the result of various components interacting positively. If your project is to arrange and run a book sale to raise money for your school, you'll need to divide up the tasks. First determine the scope or size of the project. Does the budget set forth by the sponsors (the PTA) allow for you to buy 300 children's books to sell over two days, or 3,000 books to sell over two weeks?

Next, evaluate your budget. If $2,100 has been allocated for purchasing the books and you can purchase the average children's book for $3, then you are looking at about 700 books. If previous book sales indicate that books sell at an average of about 250 a day, you'll be looking at a three-day sale. Keep in mind some of the parameters may have been decided beforehand. Make sure the numbers work. If, for example, the sponsor wants you to buy 700 books for a one-day sale, then you'll have to find a way to maximize sales by choosing a bigger location, using better promotion throughout the school, and having more volunteers on hand to sell books. You might, however, also propose a three-day sale to the sponsors, using your research (past figures) to illustrate the possible benefits of an alternative plan.

ALERT

Often projects fail because key details were omitted from the project plan. It may help you to remember all the factors if you start listing everything you can think of. Once you have your team in place, they will be able to fill in the pieces you may not have considered.

Once you've determined the overall scope, you can start addressing the details. On smaller projects, you may be able to do several of the tasks yourself. Nonetheless, even for your own organization, it's important to have a list of all the details involved.

Using the PTA book sale example, here's what your list might look like:

- Set the date of the sale.
- Set timeline of interim deadlines.
- Get volunteers.
  - Those who will help you plan and promote the sale
  - Those who will help you sell books
  - Those who will help clean up after the sale
- Find the "in-school" location for sale.
- Determine how books will be brought to the school and where they will be stored until the sale and after the sale. Are you buying books that can be returned to the publisher? Are you buying books on consignment? Are unsold books being donated to the school library? Always think about what happens to resources after the project.
- Arrange for all necessary supplies, including cash register or cash box, receipts, etc.
- Consider other items for sale, such as bookmarks, etc., but stay within your budget.
- Set up day-of rules and guidelines; for example, "no refunds, but books can be exchanged on same day as sale," "cash or personal checks only," etc. Also determine who is responsible for being the cashier and handling the finances.
- Coordinate all setup, including day-of and cleanup activities.
- Day-of: Set up and price the books (you may have already established a set formula for pricing, such as x percent above cost to you).
- Sell books.
- Shut down and clean up. Break down at end of sale; return books to storage or wherever they are supposed to go. Don't forget to think about this part of the project.
- Make sure money is accounted for and in a safe place.
- Turn over funds to PTA treasurer.
- Meet to debrief. While the event is still fresh in your (and your sponsors') mind, evaluate the success of this year's sale. Consider what you did differently that was better, what you did the same that always works, and figure out what didn't work (and why). Documenting this process will give next year's project manager a great foundation.

It's important that you cover all bases in your detailed plan of action. Your team will help you find gaps, if there are any, in your plan. They may also make additional or supplemental suggestions, such as, in the previous example, "How about having some refreshments on hand?" This was not a significant detail, as the project could proceed without refreshments, but it was evaluated nonetheless. Considering the limited space, and manpower needed (or willing) to clean up, refreshments would not have been the best way to use the project's resources.

If, at the end of the book sale, everyone started walking out, and someone turned around and said, "What are we supposed to do with all of these extra books?" one of two things could have happened. It could be that no one planned the follow-through and closeout details, or the details weren't clearly communicated (or understood). In either case, it's clear that someone didn't accomplish his or her task regarding breaking down the sale.

ESSENTIALS
Plan the delegation of tasks carefully to avoid any overlap. You don't want three people in charge of ordering bookmarks, or you'll have way too many. Review all of the details with your team beforehand to make sure every task is covered and everyone knows what their responsibilities are.

Some projects will be broken down into numerous levels of details. You may have someone doing a task, and someone else doing a subtask, and someone doing a sub-subtask, and so on. Often, the more details you're working with, the more you may need to subdivide. Breaking down a project into smaller tasks is called a "Work Breakdown Structure." It is a systematic, prioritized account of all the work necessary to be completed including the fine points necessary to plan, carry out, and track the project.

Some people are comfortable handling an entire task but may feel more comfortable if the task is broken down into multiple parts. As a project manager, you can break down a task in any number of ways— whatever is most efficient in terms of time, money, and effort. For example, the person ordering the books can order storybooks on Monday, nonfiction books on Tuesday, and reference books on Wednesday. On the other hand, she may order all books from publishers ABC and DEF on

Monday, from GHI and JKL publishing houses on Tuesday, and MNO and PQR publishers on Wednesday. She could also get all the books she can from a distributor one day and from Internet sources the next. It's important that you divide tasks realistically. Buying 600 books on Monday and 100 on Tuesday morning is probably not realistic unless your volunteer works for a publishing house.

Many factors must be taken into account when dividing a project into tasks and sub-tasks. Make estimates regarding the resources you have based on all logical and reasonable factors. For example, even if someone works for a publishing house but would clearly lose his or her job by ordering 600 books at an employee discount without prior arrangements, you cannot make this a realistic task.

Detailing tasks is helpful because tasks can be easily understood and accomplished. The majority of people work better when they are working on smaller, more manageable tasks. However, it's important (and not always easy) to determine how much breaking down of a project you need to do. Yes, you may have a list of tasks and an order in which they should be done. You may have it broken down by days, perhaps by morning and afternoon. Should you then break each task down into how many hours or even minutes it should take? It depends on the overall time structure. If the project requires you to do a complete inventory of your business in one day before the potential new buyer shows up, then you might have to break down the project into an hourly schedule.

You can determine how many pieces of the puzzle there need to be by evaluating the following:

1. The overall time frame of the project
2. The complexity of the project
3. The expertise of the person doing a particular task
4. The complexity of the task

The last two items on the list are perhaps the most important. If a person is new to the job he has been assigned, you may have to detail the task more carefully. For instance, if someone ordering the books for the book sale has never ordered books before, you might detail who needs to be called, what needs to be filled out on the order forms, and how long each order should take. The complexity of the task will also be factored into the equation. More technical or detailed tasks such as those found in an engineering project may need to be further subdivided. This will tie in to the skill level of the team members.

ALERT

When estimating how long a task will take, always allow extra time for external factors. Projects have been delayed by power failures, technical glitches, weather, illness, and various other factors. For every story about how a computer has facilitated the completion of a project much faster than it would have been done a decade ago, there's a story about how the computer crashed, lost a file, or otherwise caused a project delay.

The person planning the project needs to find team members who can work at the rate required. Sure, an author who works at a slower pace could easily handle the job with a six-month due date, but not within this particular time frame.

Sometimes the project sponsor will ask you how much of a given resource you need. If you are a contractor working with an assistant, you might have the opportunity to assess the project and give the sponsor an estimate of how much time it will take (this may also hold true for cost). You may not get the project if your estimate is not in line with standard rates and time estimates for the job you've been asked to do. If you're in the position of being able to set parameters for a project, get an idea of what other people would ask to do a similar project.

Three Common Mistakes

As is the case with any skill set, learning project management skills takes time and practice. During the course of a project you will inevitably make errors and mistakes, but learning from them will help you hone your skills. Following are some common mistakes that occur while managing activities, setting up reward systems, and prioritizing tasks and activities.

Too Many Pieces of the Pie!

One of the mistakes project managers frequently make is breaking down or subdividing activities into countless smaller tasks or chores. When the pie goes from slices to crumbs, you're in trouble. An endless list of step-by-step details though hundreds of tasks broken down by hours or even minutes can be problematic. First of all, at that level of detail, the project manager has left no room for changes in this tight and lengthy schedule. There is also no room for skilled professionals to take the ball and run with it, which in many cases produces faster, more effective results. A Work Breakdown Structure that is too rigid and too detailed leads to micro-management, which doesn't usually enhance the team spirit. The other problem with breaking down everything into an overly specific, lengthy list of detailed tasks is that the process is not an effective use of your time. You don't want to hold up the project because you are up to detail number 1,376 in a list of 2,700!

By using a broader Work Breakdown Structure, you can list the tasks necessary for each person to perform, but look at end results rather than each nut and bolt. Naturally, if a safety inspector is going to review your project, you may have to detail many of the nuts and bolts, but for most projects it's advantageous to allow people to aim for results.

Misdirected Rewards

Often projects are measured improperly. How often have you seen quantity rewarded over quality? How often has the loudest, most boisterous sales manager gotten his plan approved, while other sales managers with excellent ideas are overlooked because they aren't as loud or aggressive? Consider these other examples of misdirected rewards:

- The head of sales receives an all-expenses-paid vacation because sales are up, despite the fact that the company's reputation gets dragged though the mud by disreputable sales practices.
- The girl who sold 4,000 boxes of cookies for her school wins the award, even though she played hooky for a week to sell them during school hours.

- The player who scored the most baskets makes the All-Star team even though his lack of sportsmanship and teamwork cost his team a victory in nearly every game.
- The computer programmer gets a bonus for writing the most program codes, nearly all of which had nothing to do with helping the project.

It's important to have a justified reward system if this is how you intend to motivate your team. But often other conditions need to be considered in the bigger picture. Reaching a goal while jeopardizing the reputation of a company or organization is not really an achievement. Suppose the goal is to provide an improved, user-friendly e-commerce component to your company. If you reward the programmer who wrote the most codes, this reward is only justifiable if the codes ultimately improved the e-commerce system. If users find it easier to navigate the system, and sales are up, then indeed this programmer deserved to be rewarded. If, however, you simply said, whoever writes the most program codes gets a reward, you may be rewarding someone who simply wrote plenty of codes that effectively did nothing to improve e-commerce navigability or sales (the desired goals of the project).

FACTS

In Major League baseball, the most valuable player is not just the player with the best statistics, but the one whose team most benefited from that player's presence. Likewise, your most valuable team member doesn't necessarily have to produce the most, but has to be significant in the success of the overall project.

Rewarding a job well done may not only mean quality over quantity, but staying within set boundaries. This means you, as project manager, need to set standards that are worthy of rewards (ones that help achieve a successful project without jeopardizing the business, other projects, or people). You can then reward measurable achievements, such as improved sales or better customer relations.

No (or Unclear) Incentives

Let's face it, most people operate with a "What's in it for me?" approach to life. As a project manager, you may be in the position of establishing incentives and rewards. This can range from popcorn for a youngster to a bonus and promotion for a corporate team member. Not all projects require you to present a reward, but some incentive will generally provide a reason for team members to put forth that much more effort.

If there is a reward offered, it needs to be in proportion to the task at hand, and should be realistic in scope. Promising a child an expensive train set for passing a spelling test is a bit excessive. You are limited to the confines of your budget and an incentive plan that will encourage, not detract from, team spirit. You also want to set reasonable expectations—don't set a precedent that you cannot maintain in the future. With all of these variables to consider, it's no wonder project managers often do not offer any incentives or rewards for a job well done.

Volunteer groups are often the hardest to reward. A pat on the back, words of praise, or simply acknowledgement of a job well done is often the best appreciation you can offer a volunteer. An even better reward may come from the satisfaction of having a positive impact on something the volunteer personally supports, encourages, and believes in.

On the opposite side of rewards and incentives are consequences for a job done poorly. Yes, many people work hard not to get fired, not to fail a test, or not to be excluded from a group. While this is a form of incentive, it doesn't always produce the best results. A person working just hard enough not to fail isn't really working to exceed, but just to "get by." There is always one student trying to get an A and another student happy to simply pass with a D. Positive incentives and rewards give people more to strive for and produce better results.

Prioritize

As you begin your project, make sure you have a list of priorities. Number each task and priority from one to five, with one being low in priority and five being top priority. Sort all the ones, twos, threes, fours, and fives together, then start prioritizing within each group. Ultimately you'll have a prioritized list of what needs to be done. The top-priority tasks are those that will lead most directly to the success or failure of the project. These are your core tasks. Some tasks may seem lower in importance, such as finding a rehearsal hall. However, you can't proceed to rehearsals for the original theater production of *Phantom of the Car Wash* without a place in which to practice. Therefore, larger tasks (like three weeks of full-day rehearsals) are sometimes contingent on smaller ones being completed first. This makes those little tasks high on the priority list.

A prioritized list of objectives will help you eliminate certain tasks if sticking to your budget or completing the project on time is becoming an issue. Priorities will also help you if your need to reorganize the project. You will know which tasks and objectives will need more attention. The same holds true with shifting team members. If two people are working on a low-priority task, such as printing the program for the theater production, and there's a need for more assistance on higher priority tasks, like costumes and lighting, you'll be able to make the proper adjustment.

FACTS

Priority does not mean task order. Sometimes the most important task is done last, after preparation. In other instances the most significant task is that which begins the project and everything else plays off that task being accomplished.

Throughout the subsequent chapters there will be further discussions about resources, objectives, working effectively with the project team, making decisions, and adhering to your priorities. A project manager must remember that these areas are not mutually exclusive. A project has a life, and like any living thing, there is growth and change throughout the process. There is overlap, which means determining what you will need (the "stuff") and who you'll need (the team players) go hand in hand. As you read further, you will see that project management means keeping tabs on the whole project by monitoring the numerous parts. Your doctor keeps tabs on your overall health by checking out all your vital organs. Likewise, you will be doing similar checkups on your project.

CHAPTER 3

Assembling the Best Project Team

W hen a team wins a major sports championship, it's generally due to the efforts of the team as a whole, not a single player. As bright and shining as a star may be, other players need to step up and fulfill their roles for a team to win. Likewise for your own project, it is unlikely that there is no need for interactivity and coordination among various aspects of the project. The bottom line: A good, well-organized team gets the job done right.

Your Team's Core Members

At the center of your team are core members, those who were involved in initiating the project and laying out the parameters. Some of these are stakeholders, who will move into active roles in the project. The degree to which initial stakeholders and sponsors get involved in the actual project may vary greatly. Team members will become stakeholders as this becomes their project. Sponsors are very often not involved unless it's their own project—they're paying everyone involved, and they want to do a lot of the work themselves.

There are various levels of involvement by the sponsor. Someone may begin a project by handing you instructions and a budget, and saying, "I'll be back in six months, good luck." You may sit down with upper management and find that although you are project leader, many of the other managers who worked with you in getting this project off the ground are planning to stay involved in various capacities. Your friend who got you to head the community theater's production of *Phantom of the Car Wash* may have initiated the project to raise money for charity, but also plans to stay on as director.

FACTS

With more and more people working off-site via technology and the Internet, there are projects in which the team members never meet. Even in these circumstances communication is vital, and team members usually establish an e-mail relationship with one another.

Sometimes core project team members are found and sometimes they are already attached to the project. The team that works to plan the project is generally a core team, a starting team designed to get things lined up and set goals, objectives, and parameters. Some will continue on to the actual project team, while others won't.

Selecting Your Project Team

Your project team will do the tasks necessary to bring the project to fruition. Unlike professional sports, you won't have the luxury of scouts telling you who the best people are for the jobs. You will have to act as your own scout, seeking out the people who best fit the positions you need to fill. Although you may begin by assessing contractors to help you build that new family room on to your house, you will also need to decide who will paint the room, furnish it, and so on. A task breakdown sheet will help you assign the right people to the right project tasks. This can work in conjunction with your master plan on your work breakdown structure, which is your overall project blueprint including all tasks organized in a hierarchical chart.

Team members come in all shapes and sizes. They may be top professionals or your eight-year-old who is helping you plan that big summer trip to Europe. As long as each one brings something to the project, he or she is a valuable team member. What can your eight-year-old bring that you don't already know? He or she can give you the expectations of Europe through the eyes of a child. Instead of museums and famous landmarks, he or she may be asking about amusement parks or going to the beach. Children look at the world differently, and present ideas that they would enjoy. Rest assured that successful project managers at toy companies have consulted with children at some point.

The right team members:

- Are reliable
- Are trustworthy
- Are available
- Are flexible
- Have something to contribute

- Make an effort to get along with other team members
- Abide by the rules and parameters of the project
- Ask for help when they need it

The wrong team members:

- Show up only when they feel like it
- Are not honest about their skill level
- Must do everything their own way

- Make no effort to work as a team
- Complain frequently
- Think they know everything

It's up to you to carefully pick the right team members for the actual work on the project. You will need to look at your work breakdown structure and determine which positions you want to fill first. For example, if you're planning a wedding, do you hire the caterer or the wedding coordinator first? On some projects you can have several people come on board at the same time, while on others, team members will join at various intervals as their responsibilities dictate.

Assessing Skills

To start building your team, you'll have to assess the skills of each potential team member. Do you need a professional publisher with ten years of publishing experience to put out a newsletter for a small business? Probably not. Should you hire someone who's never catered a party for more than twenty-five people to cater a wedding for 200? Nope. Does someone need to play golf well to run a tournament for your local club? No. Do they need to know something about how a tournament is run? Yes.

ALERT

Project managers seeking team members often have a laundry list of qualifications they're looking for in a person. In fact, only a handful of those qualifications may be necessary to perform the task. Don't make the mistake of searching for Superman when Clark Kent will do!

Besides having a task breakdown sheet of all the tasks that need to be done by each team member, you need to determine how proficient a team member needs to be and how much experience he or she should have to fill a role. It's very important that you don't sell your needs short, but equally important that you don't mistakenly believe that only an expert will do.

If your business depends on building a Web page that will be easy to navigate and can handle a high volume of e-commerce, then your nineteen-year-old nephew may not be your best choice, no matter how skilled he is. On the other hand, to build a small Web site, you need not hire a team known for designing sites for multi-national corporations.

Two very common mistakes that subvert effective teams are:

1. Hiring someone who's underqualified because they are:
    *   Charging less money for their services
    *   A friend, family member, friend of a family member, or someone else for whom you are doing a favor
    *   Available now, and you need someone right away
2. Hiring someone who is overqualified because:
    *   You feel their credentials will impress your stakeholders
    *   You believe that a higher level of expertise is needed when it's really not

You need to look for the right person and have a fairly good estimate of your actual needs. Fill real jobs, not ideal ones.

Assessing talent often relies on an intuitive feeling that the candidate has a keen understanding of what the short-term task and long-term project is all about. Often a resume or background information will tell you only what the person has done; it won't indicate what else he or she could do using past experience and overall knowledge. Try to get a feel for the quality of someone's work. Just because a person has done a certain job over the past ten years doesn't mean he or she has done it well. Again, some people excel and some people just get by.

Following are ten things to keep in mind when choosing your team members:

1. If your expectations are unrealistic, you will waste a great amount of time seeking the perfect person.
2. If you find someone overqualified, he or she may very likely become bored with the project and lose interest along the way.
3. Individuals with general experience in an area are often more valuable to the team than someone who specializes in only one specific task. Generalists can also provide help in other areas. Naturally, if the task requires a specialist, it's worth your efforts to find one.

4. The hot, trendy, young technological genius fresh out of school may know a lot, but does not always have the actual hands-on experience necessary to do the job in the real world. Don't be sold only on the basis of a graduate degree—experience in the workplace is very valuable.

5. Are team members willing participants or are you hoodwinking them into participating by withholding bonuses or threatening to ground them for a week? Willing team members are more valuable than those who have been coerced, threatened, or cajoled.

6. Someone with a high profile may also have a big ego. You don't need a prima donna on your team.

7. Technical or sales skills are great, but can the person get along with others? You need team members with people skills.

8. Seek out people who have worked on similar projects before, even if it was on a lower level or smaller scale.

9. Think in broad terms. A person might not be good for one task but might fit another task perfectly.

10. Find people who are trustworthy and loyal, which isn't always easy. You'll find that it's important that people have some sense of dedication to the project. You don't want them running off mid-project and leaving you high and dry. Look for some sense of commitment.

R-E-S-P-E-C-T

In any project, whether you're working with top level executives or top level family members, you need to have respect for your team and you should expect the same in return. If you treat people in a polite, easygoing manner, you will most often get better results than if you are the stern taskmaster. Following are some tips on how to win respect and influence team members:

- *Listen to everyone's ideas.* If someone offers an idea that will work, thank the person and give credit for his or her input. If an idea isn't suitable for the project, explain why it may not work this time, but how it may be worthwhile in the future. Never be demeaning or condescending.

- *Do not embarrass team members.* If you need to discuss a problem or something that was done incorrectly, do it in a private meeting (see Chapter 4).

Remember that no one is perfect; mistakes and accidents will happen. Your time is better spent learning from the mistake and correcting what you can than delegating blame.

- *Reward team members for a job well done.* Often just saying the words "good job" is a boost for the team's morale—and it costs you nothing.
- *Treat all team members equally.* Showing favoritism will cause dissention within the group.
- *Lead by example, and treat yourself as you would a team member.* If showing up late for the family patio-planning session warrants an extra chore, give yourself an extra chore.
- *Talk to people, not at them.*
- *Be accessible.* When you are not, have an adequate system for getting all messages. If the kids are working on a family project while you are at the office, let them know how they can reach you, and make sure your secretary, assistant, or answering machine is taking all messages.
- *Return all phone calls and e-mails promptly.*
- *Don't gossip!* It can be tempting to talk about other people. But while gossip is not advised at any level, it is certainly not something that should be done by the project leader.

Mutual respect includes understanding that each team member, including you, the leader, has multiple responsibilities. Each team member needs to remember that there are other aspects of the project, and that you may not be able to respond to each request immediately. Team members also need to understand that there is a priority system and that you may have more pressing issues that need your attention.

Where to Find Team Members

On smaller projects, team members are probably all around you. Friends, family, and neighbors may be available to pack boxes when you move. Club members are usually willing to help plan the year-end holiday party or summer blowout. Your sales staff is ready, somewhat willing, and hopefully able to help you complete your store inventory. And with competent direction, your department is going to help you bring your corporate project to fruition.

You may have to move people in and out of a couple of possible jobs until you find the best fit for their talents. If you have three people who are all good at one task and nobody to fill another, you may have to re-evaluate the assignments. Depending on the scope, complexity, or detail of one task, perhaps two people could share one responsibility. When putting together the new company softball team, or the neighborhood little league team, you might have three people who want to play first base and no one who wants to play third. While all of them can handle a groundball or catch a popup without too much trouble, you'll need to determine which, if any, can actually throw the ball accurately. Strong throwing is necessary for a third baseman, so you may need to assess that skill from these three infielders. If none of them can throw accurately, you'll need to find someone else.

Try to determine what "other skills" a person can handle. Someone with multiple skills may be very valuable to your team. When the pianist took ill and couldn't make it to the cocktail reception one project manager had planned, his backup turned out to be the Senior Vice President in charge of sales. The project manager had no idea the executive loved to play the piano and was, in fact, more than happy to take over the role. You'll find plenty of surprises in your initial talent pool. Aside from the qualities and attributes you know about, make an effort to ascertain secondary skills so that you have versatile team members. This will come in handy when you suddenly realize that you need more people on one end of the project, or you need to replace another team member.

If you need a specialized resource, such as a consultant or contractor, you'll probably need to look outside of your immediate circle of friends, family, or co-workers. You, and others on the team, may have to bend a little to accommodate a specialist who may be tightly booked, or has a personality that doesn't lend itself to winning friends and influencing people. One organization often referred people to an attorney who specialized in a very specific aspect of law by saying, "You don't need to like him, but he'll do a good job for you."

SSENTIALS The team/project manager relationship is a give-and-take situation in which both sides need to treat each other as they would like to be treated. The same holds true for the relationships among team members. A team that respects its members will function much more efficiently.

Be creative—think about how you would either promote yourself or find opportunities to be a team member, and do your searching with that in mind. Potential participants for your project can come from a variety of sources, including the following:

- Other departments in the company, or other groups or committees in an association or club
- Networking or word-of-mouth (often the best and most widely used source for smaller projects)
- Newspaper, newsletter, or trade journal articles and advertisements
- Personnel agencies

When borrowing people from other committees or departments, or if neighbors help on an otherwise family-based project, keep in mind that these people may still have other projects that they are working on. Make sure they can afford the time to help you. Despite the best intentions, if he or she is overloaded with other projects, the overall quality of work (and therefore your project) may suffer.

Finding team members through networking is always desirable. You'll avoid advertising and agencies, which will save time and money, and you'll get a recommendation that (hopefully) comes from someone you trust. Sometimes the best way to find additional team members is to ask those who are already on board. If they've worked on similar projects, they may know of other good resources for your project. Keep in mind, however, that even if another team member recommends someone, you should still check that person's qualifications. Sometimes friends and family members have exaggerated opinions of people they recommend.

Someone you know and trust may be ready and willing to become a member of your project team, but that's no indication of whether he or she is *able* to do the job. Be fair to yourself (and to others) and get qualified people for the job.

When finding team members through outside sources, such as advertisements or an agency, you may have to pay top dollar. Make sure you know exactly when to run the ad or call the agency, and when you need to have this person start. Don't hire someone at a high rate for two weeks when they only have three solid days of work to do. You don't want to pay people to sit around, especially someone getting high hourly or daily rates.

Getting It Down on Paper

Not unlike when you post a job in a newspaper or on the Internet, you'll need to provide a job description to team members, particularly for complex tasks. In this case, you'll have to be more specific about the actual tasks and responsibilities of the particular job. It always helps to put it down on paper, whether formally or informally. List what you want the team member to do. The degree of detail will depend on the job and the person expected to perform it, but it's always advantageous to lean toward the side of caution by being more specific. You can always lead in with, "I'm sure you already know most of this, but . . ."

Writing down important details sets clear expectations. On an important or large-scale project, whether it's personal or professional, make sure you have the work agreement in writing. An informal project or a family project can have an informal contract, which simply brings everyone together on the project.

The formality of the agreement should match the significance (not the scope) of the project. A small project (in scope) that may take only a few hours could be critical to your business or your personal investment, and your expectations need to be clearly communicated.

A written job description does the following:

- Helps you find the precise abilities you're looking for
- Ensures that you will remember all the tasks to explain to each team member
- Provides stakeholders with a document detailing what is expected of each team member
- Assists in settling disputes about what work did or did not need to be done

Job descriptions may be part of your work breakdown. For example, if the work breakdown requires computer use, you might note that you need someone proficient in a particular program.

There are various ways to structure your list of team members and tasks. Often it's best to start by listing the tasks, then fill in the team members along with their skills. Keep in mind that as you start working with your team, you may need to reassign tasks and responsibilities. Either use a pencil as you change your records, or create new computer files as your plans are modified.

Following is an example of what your list might look like if your project involved developing a Web site for a home-based business:

Tasks

Applications Development	Phil E.—System integration background
Web Architect	Mike J.—Graphic design background
Layout and Design	Steven F.—Web design & IT consulting experience
Content Editing/Writing	John M.—Journalism experience/Web content
Advertising and Sales	Abigail M.—Former advertising account manager
Marketing	Lauren H.—Former corporate marketing manager

After filling in your first list, you might discover that Steven F. has a better technical background and has worked more closely with Web architecture than Mike J., so you might move Steven F. to Web Architect, and Mike J. to Layout and Design.

Before filling in the personnel for the specific tasks, you might fill out a skills chart like the one that follows. In this chart the candidates are rated, showing their proficiency in that area based on their backgrounds. Next to each person is a number. In some cases the number is in parentheses, which indicates that the person does not have experience but has trained in that area by taking classes or a special training program. Sometimes you'll find someone fresh out of school who has taken top level courses and displays the necessary knowledge to perform the task. You will have to assess the training program as well as talk to the individual to help determine his or her ability to apply the skills to your project. Often it will be necessary to check with other people and outside sources to evaluate someone's background and knowledge. You may, for example, look on the Internet to find out whether a degree from the John Doe Computer Design Institute is worthwhile or if it is a fly-by-night operation.

Skills Chart

The ratings are based on a 1–5 scale, with 5 being excellent and 1 being poor. A dash (—) indicates that the person does not work in that area.

	Mark	Karen	Gladys	Fred
Technical skills	5	—	(2)	—
Layout and design skills	3	3	—	—
Writing skills	—	2	4	—
Sales skills	—	—	—	5

What can we tell from this chart? Mark's experience shows that he clearly excels in the technical areas necessary, but Gladys has enough courses or training under her belt to possibly be of some assistance. Karen or Mark could handle layout and design equally well, but since Mark is needed for the technical end (his top strength) Karen will take on the role of layout and site design. She has a good background in the area but is not an expert. Gladys clearly has the most proficient writing background, but Karen has done some content writing and editing, and can fill in if necessary. Fred is a crackerjack salesperson but lacks the other qualifications necessary for this particular project.

ESSENTIALS

If you expect to manage future projects that will need team members, put together a skills directory. In a skills directory you can build a list of potential individuals, cross-referencing names and skills. The directory will be a great resource for yourself, or for networking purposes.

A skills chart should tell you who does what, how proficient they are at particular tasks, and, in some cases, how much background they have. For example, you might list college or post-graduate degrees next to the names. You can also learn who might be a good candidate for training in a particular area. Consider adding a column for noting what type of supervisory experience someone has in the event that you need to have supervisors.

But Will They Get Along?

When you sit down with all of the project's key players individually, you may not get an accurate assessment of how well they will interact in a team environment. It's easy for someone to tell you he or she is a team player, but you won't find out for sure until the project gets under way. No ballplayer is going to say, "I hog the ball every opportunity I can," although that may turn out to be the case. In the sample team, Fred may not be the ultimate team player, but if his role is more independent on a daily basis, it may not matter. Also, he's the only crackerjack salesperson you've got, so you all may have to deal with a little more "attitude" when he's in the office. While you hope everyone is gracious, people who are harder to replace are sometimes aware of that and can be more demanding. If you don't have other, more suitable resources, accommodate "difficult" personalities unless they threaten to bring down the whole project. (There is more on dealing with difficult personalities in Chapter 10.)

ALERT

Learn which members of your team need to be praised often, who can work contentedly on their own, who needs handholding, and who will be a constant challenge. Keep these assessments to yourself—they should not be shared with other members of the team!

It's very important to try to create an atmosphere in which everyone puts the overall goal ahead of their personal agendas. This, of course, is easier to do if the incentives are high for the team members. Incentives can range from a corporate promotion to a prize or ice cream sundae for your kids for helping on the family project. While it's always important to create a good working environment, it is obviously easier when team members interact less with one another. For example, your technical staff working on site to develop your Web site does not need to work closely with your freelance writers or graphic artists. In this case camaraderie is not as crucial as it is in a project in which you are moving from one office to another and everyone must pull together.

Keep in mind that more team members mean a wider variety of personalities. As project leader you will need to look for the strengths and weaknesses from a personality standpoint. Someone may be a marvelously talented designer, but is quite shy and says very little at the meetings. You may have to gently draw this person into the group dynamic. A salesman might be very outspoken at the meetings and intimidate or even turn off other team members with his or her approach. You'll have to try to channel this individual's enthusiasm into his or her work and limit their participation at the meetings—tactfully, of course.

Occasionally, there will be team members who are recommended or assigned to the project by a third party. Most often, however, we are familiar with the other people on the project—they are selected because of their skills and their personalities. After all, it's hard to separate the two.

Take a look at the following skill/personality assessment matrix. In the same way you build a team with complementary technical skills, you should build a team that will complement each other interactively.

Skills	Personality
5—Expert	5—Gets along well with almost everyone
4—High	4—Strong in a positive sense
3—Average	3—Average, generally agreeable, perhaps mild mannered
2—Below average	2—Strong in a negative sense (grating or condescending)
1—Poor	1—Difficult to get along with

A 5/5 in the two categories might seem perfect, but be realistic. Not only is that combination unlikely, but keep in mind that there can be too much of a good thing. You'll have many 3/4 or 3/3's on your roster as well. A solid cross-section is fine, as long as you have a blend of thinkers, talkers, listeners, and doers.

And what about the extremes? 1/5 (poor skills but great personality) is not desirable unless you need someone to boost morale or bring in new recruits. Some organizations (usually not in business) have a key role for someone who does basically nothing, but gets along well with everyone and puts a smile on people's faces. In reality, then, he or she is actually doing something—although it may not be a defined task—by helping to keep team enthusiasm and motivation up. The other side of the coin is the 5/1, an expert whom you cannot replace even though his conduct is not always beneficial to the team.

Determining Availability

Just because you want someone to work on a project doesn't mean they can do it. You might not be able to get your kids to pitch in on the yard clean-up project when they have final exams. Likewise, your brother-in-law might not be able to help you run the camping trip for your lodge because he's an accountant and it's tax season. In business, people have other work to do and may be part of other projects. While you can't simply delay your project or work around everyone's schedule, you may need to be somewhat flexible if you want certain individuals involved. You'll need to weigh the level of help a person can provide and determine whether it is in your best interest to try to be accommodating or simply get someone else whose schedule is not as tight.

Coordinating Staff

Once you've drawn up your work breakdown structure and listed your personnel on a task breakdown sheet, you'll have an idea of who will be needed at each stage of the project. This may also be flexible. If the flowers for the wedding are ordered a week later than planned, as long as they still arrive on time for the big day, it doesn't matter. On the other hand, if the computer systems are not set up for a week it will throw your entire inventory schedule off. Some things can wait and others cannot. The project comes first, so if you need to replace the person because the task cannot wait, then do so. The more advance planning you can afford yourself, the easier it is to book prospective. people onto your project.

Picking up the Slack

Keep in mind that there are instances when you, as team leader, will have to assume some of the work yourself. On smaller projects with fewer resources and fewer people involved, this should go without saying, particularly if you are the initiator or major stakeholder. After all, if it is your small business, you need to be in their doing some of the work. On larger projects, you may take on a role in the project, but you may also have a full-time job managing the project. If you have more than one project to manage at a time, you most likely won't have time to roll up your sleeves and get involved. Don't over-extend yourself. Don't forget you still have the job of project manager.

Ancillary Roles

Besides doing a particular task on a project, you'll need individuals to take on secondary roles, often involving the overall team. For example, someone handling the money at the school bake sale, by watching the flow of traffic, might be able to give you an assessment of how it might flow more smoothly. Perhaps you need a monitor stationed near the check out-area directing traffic. Other people may serve as critics, giving you their opinion of how a project is running and how it might be improved. While doing their own job, people may see other areas or have ideas about how things can be improved. Someone writing Web content may be able to assess how the overall layout looks or how easy the site is to navigate, since they are also working on it in a different capacity.

FACTS

Full-time, professional project managers working on corporate projects have little time to do anything else besides manage a major project. They generally aren't expected to do much beyond that, since project management is their area of expertise.

Besides having their roles in the project, members may have a team role as well. The first baseman of the ball club may also be co-captain of the team. The same holds true on a project. The person in charge of creating your marketing plan may also be in charge of setting up an after-work get-together to help boost morale. Team jobs may co-exist with project jobs. You will have team members critiquing the project, inspecting the work to make sure it meets the high necessary standards, coming up with new ideas, and helping maintain team spirit. Various team members will do the team jobs in addition to their assigned project tasks.

Who Has the Authority?

Everyone asked Marjorie how many books to order for the school book sale. She gave them the go ahead to order 500. Janet, the head of the PTA and project leader, was a bit taken aback, explaining that the PTA's budget would never afford them more than 250 books. The problem was that everyone involved was under the mistaken assumption that Marjorie had the authority to okay the number of books to be purchased. She didn't.

It is very important that everyone involved in a project understands who has authority to make decisions and who doesn't. It's also important that those with authority document their decisions for discussion and future reference. People who are put in positions of authority need to know how far that authority extends. Being the person in charge of ordering the books does not automatically mean you have the authority to order the computer software as well.

Set the Parameters

Carefully clarify each person's authority—both for the individual and the group. For example, you may allow your brother to order all the wood for the new tool shed you're about to build, but only up to $400. Any spending beyond that, he'll need to discuss with you. If everyone knows who has authority from the start, then people will know whom to turn to when they need something done—they will also know who is making (or approving) decisions that are not within their clarified responsibilities. If everyone knows (or can find out) the parameters, there are fewer opportunities for misinterpreted authority.

Sometimes there are layers of authority. For example, only two people in an association may be authorized to sign checks, the president and the treasurer. However, they may not be the people to authorize the purchase of a new basketball hoop. The sports coordinator may need to give the okay and then talk to the treasurer for funding. Everyone needs to know the chain of command in an organization, group, or company so that they go to the right person to get approval for their needs.

Delegate Responsibly

As project manager you need to know when to delegate authority. You delegate authority to relieve yourself of some of the workload and responsibilities. However, you only want to delegate responsibilities and authority to people who won't abuse it, who are responsible and can handle the decision making process, and who have a clear idea of where the project is going and how to get there.

Anyone who is in a position of authority must maintain that authority only for the good of the project and not for personal gain. Potential abuse of authority and power calls for parameters to be put in place for everyone in authority roles. Set up those parameters and let your team know that abuse of power will result in some manner of "big trouble."

A checks and balances system will often let you know how well people in a position of authority are doing. You might distribute a random, anonymous questionnaire to team members asking them to assess how working with various people has been: good, fair, or poor. If someone in a position of authority is receiving a number of complaints then you need to address the issues with this person. Likewise, if someone in authority is receiving great praise, you need to compliment him or her. Let the person in any leadership or authority position know that he or she may be monitored. Sales representatives working on phone sales calls often inform you that the conversation may be taped for review purposes. This ensures that even though they have been given a position of authority to make sales, they cannot abuse that position by offering you something beyond that which they are selling, making a subsequent deal, or abusing their position in any other manner.

Keep in mind that as project leader you can delegate authority, but ultimately you are still responsible for the work getting done and for the people you have designated as having authority. This means you may have to intercede or get involved in some manner to make sure something gets done. While you don't want to embarrass anyone, there may be situations in which you have to overrule someone else's decisions. Explain why, and that it is not personal, but a matter of doing what is best for the project.

Building Commitment

Getting people to work on a project out of the goodness of their hearts is wonderful in volunteer organizations. The problem that such organizations often run into is that someone doesn't do what she said she would, and because it's a volunteer organization you really have no recourse—you can't fire a volunteer. In such organizations you need to build a good rapport with other volunteers and provide extra pats on the back and praise for a job well done. After all, appreciation is a form of reward.

To ensure that those around you will participate in a personal, family, or neighborhood project, you may need to trade favors or remind people of what's in it for them. In business, participants can move up the ladder, receive raises, or other such perks. Team members have a much better attitude if they know what they can gain, rather than working so as not to get fired or booted out. Sales projects, such as those in the Boy Scouts, Girl Scouts, or schools have rewards for those who have sold the most boxes of cookies or rolls of wrapping paper. Similarly, a shining star on a project team may be selected for a vacated management position. Let team members know that their work can be rewarded.

FACTS

If you put someone in charge of a particular aspect of a project, no matter how big or small, that person is responsible to you. Likewise, you are responsible to whoever put you in charge of the project. Because you are in charge, you cannot blame your team members for things that go wrong. The sponsor is depending on you to complete the job, which includes being responsible for your team.

Once someone has agreed to work on a project, they have either a moral, ethical, or contractual obligation. This is not to say that a crisis may not interfere with their ability to complete their job. There is a level of understanding that needs to be afforded.

Finding the Right Mix

Putting together a project team is like putting together a complicated recipe. You often have to try a few variations before it tastes right. At every level you, as project manager, will need to ensure that you have both skilled individuals and the right blend of personalities. Mixing and matching both skills and personalities takes time and patience. You'll be rewriting or deleting and adding to your plan many times. It's a good idea to run your selections by others who know the individuals you are selecting. How often have you planned the seating chart for a wedding, Bar Mitzvah, anniversary party, or other significant event only to learn from someone else that so-and-so can't sit next to so-and-so because they don't get along? Likewise, others can tell you which team combinations are like oil and water.

Finding the right mix is also made more complicated by the constraints of a budget. You may have to accept someone who is not as talented in one position because you are forced to pay top dollar for someone else. Be careful not to spend too much money paying people who are less vital to the project. You don't want to run into budget problems when looking to hire the key personnel. Often it's best to work your way down, starting with the most significant positions first. Hiring from the top down is an ideal way to stick with your budget, but it rarely ever works. You might spend two weeks looking for a technical manager and lose other great potential team members because they took on other jobs rather than waiting for you.

Following is a summary of the process by which the project team comes together.

1. Define the goals of the project clearly.
2. Divide the project into tasks that need to be done.
3. Define what roles need to be filled to complete each task.
4. Define the attributes the person filling each role needs to bring with him. List the attributes that would make up the "ideal" candidate, then be realistic.
5. Determine who, if anyone, from the "process-initiating team" will move onto the team that does that actual work.
6. Make sure all key stakeholders are kept abreast of the team building process, unless otherwise directed.
7. Scout for team members. Make a list of possibilities. Look both inside and outside the group, office, family, or immediate circle.
8. Set up team rules, regulations, and parameters to which the team will adhere.
9. Review the qualifications of all potential team members.
10. Review the availability of all team members.
11. Discuss compensation and additional resources needed for team members.
12. Review your decisions with anyone who is involved in the decision-making process.
13. Meet team members individually to discuss what is expected of them and when.
14. Select team members and fill in your work breakdown chart.
15. Determine who will have authority.
16. Meet with team members together. Establish team rapport and build team spirit.

This is just the beginning!

CHAPTER 4
Effective Project Leadership

T o be effective as a leader means communicating what it is you want, need, and expect
people to do in such a manner that they
respectfully do the tasks or activities involved. Leading
people can mean directing them to perform specific
new activities or tasks they've done before. Whatever
the case, an effective leader makes people feel good
about themselves and a have sense of pride in the
work they do. Effective leadership also combines technical or subject knowledge with listening and people
skills, and takes some time to master. Organized, qualified, and successful managers will always do well.

Team Huddle

Okay, the team is ready to take the field. Do you have any final words? Knute Rockne became legendary for his pep talks before sending his team onto the football field. As project manager you will need to provide more than pep talks. You'll need to fuel the fire behind the team and then manage the team throughout the ensuing project. This will mean constantly monitoring and keeping track of what everyone is doing without micromanaging. It will mean sticking to a schedule that may need to be altered as you go. It will mean taking time out from your original plans for conflict resolution.

You may find yourself immersed up to your eyeballs in a project, or you may simply manage to squeeze it into your schedule without much difficulty. It all depends on the scope of the project, the team you are working with, and your level of expertise.

Your first responsibilities as project leader are to do as follows:

1. Introduce the project team to one another, or if they are meeting via videoconference or conference call, let others know who is on board.
2. Make sure everyone understands the goals and objectives of the project.
3. Make sure everyone is clear about his or her tasks and responsibilities to the overall project.
4. Establish clear lines of communication.
5. Set basic ground rules.
6. Establish and explain your method of tracking the project, such as status reports and meetings to discuss your progress.

What Kind of Leader Are You?

"Uh-oh, here he comes . . . let's go!" If this is the response you overhear from team members when you approach, there's something wrong with your leadership style. While you don't need to be everyone's pal, you do want the team to feel comfortable around you and seek you out with problems or questions. If you are a leader who is also part of the team, you need to have a sense of camaraderie. If you are busy managing the team and they are doing the actual hands-on work, let them know that you are counting on them and have confidence and faith that they can do the job. Refer to it as "our project," not "my project."

To determine what kind of leader you are, consider which of the following leadership styles best describes you:

- Are you a **taskmaster**? Are you focused solely on production?
- Are you a **people person**? Do you focus on communication between team members and take a consensus to get decisions made?
- Are you **Pavlovian**? Do you believe in behavior modification? If they do the work, will they be rewarded as they go?
- Are you a **micromanager**? Do you look over everyone's shoulder?
- Are you **missing in action**? Do you start and end the project but basically disappear for the duration of the process?

Most likely, you will combine aspects of the first three leadership styles on the list, while trying not to fall into the last two categories. Managing tasks, working well with people, and providing rewards for a job well done are all part of being a good leader. The project and the circumstances surrounding it, however, will dictate your primary style. Don't be surprised if you need to use a little of each approach for different situations. Often project managers, while focusing on the task in hand, will have to deal with difficult personalities and even stroke some egos to encourage particular individuals.

FACTS

To be both a manager and a leader, you need to combine the skills of planning, implementing a schedule, and monitoring progress along with effectively delegating, communicating, and listening to other people. Just as being knowledgeable does not make someone a good teacher, management skills and MBA credits don't automatically make you a good leader.

Be flexible enough to switch gears when necessary. Let the nature of the project, the scope, the time frame, the progress of the project, and the people determine which style of leadership you'll use on which day.

Consider the following scenarios. Each situation requires the project leader to tap into different styles in order to keep the project focused and moving forward. While all leaders will have a preferred style (one that seems most natural to them), the best leaders are able to adapt and use each style when necessary.

- A crisis arises—things are blown way off course! Take control, make unilateral decisions, and get the ship back on course. Be task-oriented.
- Morale is declining—the campers are not happy! Use your people skills, get everyone involved, take a consensus before making a move, ask for people's opinions, make nice until the team is happy again.
- Many questions are left unanswered—the team just doesn't know what to do next! If the problems are in the system, or revolve around aspects of the project itself, then you may need to take a more analytical approach and hunt and gather information and materials. Have your team work together to seek and find what needs to be learned. Turn all attention inward and get the structure of the project back on track and then return to project business as usual.

The Importance of Consistency

A good leader is consistent. From child rearing to dealing with a group of consultants, it's important that you be consistent. If you want something done a certain way on Monday, you want it done the same way on Tuesday, unless new technology or some unexpected events dictate otherwise. The manager who constantly changes how things are done confuses team members.

Likewise, the manager who favors one team member over others causes dissention in the ranks. The way in which you conduct yourself, your decision making, and your level of respect for your team should remain consistent. This way, people come to know what to expect of you and what you expect of them. A Jekyll and Hyde personality can hurt team morale if they don't know who they'll find sitting in your chair when you swivel around to talk with them.

ESSENTIALS   Parents may reprimand their children one minute and hug them the next, but they still consistently love them. You will consistently be there for your team, whether you have to get tough with them or have the time to talk casually and be a "people person."

Consistency does not mean inflexibility, however. Changing your style of leadership to fit a particular situation is part of the project management process. If you are used to making unilateral decisions but this aspect of the project requires a consensus, then you will have to change your approach. The same is true for becoming more task-oriented when necessary. Consistency means reacting in the same manner each time a situation arises. For example, every time the project is close to falling behind you will switch to a more task-oriented approach. You will still remain the lovable leader, but you'll have to be more focused on everyone just buckling down and focusing on their work.

First-Rate Teams

Some people manage projects and some project managers manage people. The work needs to be done, but unless your project is comprised completely of automated technology or robots, you will have to deal effectively with people. The modern employee is empowered. He or she is no longer subservient or unaware of his or her rights. But it goes beyond empowerment. The workplace is full of knowledgeable individuals who are well versed in their fields and in the companies that employ them.

Outside of the workplace, you can find people who excel in any one of numerous areas. From party planners to highly skilled contractors, there are top people available to meet any project need. And, when there are not, the training materials available on the Internet, in adult learning environments, and in books will make team members experts by the time a project is completed.

A L E R T

As the leader, you need to stay on top of the project. You should know the project inside and out—after all, you don't want your educated team members showing you up. This isn't to say you must have the skills to handle every task, but that the big picture is very clear in your mind.

Besides knowledge, you need to lead by example, which means displaying confidence. The team will follow your lead. If you are tense about getting the project finished and complain about the project, your team will pick up on your uneasiness and uncertainty, and morale will be affected. If you have serious doubts about a project, your team will also have doubts. If you exude confidence, they too will exude confidence. You shouldn't tell them everything is going well when it's not. However, it does not help to worry team members with situations that are out of their control. If other means are necessary to solve problems in one area of the project, then you will address that specific area with those involved, not have everyone needlessly concerned.

Your demeanor throughout the project is very important. You cannot wear your problems on your sleeve. Keep outside issues and project issues in their perspective places. For example, when a project meeting is called, it is to talk about the status of the project, not to whine because you weren't made VP of sales.

FACTS

Any project has both internal and external concerns. The external concerns may include how the project is shaping up and whether there are problems relating to the project's place in the real world. Internal problems can be late status reports or incompatible software. Often the internal problems will affect the external results.

Following are ten tips, besides having a confident attitude, for becoming a successful project manager:

1. Listen when others talk
2. Do your homework and be well versed on the project
3. Manage people, not just projects
4. Be ready to manage in various situations (be flexible)
5. Delegate work to others
6. Give people latitude to do their work (don't micromanage)
7. Get the opinions of others
8. Monitor work closely (take good notes)
9. Keep all stakeholders apprised of your progress
10. Know when you need to ask for help—don't try to be a know-it-all

Communication

You own a small landscaping business and have a small office. You and your staff of four people are creating a new brochure to be ready by the end of the month. Each person has his role in the project. You can literally see each person from where your desk is situated, and they can see you. You all get along fine, yet in the course of the day, you rarely ever speak to any of them. Communication on the project, however, seems to be okay. How is this possible?

Electronic mail (e-mail for short), of course. Although e-mail is a marvelous way of communicating almost instantly with people around the corner and around the world, it shouldn't be the preferred method of communication between two people sitting ten feet apart . . . at least not all of the time. Many individuals have simply gotten lazy and send e-mails to each other instead of actually talking. On a project (or in daily work for that matter) it's important to talk to one another. Human interaction helps maintain the bond of the project team. As a leader you may want to send information that needs to reach twenty-five people via e-mail—it's certainly easier than walking from desk to desk—but it does the team morale a disservice if you replace all face-to-face communication with e-mail.

Don't constantly bombard your team with irrelevant information. Limit what you communicate to data that is significant to the project and team members. Otherwise your team will have to sift through extraneous materials to find the important communications—and they may lose them in the constant barrage of e-mails.

ALERT

An effective leader leads all people equally. Be respectful of people's cultural differences and religious beliefs. Don't tolerate any sexist, racist, off-color, or offensive language, comments, or jokes from any team members. Remind team members that they need to be respectful of one another in any group environment.

When communicating with your project team, be confident, positive, and take the high road. If you believe that your project will be a success, let that come across in your tone, manner, and even your e-mails. Other communication tips include the following:

- Make eye contact with team members.
- Ask someone you trust to provide you with honest feedback on how the team perceives you and your management style.
- Don't do all the talking—listen as well.
- Be visible. Walk around the office, the warehouse, the gymnasium . . . wherever your project is taking place. Let team members see you, and stop to talk with them occasionally.
- Limit tangential conversations. However, since you are dealing with human beings, there might be an occasional brief off-project conversation. It's important to team morale to be able to discuss other things on occasion.
- Remember that people are entitled to their opinions, even if they differ from yours.
- Don't let your body language speak louder than your voice. Unfold your arms, stop shaking your head in disagreement, don't roll your eyes, stop sighing, stop fidgeting, and sit up straight. Proper body language is more important than most people realize. Be aware of what your body is saying.

Meetings

Meetings can bring people together for the common good of the project. They serve as a place for you to update everyone on new project news and make sure that previous issues have been dealt with. You'll want to meet with your team often, but not too often. Meet with everyone involved and with smaller sub-groups. Meet with individuals one-on-one. Meet formally and informally. Mix it up if possible so meetings don't become monotonous times for team members to get some shut-eye.

It's not advantageous to meet so frequently that you are disrupting the team's ability to get something accomplished. However, you need to keep everyone abreast of how the overall project is going and get feedback. Team members will see things that you don't notice and point them out to you. Elicit opinions and suggestions from everyone. Remind the team of the project's goals and see how far you have gone toward reaching them.

It is important to meet at the beginning of the project so that everyone on the project gets an idea of whom they are working with, and everyone is reminded of the project's goals. You might hold two or three meetings early on just to make sure everyone has started off in the same direction. It's better to nip any initial problems in the bud. However, don't meet regularly just for the sake of meeting.

Effective Meetings

If people are eager to attend meetings to express themselves and hear what you and others have to say, you are doing a good job at managing the team. If people dread yet *another* meeting, it's time to brush up on your meeting skills. Here are some pointers on holding effective meetings:

- Meet when everyone is fresh—earlier in the day is usually better than later.
- Only call impromptu or emergency meetings if there is a crisis or a need to immediately change plans.
- Make sure everyone is comfortable—serve coffee or snacks, make sure there are enough seats, have the heat or air conditioning on accordingly, limit outside distractions, etc.

- Distribute a meeting agenda before the meeting. Keep it brief. Prepare it a day or two in advance then go back and edit, so key points to be discussed are included.
- Make sure everyone is familiar with all those in attendance—introduce newcomers.
- Maintain order. You will need some basic guidelines with which the group should be familiar.
- Assign someone to take notes at the meeting. These can be typed up and distributed to members later.
- Focus on issues that involve either everyone present or the overall project. Hold one-on-one meetings to discuss problems that affect individuals.

ALERT

Invite only the necessary players to each meeting. Hold one-on-one meetings if necessary, but don't waste team members' valuable time by asking them to attend meetings that don't affect them.

- Don't overload people with papers. Only hand out condensed, significant information. Don't photocopy twenty-five articles and other papers that will result in people reading during the meeting.
- Interject humor where appropriate. Levity can lighten the tone of most meetings and keep people feeling good. Keep all jokes in good taste— think about potential repercussions before telling the joke about the rabbi, the priest, and the door-to-door salesman.
- Try not to cancel meetings or reschedule them unless it's absolutely necessary.
- Check all cell phones and pagers at the door, or at least ask everyone to turn them off.
- Never embarrass anyone at a meeting—criticize ideas, not individuals.
- Maintain a pace. Don't let the meeting get bogged down over one detail. If someone goes off on a tangent, nudge him back to the agenda. If an issue remains unresolved but you have to move on, make it an item for your next meeting.

- Be respectful and don't interrupt others. In turn, they should afford you and other team members the same respect.
- Have a set time when the meeting should end and stick to it. Short meetings are better than those that drag on.
- Change the scenery once in a while. Meet somewhere else after the first several meetings. Perhaps treat everyone to lunch.

Off-site Participants

Modern technology has made it quite easy to meet via conference call or through other high-tech methods. If you've been called to Zurich because of work, you may not have a choice but to be on speakerphone when your lodge brothers are working on the nominations for next year. However, if you can meet someone face to face, it's always advised—use high-tech alternatives only when there is no way to meet in person.

SSENTIALS

Ask broad, open-ended questions to encourage everyone to offer feedback on the project: "How might we improve our method of communication on this project?" "What type of feedback are you getting from our clients?" "Is anyone having any technical problems they want to discuss?"

Individual Meetings

One-on-one meetings are very important in any project. They allow you, as project leader, to communicate clearly what you feel the person needs to do. They also allow you to communicate why you chose this individual and what you hope can be accomplished. They allow the individual to ask questions and present any issues that need to be resolved.

In business, individual meetings may be regularly scheduled or scheduled when there is a need to address particular issues, such as performance issues. You might have an open-door policy in which team members can talk to you when necessary. In the case of large projects, you might establish a system in which team members can e-mail you and let you know that they would like to schedule a meeting. You can also have informal meetings on a one-to-one basis if the situation presents itself.

In family or neighborhood projects, you might call such meetings on a more spontaneous basis. Either way, you want to make sure all is well from a project and a personal standpoint. One-on-ones open the lines of communication and give people a chance to discuss the goals of the project on a broad level or evaluate project specifics. For people who are uncomfortable speaking at a larger meeting or feel what they have to say would be inappropriate at a team member meeting, this may be the place where they can best open up and communicate their thoughts, concerns, or ideas.

Along with the first team meeting, the first individual meeting can set the tone for how you and the team member will communicate throughout the project. Don't forget to listen well and even take notes.

You should also encourage individual groups within the project to meet. For example, the entire conference committee for a nonprofit group held meetings for everyone involved in organizing and running the upcoming conference. Subsequently, the membership, planning, programming, and hospitality committees each held individual meetings to discuss their distinct roles in the overall project.

Can Everybody Hear Me?

An often-overlooked detail by project managers is preparing to address the troops. Meetings require planning. It's important that you prepare yourself ahead of time with notes and an agenda to distribute to everyone. This way you will cover all of your key points and avoid rambling on and on. Too often people are ill prepared and end up on an endless stream of consciousness, sometimes only getting to the point by chance. This is a great way to lose your audience.

CHAPTER 5
The All-Important Budget

Money. It may be the root of all evil, but it's also the backbone of nearly all projects. In an ideal world, we'd start a project with a series of blank checks, and whatever we spent would be just fine. But unless you've got a billionaire funding your project, you've got to keep tabs on where your project is in relation to your budget at all times. The majority of projects begin on a "tight" budget, yet your "soda pop" allowance will often have to accommodate someone's champagne tastes. You might be able to handle that if you keep one eye on the budget throughout your project.

Ready, Set, Budget

In many corporate projects, you are essentially told what your budget will be without participating in the process. However, when starting a personal project or a project in your own business, you have to put together your own budget. You can use software and other technology as a guide, but you'll still be responsible for the actual money behind the numbers. It will still be your call as to exactly how much you can set aside for this project.

Budget building requires certain skills, including being very well organized and meticulous in your planning. Putting together a budget for a month-long family trip to Aruba or a budget for building a new warehouse for your business means breaking down the project into each component and determining the cost. It is a demanding process in which you need to visualize the way each task is to be completed. If, for example, your project is to plan a fiftieth anniversary party for your aunt and uncle, you'll need to start out at the beginning and think your way through all the details. Ask yourself questions as you proceed:

- How many people will attend?
- How much will you spend on invitations and postage?
- How much will the facility cost?
- Is catering included? If not, how much more will it cost?
- How much will decorations cost?

- How much will you need to spend on entertainment?
- Will you need to pay hotel costs for out-of-town guests?
- How much will you spend in transportation for guests? For the happy couple?

The list will continue through all of the details with an approximate amount based on research and acquiring cost estimates.

Often the budget builds as you answer these questions. Using the previous example, once you determine how many guests will attend, you can determine how many invitations you will need. Of course, a party for twenty will cost less in each area (invitations, food, etc.) then a party for 200. You'll find that the different elements of your project, scope, and budget will drive each other.

The need to combine resources with manpower is essential in putting together a budget. If you're leasing or renting equipment, you'll need someone to operate it. You don't want equipment sitting around unused. Likewise, you don't want people on the clock for an eight-hour day if the equipment is only available for three hours. Coordinating resources and manpower takes careful planning. Make sure they go hand in hand.

It's also important that you have enough work to keep full-timers working full-time. If you're hiring someone for a thirty-five-hour workweek (and paying them a weekly rate), you'll be spending extra money if you only have twenty-two hours of work for them to do. You might hire someone on an hourly basis instead. However, if you are paying this individual $2,000 for the week and the rate of $100 per hour would put you at $2,200, you would actually be saving money with the weekly rate, even if the person isn't busy all the time. If you have this person on your payroll, he or she could be doing another task during those extra hours.

QUESTIONS?

What are the elements of a budget?
Similar to resources, budget elements are the people, materials, and tools (along with anything else) necessary to complete a project. They are the individual aspects of the budget to which money will be allocated. The anticipated project cost at the start of a project is known as the budget cost.

Use either/or scenarios to determine which is the most cost-efficient way to run your project. Often a place will rent equipment thinking that they will only need it for a short time so they will be saving money. In the end, they need the equipment for a longer time frame and end up spending more money than they would have if they had purchased the equipment. Therefore, it's important to judge your needs in terms of equipment and time frame. No, you need not buy a forklift (which you'll probably never use again) for a two-week job, but if you buy a computer for a two-week job, you'll probably use it on your next project and the one after that. Keep in mind the practicality of buying versus renting for long-term usage.

It's also very important that you know the going rate for consultants, experts, or any specialists you may require. If the going rate is $75 per hour and you have found an expert looking for $175 per hour, guess who you shouldn't be hiring? But while you want to keep costs down, keep in mind that if this expert is the only one available, you may need to pay the higher rate, and factor it into your budget.

Don't sell your project short by hiring inexperienced personnel for low pay. More often than not, you will be left with substandard work.

Let's say you're building a patio. For this project, you might estimate spending $2,500 on wood for the patio plus $75 an hour for the contractor for ten hours, assuming this is the estimated time he assumes he needs to do his part of the job. This would give you $3,250 in the budget for the patio ($2,500 + $750). Add to that $500 for paint, assuming you'll do the painting yourself (which saves you money), and $300 for additional supplies including screws and tools. This gives you a budget of $4,050. Tack on an additional two hours for the contractor, in case he underestimated his time, and you'll be at $4,200. If you know you have $4,500 in available funds, you could put aside the remaining $300 for miscellaneous expenses—all those extra items that come to mind after you've put your budget on paper. Try to think of everything up front so you don't need to dip into those miscellaneous funds too often. In business, the extra funds, or a small portion of the budget, becomes "petty cash," which usually disappears quickly.

When determining the cost of anything from renting office space to planning a catered meal, have an estimate of the size or quantity you'll need. Don't rent an office space for twenty if you only have five and aren't expanding. Similarly, don't plan a buffet for fifty when you've only invited twenty-five. The size of the party, office, room, or any other space you will be renting or buying is a factor in estimating the cost. The more accurate your estimate, the less money you'll waste on too much space, or too much food. Track RSVPs or confirmations as they come in to be sure your estimates stay realistic.

Another important aspect of putting together a budget is research. After all, how are you expected to know the costs of all materials and rates for services rendered unless you do your homework? You'll need to check with associations, network with professionals in the field, review similar project budgets, use the Internet or the library, and ask whomever you know what the going rates are for resources, especially when it comes to hourly, daily, or weekly pay rates.

FACTS

When starting a project, you might decide to buy a copier to use for the project. The copier, purchased for your project, is considered a *direct cost*. If, however, you lease a copier for general office use, your budget would include a percentage of the overall cost based upon your use of the copier for the project. A cost not directly applied to a project (or function) is an *indirect cost*. It's to your advantage to utilize resources for multiple purposes and multiple projects.

You may get significantly different quotes from vendors. There must be a reason. Before you jump at what seems to be a bargain, make sure you aren't missing some important information. Are you getting an authentic reproduction of what you believe to be an original? Is the material substandard? Poor quality? Illegal? Remember, a deal that sounds too good to be true probably is.

Affecting the Bottom Line

As much as budgets are one aspect of the project you're managing, they are also a project in their own right. You must have time to plan and research, you need documentation, and you have to identify your resources—which may include either a financial planner or a small loan.

Time

Time plays a key role in your budget in two ways. First, you need adequate time to cover all your bases when preparing the budget. This can be very difficult if someone wants it done yesterday. If you're under great pressure, overestimate the major areas so you'll have some money in reserve when details in those key areas rear their ugly heads. For example, if you're installing a new computer system, you may budget for overtime and incentives under staffing costs. If you're not familiar with the new system, or who you will assemble as your team, it would be a good idea to factor in the cost of a specialist as well. If you don't need a specialist, then the worst thing is that you've come in under budget. The more time you have to prepare your budget, the more carefully you can examine all of the details.

Time is also a factor when planning your budget. How much time do you have to complete the project? A project on a short schedule may not afford you the luxury of lower costs. A printer, for example, might be able to have your programs for opening night ready in six weeks for $600. However, you only planned to do this show three weeks ago . . . hence you'll need the programs in two weeks. This will be a "rush job" and will cost you $900. A shorter project time frame usually means higher costs. Whenever possible, try to plan far enough in advance to avoid paying higher rates or "rush charges" when something is needed in a major hurry.

Expertise

The need for experts will also affect your budget. No, you probably won't need a professional wedding planner to plan a wedding unless you don't have enough time or are anticipating an unusually lavish affair. Most often, family members plan the wedding and either the bride and groom or their parents become the project managers by default. On the other hand, you may need to hire an aeronautical engineer before you can proceed with your project to reroute a runway at the international airport. There are many levels in between these two scenarios that will require you to bring in someone familiar with the task at hand. Factor in more money for experts, knowing that in the end the job will be done right. Make sure you get a firm estimate of how much the expert charges and how long he or she will be needed on the project. Also, make sure experts communicate in language that everyone else on the team can understand.

Supplies (Resources)

Supplies are another key factor in your budget. Make sure you know exactly what you need to buy or rent before you start. Make a mental picture of whatever it is that you are building, moving, planning, or creating, and determine what you'll need as you proceed through the project. Often, when doing projects at home or with friends, family, neighbors, or in the community, team members bring in or donate the majority of your supplies. If your neighbor already has a ratchet set, and he's helping you build the tool shed, borrow his if you can. Always make sure you know what you're getting. "Oh, you meant can I bring you a Mac computer . . . I thought you wanted a Big Mac," said the neighbor with lunch in hand. "I don't have one of those."

ESSENTIALS   Try to "pad" the budget by 5, 10, or even 15 percent to allow for extra cash for supplies. When things break (and they will) or you're running short on an item (and you will), you'll still have some money left to cover unplanned expenditures.

While you probably won't count every paperclip (unless the sponsor has you on a very tight leash budget-wise) you'll need to maintain a firm grasp on where supplies are going and what they are being used for. Look for places where you can double up. For example, if someone needs to work on a computer for only one hour a day, let them use someone else's computer while that individual is at lunch. It's not cost-effective for this person to have his or her own computer.

Also be aware of availability in an office situation. Just because no one has used those three offices on the third floor in six months, it doesn't mean they will be available next week. You may need to rent office space. Make sure you cover all bases and double-check all availability when renting, borrowing, or using existing materials.

Here are some other budget tips:

1. Include everything you can think of that might cost you or your sponsor money—from nuts and bolts to a city permit to importing the fake snow for the Christmas pageant.
2. Research rates and prices carefully. Get quotes. Find out what the quote does and does not include.

3. Look for places where you can beg or borrow (but not steal) supplies or materials.
4. Determine how much more contingency plans will cost you. Will moving the wedding indoors cost $2,000 more then having the outdoor affair you are planning? Are you prepared for that expense?

Let the Budget Work for You

Your first draft of the budget isn't your final project budget. You'll need several revisions before you complete your detailed budget. The budget can then help you in several important ways. First of all, you can use the budget to determine if the cost of completing the project will outweigh the benefits. If it costs more to complete the project than you stand to gain from it, perhaps it's time to stop before you start. In whichever way you are measuring the benefits, whether it's short-term increased sales, improved morale, stress reduction, or long-term increased property value, the budget gives you one side (in black and white) of your pro and con sheet for doing the project.

If you are not financing the project yourself, make sure you get the budget approved by whomever is putting up the funding. Get the first completed budget approved as well as any revisions that need to be made as you proceed.

The budget also lets the sponsor determine from a financial perspective whether outside assistance is necessary to finance the project. The budget keeps the flow of funds going into what is most necessary for the project's success. And finally, you can look at the budget as one way of monitoring the progress of the project.

Once the project gets started, the budget will be a key factor in determining how well the project is going. Too many projects go over budget and are axed for that reason. Get a good grasp of the budgetary needs before you begin.

Let's look at a sample project of creating a guidebook for tourists visiting the local museum. The curator has hired you to manage this project, which entails putting together a small printed book with photos to sell at the museum gift shop. He wants the guidebook to capture the key exhibits of the museum and would like it to be ready in three months, before the spring tourist season begins. You ask him how many he wants to print but he is not yet sure. You ask him if he wants you to work on site or off. He doesn't have any office space available, so you'll have to use your own office, which you already have.

You look through the museum and estimate how much needs to be written to get about forty pages. You take note of approximately thirty ideas for photographs.

You contact printers and get estimates of how much it would cost to do a forty-page book with color photos, and one with black and white photos. You get estimates of how much it would cost to print 5,000, 2,000, or 500 copies. You discuss possible turnaround times. You also get price quotes for an illustrator (in case you use one for the cover), a writer, an editor, a graphic designer, and a photographer. You get an estimate of how long it would take each of them to perform their tasks.

You return to the curator with what you have found. He decides that 2,000 copies would be sufficient, judging by the last tourist season attendance figures, and that a forty-page book would be fine.

Next you draw up a rough budget based on your findings:

Sample Project Budget

Expense	Cost
Writer ($40 per hour x 60 hours)	$2,400
Photographer ($50 per hour x 8 hours)	$400
Photographer expenses (travel, film, etc.)	$100
Editor ($25 per hour x 10 hours)	$250
Layout and graphics	$400
Cover design and illustration	$250
Printing (2,000 at .90 each)	$1,800
Indirect cost to use your office/computer	$1,000 (% of rent + computer usage)
Travel (to and from museum/printer, etc.)	$50
Miscellaneous	$350
Total project costs	$7,000

The museum could have 2,000 guidebooks available for the tourist season for $7,000, or $3.50 each. If the museum sells them at $7.00 each, they will make a 100 percent profit, or $7,000 for the museum. If the curator sees this as a cost-effective project that will have a benefit to the museum, then he or she will give you the go ahead.

QUESTIONS?

What is the difference between budgeting from the bottom up or from the top down?
If you start with an overall estimate for the project and then allocate funding to various areas of the project or to lower-level managers, you are budgeting from the top down. However, if you start with team members and the tasks they do and work your way up to the total budget by adding the sum of the parts as you go, you are budgeting from the bottom up.

And the Project Goes On

As the project continues, the budget will change. You'll find yourself needing $500 less for flowers and $500 more for centerpieces, or the contractor will need $1,000 more to finish the job. You'll need to move the numbers around accordingly. Of course, the problem arises when there are no numbers to move! (We'll talk about juggling in the next section.)

The other situation that you will need to pay close attention to is the schedule with regard to the budget. Allocating $10,000 to a project that needs to be completed in two months doesn't necessarily mean you need to spend $5,000 each month. You may have greater start-up costs and find you'll spend $7,000 the first month and only $3,000 in the second month. However, if you've spent $9,000 in the first month, you'll be in trouble in month number two.

A budget need not be evenly distributed across your schedule. You do, however, need to know if you're falling behind whatever pace you have set for yourself. Set up a system by which you will monitor your budget as the project proceeds. It's important to subtract money as it's spent, but it's also important to keep track of expenses that have been agreed upon, but not yet paid. If, for example, you've ordered the supplies for the new office but have not paid the bill for the supplies, you would have to make a note that your $10,000 budget to move the office is now down by $3,000 for new supplies, or at $7,000 remaining in actual funds. Chances are, a lot of that $7,000 is earmarked as well. It's similar to balancing your checkbook. There are checks that have cleared your account and outstanding checks that you have just written.

Making sure that everyone involved in the project fills you in on all financial commitments is just as important as tracking actual expenses. Have team members keep written records of their expenses and any vendors or outside sources who are still to be paid. Get photocopies of signed agreements or contracts. Make sure each person on the team is aware of his or her budgetary limitations. When a team member is buying materials, you need to set a maximum amount that he or she can spend. Likewise, you can set maximums for what can be spent on consultants' fees or other hiring costs. Make sure it is clear that this is all that is in the budget before the individual begins the work. Make it clear that you, or whoever is paying the bills, will not pay more than the maximum. This may also mean having people record their time.

ESSENTIALS

It's easy to maintain control over the budget if you limit the number of people who can spend money or make financial promises or agreements. Make sure anyone operating under a budget understands the ramifications of spending more than their budget allows.

Depending on your relationship with the team members and the nature of the project, you may have a system worked out that allows each team member x dollars with which to handle their tasks. They are expected to stay at or below that total. On the other hand, you may have a centralized budget and each person may need to get an okay from you, the treasurer, or whoever is keeping track of the budget, before making any financial commitment.

When working on a conference, the chairperson of the speakers' committee promised several out-of-town guest speakers that the organization would pay their travel expenses. His budget was only $3,000. After making this promise to several people, he was asked to provide an estimate for those travel expenses. He researched the airfares and it came to $8,000. He had therefore made promises that would cost $5,000 over his budget. He had two choices: either call back some speakers and rescind his promise (at great embarrassment to the organization), or help locate $5,000 in another part of the budget. Ultimately the $5,000 was found elsewhere. What this committee chair should have done was added up the costs as he went along and stopped at $3,000, or asked if there was additional money in the budget before making the promises.

A Juggling Act

Juggling the budget is essentially taking from line "A" to pay for items on line "B." The problem with this is that while you may still have the money sitting there on line "A," it is most likely earmarked for another significant part of the project. Otherwise, why would you have budgeted money on line "A" in the first place?

ALERT

Monitor your project closely. Try to foresee any and all reasons to change your budget ahead of time so that you are ahead of the budget and it's not ahead of you!

Essentially, the only way to avoid getting into budget trouble is to plan your budget very carefully and stick to it throughout the project. If you need to juggle, you'll need to take money away from the lowest priority area of the project and place it into a higher priority area. That may mean you'll have fewer new lounge chairs on the new pool deck, but at least you'll be able to pay the contractor to finish building the deck!

Inevitably, there will be decisions that need to be addressed throughout the life of the project. Unforeseen circumstances may mean spending extra money. For this reason, it's wise to look for one area of the project where you can cut costs early on. This may give you a place to turn when such emergency funds are needed. Look at the lowest priority items first and consider them your "luxury" items, those that will be there if the budget allows and nothing unforeseen takes the money. Perhaps you want a hotel suite on your trip to Paris. You may have to settle for a more standard room if you're stuck paying a speeding ticket because you were late leaving for the airport. Expect the unexpected and be glad if you can afford any luxuries in your budget.

Budget Busters

Budgets go off-course for various reasons. Don't tuck away the budget and say, "We'll look at it when we're done and see how well we did." To avoid blowing your budget, you need to pay careful attention to all the details. Among the leading causes of such monetary mishaps are as follows:

- Inadequate budget estimations (underestimating costs)
- Lack of properly researching pay rates and resource costs
- Basing costs on old price structures
- Failure to include all significant details
- Poor communications with team members about their responsibility to stay within the budget
- Failure to properly document expenditures
- Not properly addressing emergencies and other changes as they occur throughout the project and impact your budget
- Falling behind on your schedule and needing to spend more to meet last-minute deadlines

These budget busters can be avoided, but others cannot. For example, technical glitches can turn into nightmares that can wreak havoc with your budget, or materials you ordered may be delayed. Consultants and experts may also need to put in more hours on the project to overcome potential pitfalls. Whatever the reason, many well-intentioned projects have been scrapped or run into the ground because of budgeting disasters. Look at

New York City's long-anticipated Second Avenue subway. Every city has its share of projects that simply didn't have the budget to either get started or completed. Many companies and new businesses run into similar problems trying to introduce new products or ideas. Sometimes the project is delayed and sometimes it comes to an abrupt halt.

FACTS

There's nothing wrong with letting the budget do what it's intended to do—set boundaries. If funds were unlimited, you'd love new uniforms or a fancy restaurant reception, but they're not. Let the budget say no for you: "I'd love to have custom-made uniforms, but it's just not in the budget." "I think the cocktail reception would be great at a restaurant, but the budget limits us to the hospitality suite here at the hotel . . . my hands are tied."

Even personal projects may be scrapped because the money is no longer there. For example, you may have planned and budgeted to make home repairs as your fall project, only to find you needed to spend the money to repair the car after an accident.

Remember, the budget needs to be carefully planned, reviewed, and monitored throughout any project. Expect that there will be changes. Make sure you work with a system that you are comfortable using. Don't work on a software program that you are don't know, and if you prefer to use a notebook or any other manner of maintaining the budget, that's fine, too. You want to avoid making errors on your budget simply because you couldn't figure out the calculations on the program or on the page. Spreadsheets, software or actual, are just that—places where you can spread numbers out. Do it.

Also, keep a separate budget for the project. If you incorporate it into another budget or use the budget for other things, you will only confuse yourself and jeopardize the project. You can always set up a separate project account for your personal or small business projects.

CHAPTER 6

Creating the Schedule

W hether you call it a roadmap, outline, or blueprint, you'll need a plan of action to get your project from the drawing board to completion. Your schedule is critical for the success of the project. Most often, on medium to larger projects, you will have a combination of graphs, charts, and diagrams laying out the tasks to be performed and their time frames. You will want to be able to view tasks relative to each other, to the allotted project time, and to the budget. Maintain graphs and charts to measure progress, and as tools for reporting back to your team and other stakeholders.

In the Beginning

The schedule should provide a variety of ways of measuring success as you monitor your project. You will start off with your baseline, which will be your initial project schedule for a specific time. This baseline schedule remains fixed and is used for comparison against your current project schedule. Baseline dates are, therefore, the initial dates for starting and finishing a task. These will be used with your current schedule for comparison purposes to see if tasks are being performed on schedule. This can also be used to calculate where your project costs are in conjunction with the budget.

As you plan your schedule there will be several key dates, including your project start date, the start dates of individual tasks, and the completion dates of the tasks and the project. You will see as you build your schedule that there will be some variance regarding when you can start and finish specific activities. You will have designated start and finish dates as well as earliest feasible start dates, which mark the earliest date on which the activity could be scheduled to start based on the scheduled dates of all its predecessors (other activities that need be completed first). This date is also calculated by resource scheduling, meaning that the date cannot be set if resources have not been purchased or set up for this activity. You'll also find an earliest finish date lurking on the other end of the activity. This date is based on the calculated start date.

The Network Diagram

A network diagram is essentially a flow chart that includes all of the project elements and how they relate to one another. It is widely used because it is easy to read and depicts not only the sequence of activities in the project, but shows parallel activities and the links between each activity. Network logic is the collection of activity dependencies that make up a network diagram for a particular project. In other words, certain tasks are dependent on one another to complete the project. This creates a logical stream of events that will lead to completion of the project.

You'll need to analyze, organize, and put into sequence the activities that need to be completed. You'll also need to carefully determine how long it should take to complete each task and in what order they will be performed. Setting up dependencies, or tasks that depend on the previous one being performed, will be vital to a smooth flowing schedule. Setting deliverable dates—when tasks need to be completed or products delivered—will also be part of the equation.

Lining Up the Pieces

Even when doing a smaller personal project, it's important to have a schedule. You may be able to get by with a "To Do" list when planning a vacation or a party, but there is still a need to organize and prioritize. For example, you can't plan a trip to France without a passport for each family member. Because of the length of time it takes to receive a passport, this will need to be a high priority item, scheduled early on in the sequence of events leading up to your trip. No matter what the project, the sequence of events is significant to completing the project.

FACTS

A good project manager wears many hats. Identifying stakeholders and defining their roles, clarifying project objectives and goals, doing plenty of research, assessing skills, putting the team together, promoting effective communication between team members (and everyone else), monitoring the project, and about ninety-nine other tasks fall under your jurisdiction.

Determining dual tasks is also important. If a project has fifty tasks that would each take a week to complete, your initial estimate might be that the project would take one year to complete. However, if five tasks could be completed simultaneously every week, you'd have the project finished in ten weeks. Therefore, you need to carefully determine which tasks can be done simultaneously.

Refer to this diagram as you read through the chapter. As a visual and organizational aid, the diagram will help you plan and track dependancies and concurrent tasks.

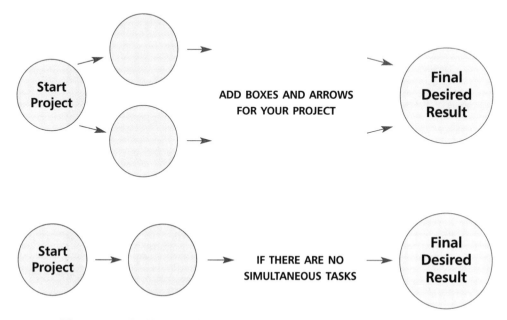

The network diagram lets you do the following:

- Define the project's path
- Determine the sequence of tasks to be completed
- Look at the relationship between activities
- Determine the dependencies
- Set up simultaneous tasks
- Monitor your project by establishing benchmarks, milestones, or deliverables—these are markers to determine whether your project is on, ahead of, or behind schedule
- Make adjustments as tasks are completed
- Take a broad look at the project path and clearly see the relationships and dependencies between tasks

There are complicated network diagrams and simple ones that you can figure out at a glance. The ease with which you can follow the network diagram depends on how complex the project is and how well you have defined everything that appears on it. You can use one color to indicate the tasks that can be completed simultaneously and another color to highlight tasks that are dependencies, or dependent on the completion of a prior task.

FACTS

Elapsed time or duration is how much real time is needed to complete an activity. A consultant may estimate he'll need twelve hours to do a task, but he probably won't work twelve hours straight. If he works four hours a day for three days, the duration or elapsed time is three days, so you'll need to factor three days into your schedule for the task to be completed.

Your network diagram will have a critical path, which is the route from start to end that must be completed to finish the project. This is the spine, or what drives the network diagram. The activities that need to be completed along the critical path and all other paths (which ultimately connect to the critical path) are typically connected with lines and arrows. Then you will label the activity. As activities are completed, you should clearly mark them "completed" or highlight them in another color or manner. Each activity should include the number of days it will take to complete the task.

The benefits of the network diagram are that you can not only see the tasks that need to be done, but how long they should take to complete and where they are in relationship to one another. Each task is defined in a box and the boxes are laid out horizontally to show the sequence of tasks. Two rows (or more) of parallel boxes indicate that these tasks are taking place simultaneously.

A good network diagram, like a treatment for a screenplay, blueprints for an engineer, or a game plan for a football team, includes all the details that need to be taking place. This allows you to get a good estimate of how long the activities should take and helps you monitor the flow of the project on a task-by-task basis. You can easily see where you might have to add more time or manpower, or where the flow of activity in one area is ahead of another. When putting together the museum guidebook that I mentioned in Chapter 5, you might have writers creating copy while photographers are taking photos. You'll be able to see that the photographers have completed taking the pictures, while the writers have not yet completed their first drafts. Therefore you may need to call in another writer.

FACTS

The network diagram doesn't place tasks in order of what is more important or more costly to complete. Sometimes the most important task (which might be judged by difficulty to accomplish, significance to other tasks being completed, or simply by time or cost) comes at the beginning of the project and everything else is the icing on the cake. In other projects, all the preliminaries, such as planning the wedding, lead to the main event.

Building Your Network Diagram

No matter what the scope of the project is, unless it's a one- or two-person operation with few individual tasks involved, it's helpful to have something on paper. Build yourself a little network diagram and use it as your guide. If nothing else, it will give you a sense of accomplishment as you color in each task en route to your conclusion. Anyone who has ever tried a serious diet (one approved by a doctor and not a "fad" diet) knows the benefit of celebrating milestones along the way to achieving their project goal. If your goal is losing twenty pounds in a month, then every five pounds lost may serve as a milestone along the way.

While a diet is a uniquely individual project, you can set it up for yourself horizontally on a network diagram just as you would for any business, community, or home-based project. To set up the diagram, you take the list of all the tasks involved, see which ones must be accomplished before moving on to other tasks and which ones can be done independently of each other. The museum guidebook, however, is more team-oriented, and its diagram would first include the tasks that the writers needed to do along with the tasks the photographers needed to do, plus perhaps a third column of tasks ad sales representatives needed to do. At first the ad sales reps are dependent on some initial copy and graphics being completed so they have something to show sponsors. Then all three—the writers, photographers and sales staff—can work simultaneously until the material needs to come together and be presented to the printer. Along the way, you might want to select specific milestones, such as an outline from the writers, a list of photos from the photographers, or a list of local retailers to contact for advertisements.

QUESTIONS?

What is a milestone?

A milestone in a network diagram is a box that defines a task or series of tasks that have been completed. These are checkpoints that you can look at to see whether you are or aren't on schedule. Milestones may, and often do, include deliverables.

If you're working on paper, use a pencil and eraser. Be prepared to rewrite your diagram a few times until you've included everything in sequential order with milestones and all. Look at the sample network diagram to guide you. On a computer program, you'll be entering and re-entering your information a lot.

Reviewing Your Network Diagram

Once you've completed your network diagram, review it carefully before hanging it on the wall like a Picasso (believe me, when you're done, it will feel like you've created a masterpiece!). Check to make sure all the activities on your detailed task list are included and be sure the sequence makes sense. Remember, you can't edit the museum guide copy if you haven't written it yet. If several tasks taking place simultaneously need to be finished before a next step can be started, make sure all arrows from the first tasks lead to second. In other words, the tasks of writing, photography, and ad sales all have to be completed before the box that says "take to the printer," so all of these activities lead to the same final box.

It's really pretty simple once you start trying it on paper. In fact, why not fill in the blank network diagram with a task you'd like to accomplish? First, however, you need to make a simple work breakdown sheet for yourself on a piece of paper listing the tasks needed to complete your project. Then start filling in the network diagram. Feel free to add more boxes if necessary and don't forget to pencil in your milestones in some of the boxes. (Remember, milestones are simply signposts that let you mark your progress.)

Verify Your Estimates

In most cases, unless you are very familiar with the task at hand, you should check with whoever is going to do the work to find out how long it will take them to complete it. If the time frame sounds unreasonable, research how long it takes someone else to do the same task. For example, if a printer says he can have the job in five weeks but you feel, based on your experience, that it should not take that long, check with a couple of other printers to determine their turnaround time. If two other places can have it done in three weeks, clarify why your printer cannot do it in that same time period. Often, team members or outside vendors like to pad their own schedule in case they have to push the work back a few hours or a few days. This is fine if you have some flexibility in your schedule. That, however, isn't always the case, especially in business.

Once you've set up the time frames in your network diagrams, go back and reconfirm that they are okay. Suppose you accepted the printer's estimate that he could do the job in four weeks because you like his work and have that much time available in the schedule. You still need to confirm that he indeed understands that you have it on your schedule to be completed in four weeks, and have that due date clear on both of your calendars.

Absolute Completion Date

When you tell your children you want their homework done by six o'clock, knowing you really want them finished by seven, you're setting one time for their benefit and a second one for yours. Likewise, you know the last possible date something can be completed on the project, but that is not the date you put down on the network diagram or tell the person doing the task. If you're printing a special end-of-year holiday brochure to come out in November, you may tell your copywriter that you need all copy in by September fifteenth, knowing that it won't be sent to the printer until September thirtieth.

Make sure team members know when their work needs to be completed. This is especially important when the start of one task depends on the completion of another.

You should have a completion date for each task and an absolute drop-dead completion date, which is when the work absolutely, positively must be finished. Promote your deadlines and keep your absolute deadline in a separate place. Just as budgets get padded, so do schedules. Often the manager or boss who must have it tomorrow, really doesn't need it until the day after . . . she's just not providing you with that information. By determining the latest a task or activity can be completed without interfering with the overall project, you have some room to maneuver when you need to make adjustments to the schedule.

The same holds true for a start date. What is the date you plan to start an activity? If there are delays, what is the absolute latest date you could start the activity and still get it completed in time to keep the project running on schedule? You may have to look at other tasks to determine this because other tasks may be dependent on this work getting started and completed at a certain time.

If you're not sure how long something should take to accomplish, get the best and worst time frames and use the average number plus 10 percent. If, for example, one source indicates that you can get all the necessary supplies to Boston in seven hours, but another source says that with heavy traffic it has taken as long as nine hours, you might take the average of the time estimates and come up with eight hours. Add 10 percent to play it safe and you have 8.8 hours, which rounds off to nine hours for your time estimate.

Cut Yourself Some Slack

Slack or "float time" is essentially the extra time between how long you've allotted for the task and how long it will take to complete it. If you've allotted ten days for a task but you actually need only six days, you'll have four days of slack or float time, which you can use to your advantage.

While you want to have some time to play with, if your project is running late, you can use the slack in the schedule to pick up the pace of your project. You may find places where you can double up your resources. For example, if you can't start rehearsals of the community production of *Death of a Salesman* until Friday when the rehearsal space opens, you might have some of your cast double up on other activities, such as putting together the program, selling tickets, or building the set.

ALERT

Don't use precious slack time for a round of golf early on in the project. It will come back to bite you later. Perhaps if you're six days ahead of schedule in the final week of the project you can hit the links . . . but even then, it's a risk!

Unfortunately, slack time is often used to solve problems, resolve conflicts, and make changes brought about by external factors. From cleaning up the mess in your new office to spending a day calming two feuding relatives who can't plan a wedding together, you'll find your slack time disappearing quickly.

Various Projects, Various Methods

The network diagram is in vogue in the business world. Other popular tools are the Performance Evaluation and Review Technique (PERT) and the Critical Path Method (CPM), both of which are more technical in nature, but basically are used for the same purpose: to schedule, chart, and monitor a project. The PERT method uses differing degrees of likelihood while CPM includes activities and circles for milestones. You'll find other tools too, but many are more complicated than necessary for the vast majority of simple and smaller projects.

No matter what method you use, you need a way to follow the progress of your project.

- Have each task clearly displayed
- Be able to see multiple parallel tasks and see their relationship to one another
- Have a clear understanding of the order of the tasks
- Know when you've reached key goals (milestones, signposts) along the way

If your method gives you a clear overview of the project and all the various components within it, then whatever you're doing is just fine.

The Famous Gantt Chart

The Gantt Chart is a well-known standard in program management that dates back to 1917 when Henry Gantt, a pioneer in the field of scientific management, invented it. The chart plots a number of tasks across a horizontal time scale. It is easy to understand and allows team members to maintain the status of their tasks against planned progress. In its most basic usage, the Gantt Chart puts tasks on a series of horizontal time lines. The time line can measure the progress in hours for a short-term project, months for a long-term project, or weeks as shown in the following example.

Project: Producing New Sales Brochure

Task	Weeks										
	1	2	3	4	5	6	7	8	9	10	11
Gathering resources (team, materials, etc.)	▨	▨									
Sales research		▓	▓	▓	▓	▓	▓	▓			
Writing			▨	▨	▨	▨					
Graphics		▨	▨								
Editing					▓	▓	▓				
Printing/production									▨	▨	▨

The Gantt Chart shows timelines for each task and the overlap between tasks. You can clearly get an idea of what tasks are being performed in any given week. You can also use the chart to gauge where you are. For example, if, in week eight, graphics are not complete, then you are behind schedule. Gantt charts are easy to read at a glance, particularly if you use different colors for each task. You can show progress on the Gantt Chart by using light colors or no colors on the initial time lines for each task and then coloring in the boxes as the work gets done.

What the Gantt Chart doesn't tell you is who is performing each task or if tasks depend on one another. For this information you will need a task member schedule or task list. Therefore, while the Gantt chart is very helpful in terms of a timeline, you'll need to use it in conjunction with other scheduling tools.

Task Schedule or Matrix

You will need to refer to your skills roster (discussed in Chapter 3), in which you will see the various skills of each team member, to establish a schedule for your personnel or team members. This task schedule, also known as a resource assignment matrix, will indicate who should be doing what and where they should be in the process. When setting up this matrix, defining the relationship between individuals is as important as the relationship of individuals to their tasks.

ESSENTIALS Do you have a communications plan? If you don't, you should. The plan indicates how you will communicate important information to your team and others, including milestones, changes in the plan, and the overall progress of the project.

Review the task matrix with team members to make sure they know when they are expected to do their assigned tasks. Make sure everyone is available during the times they are needed. If there are limits to their availability (part time employees, your children helping you after school, volunteers giving their time one day a week), make sure you schedule accordingly. Obviously a task that takes six hours a day cannot be performed efficiently by one person who is only available for three hours a day. However, if you've budgeted for six hours daily on that task and it needs to be done in x amount of time, you can solve the problem easily by hiring two people to do the task.

In business, community, and other projects, you will run up against team members' vacation schedules. Make sure you ask before the project if anyone will be away during any part of the project. Schedule their task(s) accordingly. If they need be around for the entire project, then they either have to reschedule their vacation or you need to find someone else as either a replacement or a fill-in while they are away. It's often difficult to fill in for a short time when someone is away from a project. It's best to have someone available for the duration. Remember, the project comes first.

One word of caution: It's tough enough managing a project. The last thing you need to do is create a task list or a schedule that is so complex it will occupy your day just checking off what is being done. If you're spending all of your time walking around checking off a lengthy list of tasks, you'll have no time to look at the overall progress being made on the project or address problems or conflicts that arise. Don't overload yourself with data-entry duties.

Anticipating Pitfalls

It's important to try to anticipate any potential pitfalls that could ultimately spell disaster for the project. There will certainly be surprising, unforeseen developments along the way, which you will try to deal with accordingly. After all, you do need to expect the unexpected. But there are ways to reduce the probability of problems that might occur.

Look at factors surrounding your project that could directly or indirectly impact your goal. Is there an upcoming labor strike? A change in leadership (in your company or in one that you do business with)? A change in politics? New zoning laws? Policy changes? Is the economy heading into a recession, thus affecting your sponsor's ability to adequately bankroll the project? Is there a "for sale" sign on the catering hall you just booked for your manager's retirement party?

Contingency planning needs to be part of your overall initial planning stage. Such backup plans also need to be mentioned at meetings so that other team members can suggest alternatives should problems arise. The more people you have thinking of alternative plans, the more likely you'll be prepared to handle problems and avert potentially disastrous situations. While you do not want to take time away from the project, you do need to have some backup plans in place from the start of the project. For example, if a shipment is going to be delayed, are you ready with the FedEx number handy? You may have to pay more, but your project may benefit by staying on schedule.

ESSENTIALS

How do you eat an elephant? One bite at a time. If the project is huge (an elephant), the best way to get through it is one step at a time, "bite by bite."

Not only do you need to have contingency plans ready in the back of your mind and in the minds of your team members, but you need to know how (and when) to switch to plan "B" if necessary. For example, at what point does the outdoor wedding become an indoor wedding because of the weather? When it looks like rain, when it starts to rain, or does it depend on the forecast? You also need to know who will make the changes and move the seating indoors. Who will tell the guests? Planning contingency tasks is as important as planning the project.

Sometimes projects grow. For example, the ninety-person wedding now has 110 attendees. It's not important how it happened, it's just important that the project scope changed. Can you adjust? Likewise, your promotional video, which was going to twenty-seven offices across the country, is now being slated to appear in Japan as well. Subtitles! Who will translate? Who will add these subtitles?

If you have project files in your computer, *always* back them up regularly on floppy disks. It's a good idea to make hard copies too. A project can be lost or set back several days or even months because a power failure or computer crash erases the work.

Naturally, you can't anticipate what new developments will arise, but you can have some basic plans in place. Be resourceful when projects change or grow. There's more on planning in Chapter 12.

And the Calendar Says . . .

If you're not quite ready for elaborate charts and diagrams, you might opt for scheduling a project on a simple calendar. Using a different color for each task or assigning a color for each of the three or four people on the project, you can make up an easy-to-follow schedule such as the one that follows. You might also use initials for team members.

JUNE

	SU 4	MO 5	TU 6	WE 7	TH 8	FR 9	SA 10
AJ:			TASK A		TASK B	TASK B	
DJ:		TASK A	TASK A	TASK A	TASK A	TASK B	
ST:		TASK A	TASK A	TASK A			

In this example, each "Task A" is a different activity for the project. Task B, however, might be the same color, indicating that AJ and DJ worked on the same task at the end of the week. Task B was only one day of work for DJ, but AJ had enough to complete to take her into Friday.

A calendar can be posted in a central location so everyone can check their status and note how many days are remaining in the project.

We've all seen children (and adults for that matter) mark off a calendar with how many days are left until vacation. In this case, you're marking off how many days until the project is complete. Just make sure each day's task is complete before you mark it "finished."

Add milestones to your calendar or create a milestone schedule. You can highlight important events by circling the date on the calendar or pasting a gold star next to key tasks that you have completed. These will indicate that you have reached an important point or a milestone en route to completing your project.

In some cases you might not list tasks on a daily basis, particularly if they are repetitive by nature. You can simply include the milestones that need to be reached on certain days. For example, someone might be painting six similarly sized offices over the course of two consecutive weeks. You can make a line for a continuing task as in the previous example rather than writing "paint office" in each box. At the end of the first Friday, you might mark down "Finish painting three offices" as a milestone or marker.

A milestone version of a more detailed schedule can give stakeholders who are not actively involved with the project on a daily basis, or the sponsors, an idea of when key goals within the project have been reached. For example, the backer of the film will know when shooting wrapped and the post production phase begins.

CHAPTER 7

Monitoring Progress

As the project moves forward, you will need to establish how you monitor your progress based on a number of criteria, including time, cost, and performance. Your system must highlight potential problems so that you can steer the project back on track. You may come upon a detour and you'll need to find another route in order to arrive at your destination on time. Naturally, the sooner you find out about upcoming roadwork, the sooner you can plan an alternate route. Likewise, the sooner you discover potential problems, the sooner you can make plans to circumvent them.

Why Monitor?

Monitoring a project is vital because it lets you communicate to stakeholders, sponsors, and team members exactly where the project stands and determine how closely your initial plan of action resembles reality. It allows you to validate any decisions you will make in regard to implementing changes. Your data will benefit anyone who has an interest in the potential outcome of the project. Monitoring your project also allows you to make the necessary adjustments regarding resources or your budget. If you learn, for example, that you have more people than you need on one task (which is way ahead of schedule) but need someone in another area that is lagging behind, you can make the adjustment.

FACTS

Regular monitoring helps you avoid disasters. Just as checking the gas gauge in your car as you drive helps you see how much gas is left in the tank, monitoring your project helps you avoid "running out of gas" before you reach your goal.

As your project comes to life, keep these questions in mind:

- Are you on schedule?
- If not, how far behind are you, and how can you catch up?
- Are you over budget?
- Are you still working toward the same project goal?
- Are you running low on resources?
- Are there warning signs of impending problems?
- Is there pressure from management to complete the project sooner?
- Is there public opposition or any other opposition to the project being completed?

These are just a few of the many questions you should ask yourself as you monitor the progress of your project. Monitoring will allow you to make comparisons between your original plan and your progress so far. You will be able to implement changes, where necessary, to complete the project successfully.

How Often to Monitor

Do you keep progress reports on a daily basis? On a weekly basis? Do you need frequent review meetings? How often you monitor a project depends on several factors:

- The scope of the project
- The number of people working on the project
- The skill level of the individuals working on the project
- The schedule/time frame of the project
- The familiarity of the project (are team members taking on tasks that they have not done before?)
- Communication needs (are stakeholders, upper level managers, or others waiting for, or expecting, regular updates?)
- The complexity of the project (are there numerous technical details?)
- The level of risk associated with the project
- The resources associated with the project

Let's look more closely at each of these factors to help determine how often to monitor a project.

Scope

Larger projects will generally require closer and more frequent monitoring, since numerous activities are taking place and there is a greater likelihood that some areas of the project will fall behind or that a problem will arise. A larger project will need a more formal system of monitoring while a small, or family, project can be monitored informally.

Number of People on the Project

When more people are involved, the chance of human error is greater, no matter what the overall scope of the project. Unless everyone is doing the same task, it takes closer monitoring to make sure each person stays on track. (Don't overdo it, however. More on this later.) Usually, more people will mean more monitoring. However, fifty people performing the same activity may be easier to monitor than ten people doing ten different tasks, because you will be able to use the same baseline criteria for the fifty people.

ESSENTIALS Get to know more than one person at the company (unless it is an individual subcontractor). If you can't reach one person, or if your contact leaves the company, you can still get in touch with someone who can find out what part of the work is completed and what needs to be done.

If outside contractors, suppliers, consultants, and others are necessary to help complete your project, it may be hard to keep track of their progress, especially if they are working off-site. It's to your advantage to include them in aspects of the project. Keep them updated on the project's progress, include them in team get-togethers, etc. The more involved they become, the more accessible they will be and the easier it will be for you to get the updates you need. You can set up the "how" and "when" of supplying you with a progress report, but you'll often get better results by establishing a good rapport with outside vendors and resources.

Skill Level

You may have experts who have done the same activities many times before. These individuals may not need to be monitored as often or as closely as people who are doing a task for the first time. So as not to micromanage, you may simply set up more frequent "check points" in the process or have more meetings to closely monitor individuals who are less familiar with specific tasks. You can also make it clear that people should be able to approach you with questions or problems, especially if they are being trained or are new to a specific task.

Schedule

If the project requires presenting deliverables every couple of weeks, you will want to monitor on a weekly basis (at the least). A longer project with more time committed to each task and no deliverables until the end result may allow you greater intervals before you'll need to monitor the progress. You can judge your progress based on when the team reaches specific milestones on your original schedule, which is a very common way to monitor projects.

Remember, each person needs to stay on schedule. The farther behind the project falls, the more closely you'll have to monitor progress. Generally there's a little slack built into the schedule, but the further behind you fall, the less slack there is to play with. If, for example, you know that the project can run three days behind schedule, and you're already two days behind and not even halfway finished, you'll need to monitor more closely to see where you can pick up the pace.

Familiarity of the Project

If you've never done this project before, you'll need to monitor more closely to make sure you haven't veered off course. It will be important to have a prototype or some form of blueprint or document on which to base your project. If, for example, you're setting up a backyard swing set for the kids, you'll have to check the diagram more closely as you go and double check for safety each step of the way. When a team has done a similar project in the past, you can monitor more loosely.

Communication Needs

If stakeholders, or others, expect monthly, weekly, or daily updates or reports, you have to furnish them with the latest project news. That news will come from monitoring your project to respond to their needs. Make sure you address the needs of the individuals waiting to hear the latest developments. High-profile projects, such as the building of a new bridge or a new convention center, will often require you to provide frequent updates to numerous media sources as well as politicians and other government offices.

Complexity

The more "nuts and bolts" there are involved in the project, the more closely you'll need to oversee what is going on. Complex projects are more likely to have potential for error, so they need to be tracked more closely. These may include numerous tests for quality assessment.

Risk

"Risk" is a relative term. Building a power plant takes much closer monitoring than planning a convention. A project that can be potentially detrimental to "the world at large" obviously requires much closer monitoring than building the backyard pool. The risk that your new corporate offices will not be ready on time does not affect the world at large. However, it does affect the success of your company and the jobs of many people.

Don't assume that because a team worked on a similar project a month ago they won't need any monitoring this time around. You'll still need to monitor for accuracy, safety, and other issues. Remember, every project is different, with unique concerns and issues.

Projects involve two levels of risk. One is the risk of the project failing in the larger picture and the other is internal risk, meaning that the project won't get completed. While your first risk is that of the project failing, the greater risk lies in the *consequences* of the project failing. The consequences of a project failing will affect the stakeholders. But how? Will the company fall behind in the market place, causing lower sales figures and costing people their jobs? Will people simply have to wait fifteen minutes longer for the bus because the new subway line project bombed? Basically, if a project fails and no one is affected by it, then there wasn't much risk involved. But if the project fails and shuts down the city of Pittsburgh for two weeks, there was significant "real world" risk involved. Monitor accordingly.

Resources

What do you need to complete the project? Resources may seem plentiful when you start out, but they can run out fast. From labor to paperclips, it's important that you keep an eye on what is running low. Do you need toner for the printer? Are you out of cement for construction? Has your art director just left for another project? Monitor what you have and what you need.

Once you monitor the project (as often as necessary to keep you abreast of what is going on), you will need to do something with the data you have gathered. The point of monitoring a project is that someone will gain insight from the information. After all, if you monitor a project and no one ever reads or evaluates the data, what is the point? Gather the information, then compare and analyze what you have gathered and make an assessment of where you stand in each area.

Performance Periods

Call them performance periods, segments, or anything you choose . . . as long as you determine a time frame in which activities will get done. Two halves or four quarters break down a football game. This allows the statisticians and analysts to review the game through an allotted time period. Likewise, companies have quarterly reports every three months to assess how well they are doing financially. Projects need the same type of breakdown. This allows you to analyze and review the project through each period. It also gives you time to review the intended goals of the overall project and discuss the upcoming phases with team members.

Performance periods will help you subdivide the overall task into more manageable segments. Select appropriate amounts of time. If your time periods are too short, there may not be enough progress to monitor. On the other hand, if monitoring occurs too infrequently, some aspect of the project can go wrong and be undetected before turning into a major problem.

Gathering Information

Once you've assessed what you'll be looking for and how often you'll be monitoring the project, you'll need to determine exactly what information needs to be gathered:

1. When each activity began and ended
2. The resources used for each activity
3. The expenses incurred for each activity
4. The number of man-hours put into each activity
5. Whether the goal of the activity was accomplished or not (this may determine whether you can move on to the next activity or task)

To make all of this information worthwhile, you need a measure of comparison. This is where you turn to your original plans. Did the start and end dates of the activity coincide with your projected start and end dates? Did you use the anticipated resources or did you run short or have materials left over? Where are you in conjunction with your projected budget at this point in the project? Did you anticipate more or fewer man-hours to this point?

All of the comparisons with your initial plan are vital to determining where you stand at any given time in the process. Compare the performance of your team with the original plan and look for reasons why there are differences. To better your understanding of the comparisons, you may want to meet with team members and get further details. In these meetings you can discuss progress, assess any setbacks, resolve issues, and evaluate performance. Team members can often provide valuable suggestions on ways to perform more efficiently. Perhaps the resources are at fault for the delays.

Prior to meetings, you should study the details of your tracking or monitoring system to find the most glaring differences between scheduled and actual performance. If everything is running smoothly, you may simply want to tell everyone how well they are doing and keep up the team spirit by using the review meeting as an opportunity to reward everyone in a small way.

While you may not need as lengthy a discussion as you would if the project were off-schedule, it's a good idea to get some notion of why things are going well. You will want to document what you are doing so that you can repeat your success on the next project. Just as we learn from our mistakes, we learn from our successes. (And don't get too overconfident if the project is on course; things can always take a turn for the worse!)

If a team member is at the root of a problem, work on constructive ways to resolve the problem and let the team member maintain dignity and respect. If, however, someone is not performing his task or cannot do an adequate job, he may need to be replaced.

More often than not, one area is lagging behind or one task is falling behind schedule. You need to assess why. Did you underestimate the time it would take to perform the task? Are you using improper resources? Is the right person doing the right task? Whatever the reason, you need to find the source of the problem, then you need to try to prevent that task from falling further behind schedule.

Monitoring at the Individual Level

For you to monitor a project, it will require that individuals provide updates of where they are up to and how long it has taken to get there. Monitoring needs to start with team members. However, be careful not to stifle positive attitudes, productivity, and creativity by imposing too much clerical work.

Make sure team members know how you want their reports to read. Don't make the process overly complicated or team members will shrug it off or not hand in the reports on time. Remember that less is more. The less you ask of your team members, the more likely it is that they will provide you with timely updates. Get basic, but specific, information as opposed to nitpicking for details. The setting will dictate the level of formality necessary and the amount of information to be reported. Keep it simple. Let's look at a few examples:

1. Someone volunteering to make costumes for the community center theater production may simply tell you she has completed five costumes in three days and has three more to complete in the next couple of days. Since this is a volunteer position and there is no pay, you don't need an hourly assessment. You may, however, want to ask if she has all the resources she needs to complete the task.
2. Someone writing a brochure may write down that she has completed the first draft of three (out of four) pages of copy in seventeen hours. She estimates that it will take her one more day to complete the first draft of page four. This example would include hours, since the copywriter is being paid by the hour.
3. Someone on a project to assemble 200 new vacuum cleaners for demonstration purposes will have a report that tells you that between January 4 and January 8, twenty-nine shipments arrived and the first hundred of the new hydraulic vacuum cleaner prototypes had completed phase one of assembly. It took 300 man-hours at a cost of $12,395. This example may require more detail since the project has a greater scope and a larger budget. Ask team members:

   - To provide the information that you need
   - To hand in written reports on time
   - To report potential problems
   - To include milestones reached
   - To let you know if they need more resources to complete the task

You will need to evaluate reports or updates from team members, whether it's a verbal update, as in the first example, or a more detailed report. Are they on schedule? Are they within their budgetary constraints?

Is there a conflict situation brewing that you should be aware of? Can you find solutions to the problems that are presented early on, before they become large-scale problems? It's important that you address these concerns.

ESSENTIALS Getting written or verbal comments from team members can help you avert potential problems. Be sure to take notes. It's likely that people working directly on individual tasks will be able to point out key areas of concern.

You should also perform a quality check. Make sure such quality checks are incorporated into the project itself. If, for example, the costumes for *The Wizard of Oz* look like a leopard, a spaceship, and a giant stalk of corn, you won't have a lion, tin man, or scarecrow for your production. Completed work has to be quality work or it's useless!

Problems, Priorities, and Comments

When you ask for comments, you open yourself up to anything from "This project stinks" to "If we don't get more cement by Friday the entire building's structure will collapse." Comments will run the gamut from rantings to significant predicaments. You will need to determine the severity of problems and make a hierarchical list starting with significant actual problems and continuing with potential problems. If you are out of a particular resource, that is a problem. If you will run out of a resource if you keep using it at this rate, that is a potential problem. Both need to be addressed. Make sure, however, that a potential problem is real and based on the current project assessments and not on a hunch or a guesstimate.

Problems in the here and now will generally take precedence, unless they are not actually threatening the project. For example, a problem with a software package may be immediate, but an upcoming labor strike by truckers may be a more pressing problem, because without the supplies the project may be shut down completely.

Rank all current problems 1–10, with 10 being the most serious. Then number all *potential* problems as 1–10, with 10 being the most serious. Look at your lists. Those problems ranked 5–10 on your current list of concerns should take precedence, with potential problems ranked 5–10 addressed next. Then you can take care of the smaller problems ranked 1–4, and finally, address the potential problems ranked 1–4.

Comments will also need your attention. Let team members know that time is limited and that you would appreciate concise comments that pertain only to the project. Separate those that pertain to the project and those that pertain to the project team, such as conflicts between members. Rate them and prioritize them as well. Discard those that are not project-related. Also, look for consistencies. If one person says that the work area is too warm, you can suggest opening a window near where that person is working. However, if twenty-two people say they are too hot, you'll need to seriously consider a better air conditioner. A consensus of opinions can point you to key concerns of team members.

ESSENTIALS

If you see a problem on your list that you can solve with a quick phone call or flick of a switch, make the change or have someone else do it. It's always nice to knock out a few problems quickly.

Your lists of immediate and potential problems will provide significant points for discussion in project review meetings and will also give you key points to summarize with stakeholders. Depending on the problem and the stakeholder, you can determine which information to pass along and which can be solved without alerting others. For example, customers don't need to know that three of your team members have left and need to be replaced, as long as deliverables are ready on time. Stockholders, on the other hand, may want to know if one of the three people who left is also the CEO.

Determine which problems need to be communicated to others and which ones you are expected to handle. The level of authority you have, and the nature of the project will dictate your best course of action. It's very important to clearly know what is for public consumption, what is for key personnel to know, and what is and isn't for the media to sink their teeth into. Some projects will require detailed accounts or public posting of every written document. Others will require that you just make the changes and move on. Judge carefully whom you apprise of current and potential problems.

Remember: Problems can become magnified when they are communicated to the wrong people, or are *not* communicated to the *right* people. Either way your position as project manager could hang in the balance.

Some activities in a project seem to follow Murphy's Law: "Whatever can go wrong will go wrong." If you're lucky, these nightmare aspects of the project will be minimal. Any activities that have proven to be troublesome in previous projects are worth monitoring more closely. You may also have to monitor people who've been tardy or lazy in the past more closely, but first give them the benefit of the doubt—a new project might mean a new attitude.

Three Steps Forward, Two Steps Back

Once there was a beautiful, natural waterfall that flowed magnificently, taking crystal clear water from high up in the mountains down to a river below. The stream of the waterfall was continuous, flowing steadily in the same direction.

Once there was a project that emerged from a mountain of paperwork. It was designed to put the paperwork into a series of computer databanks so that work could flow more smoothly. Unlike the waterfall, these databanks would need to be set up by programmers through an elaborate technological system. The project flowed smoothly for some time, like the waterfall, until someone realized that there was trouble way back in the early stages of the flow—technological pollution, so to speak—which meant that the water would no longer flow crystal clear to the bottom.

ALERT

Don't try to play hero and do everything yourself—ask for and get help when necessary. If someone higher up in the pecking order (whether it's your boss, PTA president, or your dad) has told you to report any problems to him, do so!

The waterfall method of completing projects, which has one activity flowing into another and into another, has been proven to be *not* very effective for technological projects. It has become increasingly obvious that one needs to move forward with caution and after proceeding through one, two, or three phases, there is a need to go back and make sure phase one still works as intended. Often, changes in a project will occur at many of the early stages, affecting all the information processing that will follow. Therefore, it is often a three-step process, one step forward and two steps back, to make sure everything is still working properly.

Technology presents many complex issues:

1. The technological team needs to satisfy the needs of the potential users. Both the needs and the users can often change as the project progresses.
2. There is a need for interfacing, both within the company or business and externally.
3. The technology itself changes very rapidly, particularly in the course of a yearlong project. What was cutting edge on day one is now old news on day 365 of your project.
4. An intended goal can be achieved in many ways. Try to get a consensus on which course of action would be best to follow.
5. Testing is crucial and needs to be factored into the schedule. Results need to be clearly defined. Programs need to be tested individually and the system needs to be tested as a whole.
6. Good communication is critical.

The last point derails many projects. How often has one learned that the technical team and management did not clearly understand one another? How often has the technical team had to go back to phase one, two, or three and make changes that would affect the phases that followed? How often has someone wanted to do it his or her own way only to find out the method did not work? More often than not, a lack of clear communication is at the root of the technical problems that slow a project down.

For example, many of the dot-coms that failed in late 2000 and early 2001 were victims of poor communication between management, sales, content developers, and the technical team. Frequently someone had a great idea, or thought it was a great idea, but the technical team was not informed of all the details. In other instances, the technical teams clearly did not share the same vision with the creative team. Then there were cases where something simply could not be done, or would cost much more to achieve than was feasible. Poor management and the inability of the management, creative, sales and marketing, and technical teams to "get on the same page" was at the root of many dot-com disasters.

Monitoring Expenditures

Few projects can succeed without money. Your purchase orders, vendor bills, checks, credit card bills, and other documents will be used to verify what is actually being spent on the project. As you learned in Chapter 5, your budget should clearly illustrate the sum total of what needs to be spent.

You, or someone handling the disbursements and expenditures, should have a system in which every payment is approved, using the original invoice only, to make sure that no bills are paid in duplicate. Make sure purchases are accounted for and subtracted from your budget. Just because the new computer isn't sitting on your desk doesn't mean that $2,000 from your budget hasn't already been spent. Remember that the $150 for shipping the computer needs to be accounted for in the budget as well. Make sure any additional expenditures that were not in the original budget are addressed and noted immediately—don't even wait for the end of the next monitoring period such as the weekly status report. It's important that a $500 change in the budget on a small project be incorporated on Monday when the purchase is made and not on Friday when the status report is handed in. Someone, very likely you, needs to review and approve any and all additional expenses.

ESSENTIALS

Always plan for at least 10 to 15 percent more in your budget for large item purchases because of shipping, handling, taxes, and other expenses. Also allow for unforeseen expenses, but set a limit in this area—say, $500 under "Miscellaneous"—unless there's a major emergency.

If your accounting department is handling the payments, they may not be keeping separate records for your particular project. That means you must keep track of the project budget. If they are handling the budget for the project, you must make sure to have steady communication and know exactly what they have and have not yet included as expenditures. The best way to monitor expenditures is to set up a system at the beginning of the project that accounts for all expenses. Use software if you choose, but remember, it's up to you and your team to make sure the correct data is entered.

To judge your project's success in relation to your original projected budget, you'll need to compare how much you have spent in conjunction with how much you have in the overall budget. Using a system known as Earned Value Analysis, you can determine whether you are ahead of or behind your budget at a specific point in the project.

For example, suppose your total budget to move the office to the new location is $40,000 and you have a time frame of two months. After one month you've spent $20,000. Are you on budget? If all work to be done including all expenses (such as resources and manpower) is equal in both months, you're fine. However, this is not always the case. You will have different needs and costs at different points in your projects. You need to look specifically at the project's schedule and resource expenditures to that point . . . both actual and projected. If you had planned to spend only $15,000 through the first month and you have spent $20,000, you have overspent by $5,000 at this point, based on your projection. This is known as your cost variance.

Your proposed budget has an additional $25,000 to be spent in the second month of the project. You have only $20,000 left in your actual budget. Therefore, you will either need to ask management or whoever is sponsoring the move for an additional $5,000, or you will need to find a way of saving $5,000 in the next month.

QUESTIONS?

What is Earned Value Analysis?
Earned Value Analysis is how you analyze the progress of the project. You compare the money budgeted with the money spent and the work achieved. You can determine whether you are ahead or behind your projected budget.

If you take the actual cost of work performed and divide it by the budgeted cost of work performed, then multiply your answer by the total cost of the project, you can get a rough estimate of how much you would spend at the current rate. This is important if you are over budget and see upcoming spending continuing at a similar rate. It's a rough estimate, because there are variables that will come into play that will impinge on your budget. You may also find ways to save money.

Your earned value analysis tells you it's time to either:

- Find ways to save money
- Ask your sponsor for more money
- Eliminate a portion of the project that may be extraneous and will not impinge on meeting the goals of the overall project
- Hop a plane and leave town!

Project Evolution

As you monitor your project, you will discover changes or alterations that need to be made to your schedule or budget. Insignificant alterations are usually easy to make, while large-scale changes take more time to plan and often need approval from various sources including sponsors, stakeholders, and upper management or supervisors.

Just as a living organism grows, your project will grow and evolve into something more than just plans or blueprints. And just as your children come home and surprise you with new words they've learned from their friends at school, there are outside factors that will pop up during the growth of your project that you will have to address. No matter how much you monitor, you will never be completely prepared for every unforeseen event, such as new shipping charges, a new ordinance, or a labor strike. But the more carefully you monitor progress, the more you will be able to handle those issues that are within your control.

Be Prepared

As you make changes and alterations to the schedule or budget, make sure you keep everyone apprised. If the people working on a project don't know that the due date is now Tuesday instead of Thursday, they'll be late in finishing their activity. Keep all necessary people informed of any changes that affect their work. Also:

- Be ready to explain and justify any changes you have made
- Make sure you get all necessary approvals before making changes
- Always work within the system and ask team members to do the same

Be Clear

It is important to be very clear when you give instructions. If you ask someone to make sure everything remaining in the office is packed up for a move, the individual may pack everything up in any number of ways. Asking someone to "pack everything up" is vague. However, asking someone to pack up everything in cartons that are labeled and taped so you can easily identify and load each item onto the hand-trucks in the morning is much more specific. You need to spell out details and let the team members know what you expect to be the achievement or end result of each task.

More specific directions will result in less frequent monitoring because you've clarified the process and the desired (and expected) results of the task. Never assume people can read your mind. Let individuals know the details you are seeking and the end result (achievement). Achievement-based assignments keep things clear for all concerned.

Monitor Your Monitoring

Are you becoming a pain in the neck? Are people spending more time filling out progress reports than doing actual tasks? Do team members duck into restrooms to avoid you for fear of being given the third degree? If you are over-monitoring, you can become the project's worst enemy.

While you do need to monitor a project's progress, you also need to know when to stop monitoring the project itself. You can keep a log of project activities that does not require constant input from other team members. However, when others are involved in monitoring the project, they are using valuable time. Keep monitoring to a minimum unless you are working with complex projects or highly sensitive materials that need to be double-checked or tested very often.

Resources such as equipment and materials have a way of disappearing. You need to monitor that, so they don't grow legs and walk off the project. Short of locking up every pen, you'll have to keep a rough inventory of the tools, materials, and equipment involved in your project.

If you do need frequent updates on a more complex project, keep the updates simple. It's easier to fill out a concise form, even on a daily basis, than to have to write out pages of details. Too much paperwork will lower the morale of your team members, and that will show up in their work. You'll also find that if you require too much reporting, team members may start ignoring the reports or handing them in incomplete or late.

You don't want people to feel micro-managed. On a smaller or less technical project, you might begin by informal monitoring, such as walking around to see how everything is going and asking people informally if there's any problem. For many projects, such informal discussions or weekly team meetings and summary reports will do the trick. For larger projects you may hold team meetings on a monthly basis but still want weekly status reports.

If the people working on the project are not highly experienced, or you are not familiar with their work, you might monitor more closely at first and then once things are on track, loosen the reins a bit. It all depends on your approach and the people on your team.

The basic rules of thumb are:

- Make sure you are clear about what you expect from team members regarding their assigned activities
- Make sure people know what you want on your reports
- Monitor just enough to feel comfortable with and remain in control of the project
- Monitor to track and gain insight into the flow of information, but don't waste people's time
- Make sure monitoring is not a burden to your team

To establish the most effective monitoring process, keep status reports short and to the point. If you are working on a community, family, or small business project, you might have weekly meetings to get status updates. Ask which tasks have been completed in the past week, which ones are still in progress, when they will be completed, and how much money has been spent so far. Ask if there are any questions or if your team members anticipate any problems. Also ask for suggestions to make things run more smoothly. Remember, there are no bad suggestions, just ones that may or may not work well on your particular project.

For more formal tracking methods in business or on larger projects, you can write each of these questions down and present a stack of status forms to be filled out at the end of the week. A simple form e-mailed to team members each week is often the simplest method. Make sure there is room to fill in suggestions or comments. Whether or not you use many (or any) suggestions, it helps make everyone feel involved in the project if you ask them for feedback.

Suggestions are also helpful because:

1. You never know when someone will have a brilliant idea.
2. It keeps people thinking about the project.
3. It makes team members feel involved.

Monitoring for the Sake of Others

If you need to monitor for the sake of providing reports to outside sources including stakeholders and sponsors, let the team know that the information is needed for other sources. Make sure you are addressing the concerns of the customers, partners, stockholders, upper management, and others involved in the project. Get a clear idea of who needs to know what so that you don't have to burden your team or waste your own time gathering extraneous information. Sources seeking information on the project may include:

- Stakeholders
- Sponsors
- Politicians
- Government offices
- The media
- The community

Other reports (internal and external) may also need to include your project data, including:

- Quarterly or annual reports
- Cost-variance reports
- Supply inventories
- Operating budgets
- Marketing materials
- Compliance reports

Tools for Monitoring Your Project

For small projects and personal projects you can use notebooks, graphs, diagrams, day planners, personal organizers, or other tools to clearly post your schedule and project updates. Don't make things more complicated than necessary by using high-tech tracking devices for simple projects. You don't need an elaborate software system to run a bake sale, plan a wedding, set up a small business, or build a jungle gym for the kids. The tracking system should match the scope of the project. Many software products such as those offered by Microsoft are designed primarily for corporate, or large-scope, projects. (Several are listed in Chapter 8.) You can always use a spreadsheet program, such as Excel, on your PC if you want to track a simple, small-scope project on your desktop.

The easier the monitoring tools are to understand, the quicker you'll be able to explain them to others and read (and analyze) them yourself. A tool is only useful if it serves a productive purpose. If monitoring means being able to easily gather, read, and utilize information for comparisons, you need a tool that does this without distractions.

Monitoring Intangibles

Okay, it's easy to have everyone list how many hours they've worked on the project. It's also easy to write down what work has been completed and what work still needs to be done. It's not hard to match this information against the original plan, budget, and schedule to see if you are on course. But how do you measure the intangibles? How do you measure how well your team members are getting along? How do you measure whether communication is effective or not? How do you measure the quality of the work that has been completed?

Status reports won't tell you if the work is done poorly. After all, who's going to write down "The new roof is in place, the job is completed . . . but the roof will leak." So what can you do? Be omnipresent. The more walkthroughs, the better. Walkthroughs are those little strolls you take just to see that all is going well. No, you don't want to appear to be looking over peoples' shoulders, but you do need to know that the person in charge of hiring a stripper to strip the shingles off the roof doesn't hire a stripper in an exotic outfit. You want to remain somewhat unobtrusive, yet approachable; somewhat cheerful, yet businesslike. Don't get sidetracked by lengthy conversations; set up appointments to discuss matters that would slow down your otherwise breezy jaunt.

FACTS

Depending on the project, your monitoring may end up in the daily newspaper. Yes, the media follows projects. While only large-scale projects will make the larger market papers, a store moving to a new location after twenty-five years might be a headline in a small town paper, and you may be managing that move!

Activities not only need to be done on time but they need to be done correctly. Make sure that early on, you have a feel for exactly what task members are doing and how they are doing it. Then politely set task members back on course if they seem to be going astray. If the first page of the brochure copy makes little sense, it's not likely the next three pages will be any better.

It helps to have examples available of exactly what you want. A picture or video presentation is worth a thousand words. Explaining, "We want the pool to look like this one," as you hold up a photo of an in-ground, kidney-shaped pool, will prevent misunderstandings. Since most projects do not create something completely new and original, you can use a model to show both the quality and specifics you are looking for.

As for monitoring morale and cohesiveness, you need to make a concerted effort to note whether people are working well together or just barely tolerating one another. Although you may be tipped off by a slowdown in production or a lack of interest in planned extracurricular activities, this is primarily a judgment call. Encourage people to discuss matters with you, particularly if it they are having trouble working with other team members. Never take sides; just try to create a situation in which the two parties can come to common terms on the project and work together. You need not create friendships, just a workable partnership. Spell out what each side should expect from the other, almost like drawing up a contract as to how they can best respect and work with one another. Keep it informal, unless you see the potential for serious problems. (There's more on resolving conflicts in Chapter 10.)

QUESTIONS?

How is communication measured?
If people are asking too many questions about your requests and project requirements, you may not be communicating clearly. Measure communication from your office, or easy chair, by how many people are questioning your instructions or the number of errors in the work being turned in.

You can also measure communications by how effective the communications system is that you are using. If no one is getting your e-mails, the system is not working. If everyone is getting your memos but they are using them to shoot baskets, the system is not working. Make sure people are receiving—and reading—your communications.

Your team's communication will affect the ease of transition from one phase of the project to the next, and will be reflected in the quality of the final product. Take active steps to maintain clear expectations throughout the project. Set up meetings to ensure that team members doing task "A" and team members doing task "B" know their deliverables for the team waiting to work on task "C." Team "C" people should also have some representation at these meetings to address minor issues as they arise.

All parties need to know what is expected of them regarding the flow of information to each other and to you. Facilitate and encourage ongoing communication by having reliable and efficient systems in place—they will show your commitment to the initiative. "Please let shipping know what percentage of widgets are completed by Friday so they can prepare for how many you'll be sending down next week" is a reasonable request.

Yes, you will have to use a combination of good listening, subtle scouting, a keen overall awareness, and a little intuition to monitor all the intangibles of a project that won't show up on status reports or be caught by your software program. Look, listen, and keep your door open.

CHAPTER 8

Software and Organizational Technologies

O nce you start accumulating the data from your research, you will have to organize it and store it. Technology can greatly assist you in all of these endeavors. Computer programs allow you to set up and monitor your schedule and budget. The program will keep track of hours, expenditures, and even provide warnings as to when you may be approaching project risks. Programs can take what you enter (including resources, schedules, dates, and costs) and organize and adjust your data as the project changes. Software may even include tips on how to manage conflicts and deal with team members, but tact, people skills, and other human interactions are still left up to you.

Using Software to Facilitate Your Project

Consider the following questions when determining whether you need program management software:

- How many people are involved in the project?
- About how many tasks are involved?
- To whom are you responsible? (Is the only one involved yourself or does this project affect the entire company?)
- Are tasks being done simultaneously or one at a time?

The key is to know your strengths, and how well you can initiate, organize, schedule, monitor, and complete the project effectively. If a simple "To Do" list will work, use your word processing program and type it out. If two dozen people are involved, handling sixty-five tasks, many at the same time, it might be easier to invest in a project software package. Keep in mind that many projects were completed well before software packages ever existed. However, there's nothing wrong with making life easier, is there?

Don't make the common mistake of depending too heavily on your software programs. They are there to help you facilitate the process, but they cannot do the project management job for you. Every project needs human input.

Your tools are designed to help, but you are still in the driver's seat, especially when it comes to weighing various options and making decisions. You, not your software, are responsible for maintaining integrity. For example, the software will not tell you that someone has entered brochure copy that they've plagiarized from another brochure. Likewise, your software won't tell you why a key team member missed the morning meeting or a shipment from a vendor is delayed because someone neglected to order it on time.

Let's look at what you want from a good project management software package. You want the software to:

- Be user-friendly so you don't need to spend an excessive amount of time figuring out the program or entering data. If repeated data entry is slowing you down, then the program may not be beneficial.
- Store, sort, and retrieve all key information on the project.
- Assist you in tracking, monitoring, and updating the success of the project.
- Provide tips, pointers, warnings, analysis, and other best- or worst-case scenarios based on the data you have input.
- Help you by producing charts, graphs, reports, and other project documentation.

Software Shopping

For more complex and larger scope projects you may want a program that assists you in all key project areas. Integrated project-management software programs can help you set up your budget, fill in your task list, include all task details, set up schedules, create Gantt charts and network diagrams (see Chapter 6), and monitor all aspects of the project. From hours put in by team members to expenditures and reaching key milestones, the monitoring process should cover various project areas. In the end, the program can print out a table, graph, chart, report, or whatever project information you need.

For smaller projects you can use a basic spreadsheet program, a word processing program, or a presentation program. Basic, cross-functional programs can handle the elements of a simple project, and are easier to familiarize yourself with than the more elaborate integrated systems. Of course, if you use several different individual software programs to handle various tasks, you won't have the added feature of integrating them. You'll be re-entering data several times, and that will slow you down.

Keep It Simple

Don't make a project more complicated than it is by setting up an elaborate software program. Personal projects, home improvements, school projects, neighborhood projects, and smaller scale business projects generally won't require you to use specialized project management programs. Check out what tools you have available to you on your computer before investing in additional software.

FACTS

One of the most significant aspects of software programs is that they handle numerous details. On larger, complex programs, this is beneficial from an organizational perspective. The program allows you to clear your mind of extraneous information. Lower your stress level—let the software program manage the wealth of details so that you can handle the people problems and make the big decisions.

When deciding what software will best suit your needs, consider your own level of comfort and expertise on the computer. Some people can sit down with a complicated program and figure it out in an hour. Like an accomplished violinist, they will, in a short time, make the computer hum as they whiz through the software entering everything into the right place. For such people, the finest software systems are worth their abundance of capabilities. For the rest of us, the more intimidating the program, the more reasons we find not to use it. Every year, millions of hours are wasted by team members and project managers staring at computer screens trying to figure out what went wrong. Don't let this happen to you.

Besides data storage and implementation, what do you need from a software program or programs? Use this checklist to help you determine your requirements:

- ❏ Scheduling
- ❏ Task management listings, skills matrix, and personnel lists
- ❏ Gantt charts and other graphs and diagrams

- ❏ Budgeting capabilities
- ❏ Accounting
- ❏ Calendar
- ❏ Word-processing
- ❏ Problem management solutions
- ❏ Project tracking and monitoring
- ❏ Resource tracking
- ❏ Tracking multiple projects
- ❏ Multiple user capabilities
- ❏ "What if" risk management assistance
- ❏ Communications system (for working with team members on- and off-site)
- ❏ Creating reports and presentations
- ❏ Compatibility with other programs

Be an Educated Consumer

It's also advantageous to get a thirty-day, money-back guarantee, in case the program isn't delivering what you anticipated or the functions are not user-friendly. Allow for a reasonable learning curve, but be realistic. If the package is overwhelming and it isn't making your life and the life of the project easier, then it's not for you.

Look around for various other features, and determine what you need given the scope of the project. Be sure you factor in your computer skills and comfort level. Try to anticipate features you may need as the progress grows and changes. It's better to have an extra feature or two than to not have significant features you may need later on. After evaluating your needs, determine whether you are going to use an integrated project management program or separate organizational tools. Keep in mind that if you need more than two individual programs, the integrated system may be best. Consider the scope and the costs involved in your project, and remember that the software package should not cost more than the project!

Popular Favorites

Microsoft Project 2000

The most popular project software program comes from Microsoft. Designed for the individual user (the project manager), Project 2000 lets you easily create and categorize a database of information for your entire project. You'll be able to customize the network diagram to fit your project and make adjustments as you go. The software not only provides an overview of all facets of the project and helps you monitor them, but it is also designed to help you think through scenarios using "what if" situations. Essentially, the software is designed to provide great flexibility and help you through the process from the start of your project through each of your deliverables. An upgrade version is also available for those who already have the Project 1998 version. Microsoft Project 2000 features Internet access and a new Project Central feature allowing two-way communication. For more details, go to *www.microsoft.com*.

SureTrak Project Manager 3.0

From Primavera Systems, SureTrak features a user-friendly KickStart tool that helps you simplify the often intimidating and worrisome initial planning and project starting phase. Built-in tutorials help guide users through the process of creating project schedules and monitoring the project. PERT and Gantt charts are easy to customize and allow you to clearly examine the relationships between various tasks. You'll find specialized calendars, numerous reports that can be customized, up-to-the-moment budget tracking capabilities, team member "To Do" lists, float calendars, critical path scheduling, baseline comparisons, and an easy manner in which to distribute assignments or reports. An extremely comprehensive program, SureTrak provides tremendous flexibility and assists you from the planning phase through organizing and tracking the project to its completion. SureTrak has proven to be highly effective for beginners as well as advanced project managers. To find out more, go to *www.primavera.com*.

ESSENTIALS Make sure the software package that you are interested in is compatible with your existing computer setup. System requirements are usually clearly spelled out on the software package. If you're not sure, ask before you purchase anything.

FastTrack Schedule Version 7.0

Interactive calendars, colorful timelines, and Gantt charts make it easy to read schedules and project details on this highly rated software package from AEC Software. Plan activities for days, weeks, or years ahead on this multi-faceted, point-and-click application. QuickStart templates get you started quickly, and a new Generator feature allows you to produce up-to-the-minute reports with as much data as you wish to include. The program features drag-and-drop editing, action columns, customized timelines, and layouts and milestones. It also includes a host of tracking features such as easy schedule revising, critical path highlighting, and cost and revenue summaries. This program is available in single, five, ten, or twenty-five user versions. For details, go to *www.aecsoftware.com*.

Various Software Products

The following sections examine several other software packages you might consider for your project.

AMS REAL TIME

A suite of software products from AMS includes several cross-platform compatible programs designed to let you manage your project more efficiently. REAL TIME Projects includes cost management and critical path method analysis; REAL TIME Resources lets you organize and track all resources; REAL TIME Solo allows for interaction with team members; and REAL TIME Server serves up an overview of the project. For details, go to *www.amsusa.com*.

Artemis Views, 7000, and Knowledge Plan

Artemis offers three powerful software products. Views handles project planning, cost control, tracking, and analysis; Artemis 7000 provides a sophisticated, customized cost-control system; and Knowledge Plan is a well-stocked resource base to assist with cost estimation. To learn more, go to *www.artemispm.com*.

FACTS

Often companies already have software packages or individual programs that they use for projects. If the company already has sufficient project management software to do the job, you probably don't need to buy something new.

B-Liner Project Outliner

This project organizer from B-Liner provides a flexible, user-friendly system you can use to create your work breakdown structure, estimate costs and time, and set up your project schedule. Project analysis and technical development are included. For details, go to *www.bliner.com*.

CommonOffice

An easy-to-learn, Web-based management and collaboration tool, CommonOffice, helps you save money on IT administrative costs while performing numerous timesaving activities. Some of the possibilities include hiring talent from anywhere in the world, booking boardrooms, and finding rental car deals for out-of-town stakeholders. The system makes it easy to track and generate reports and coordinate activities with off-site team members and other key players. For more information, go to *www.commonoffice.com*.

iTeamWork.com

iTeamWork offers a simple system for creating projects, creating tasks, and assigning tasks to team members. You can check out the overall status of the project or use the e-mail notification system to communicate with team members about various tasks as they proceed through the project. For details, go to *www.iteamwork.com*.

Journyx Timesheet 4.0

A Web-based time-tracking component, Timesheet works with any operating system and browser. Wireless capabilities let you create time records and track time from anywhere. You can also track billing and payroll, or keep tabs on other aspects of your project. Timesheet 4.0 can be customized to integrate and import information to and from other software programs. For more information, go to *www.journyx.com*.

ManagePro 4.0 from Performance Solutions Technology

You can select the Solo edition or the Team edition to optimize productivity at a single or group level. Both products are designed to help all levels of product management. The Team version allows for coordination and collaboration along a multi-access shared database. ManagePro also has a beginning training video series and advanced training CD available. For details, go to *www.performancesolutiontech.com*.

Micro Planner

Micro Planner offers X-Pert and Manager to support different sized projects. The programs interface with one another to support all levels of an organization. X-Pert is used by high-level executives and can handle up to 10,000 operations (tasks, milestones, etc.) while reporting on both progress and cost performance of many projects. Manager is an easy-to-use, multifaceted program with up to 1,500 operations and up to five sub-projects per file. Data entry on Gantt charts, spreadsheets, work breakdown structures, and reports are all included. To find out more, go to *www.microplanning.com*.

onProject.com

The onProject Web-based interactive system is designed to help managers work with their team and allocate resources while bringing team members together from any location. For one low-price, you can bring as many as twenty team members together. For details, go to *www.onproject.com.*

FACTS

Many software packages offer "what if" scenarios to help guide you through a variety of events that may take place on your project. The software can provide alternative methods, find resource conflicts, and display the project at any point along the critical path from any of several desired angles.

OPX2 from Planisware

A Web-based system, OPX2 offers a suite of products for enterprise-wide project management. OPX2 Pro, TimeCard, Server, and Intranet Server will allow you to customize your project planning and reporting based on templates and business rules. Continually refine the process and optimize your production as you work with these fully integrated tools. For more information, go to *www.planisware.com.*

Plan & Progress Tracker from 4aBetterBusiness, Inc.

A Microsoft Excel–based program, available for one to ten users, P&P provides planning and actual Gantt charts. The software lets you track all the important elements of your project and provides percentage completion data and a visual warning system. For details, go to *www.4abetterbusiness.com.*

Project Exchange from IMS Corporation

Project Exchange offers a family of products designed for planning, managing, and tracking projects. Included are Resource Xchange, designed to store and maintain resource information, WebTime, ProjectExplorer, AddInfo, TaskClass, Data Xchange, TimeReview, and ProFiler. Team communication, time reporting compliance, and matrix management of tasks are all included in these comprehensive tools. For more information, go to *www.imscorp.com.*

Project KickStart3 from Experienceware

Eight steps in easy planning icons allow you to quickly start planning your project. Task lists; a library of goals, phases, and obstacles; unlimited report capabilities; sample projects; easy to maneuver Gantt charts; and free tech support are features of this comprehensive PM program. To find out more, go to *www.experienceware.com*.

QuickGantt from Tools-for-Business.com

An easy-to-use software program, QuickGantt includes a pop-up calendar, intuitive worksheet, and, of course, the popular Gantt charts with multiple features and capabilities. QuickGantt allows you to compare actual project data to the original plans, make numerous revisions, and print customized time and cost variance reports. For details, go to *www.tools-for-business.com*.

Task Manager 2000 from Orbisoft

From single- to 100-user versions, this easy-to-use program is designed to help organize any project. Task lists, budgets, "instant snapshot" overviews of work in progress, user-friendly graphic interface custom reports, and direct e-mailing features are all included in this highly rated program. For more information, go to *www.orbisoft.com*.

TeamPlay from Primavera.com

An extensive project, process, and resource management program, TeamPlay was designed as an IT software package to handle numerous projects of varying scopes. A centralized system maintains all project background and data, and can be used with other information systems. For more, go to *www.primavera.com*.

Time Control 3 from HMS Software

A widely used, state-of-the-art time management tool, Time Control 3 links with other popular time management programs and works as a project timekeeping system. Numerous features include a hierarchical data system, preprepared timesheets, and customization of the user interface. For details, go to *www.hmssoftware.ca/*.

Time Disciple from Pictdata Productions

Four core modules highlight this time recording and accounting software package. You can easily list and maintain all task details and document files for one or more projects, create numerous reports, track timesheets and expense reports, and control the parameters of the system to create a full service project management tool to meet all of your needs. To find out more, go to *www.pictdata.com*.

Time Tiger from Indigo Technologies, Ltd.

Designed to replace timesheets, Time Tiger easily tracks all time recording activities. For Workgroups 1.6 and 2.0, the program also includes invoicing and tools for current project analysis, and can support workgroups of up to 150 users. For details, go to *www.indigo1.com*.

Software packages range from $40 or $50 for a simple one-task program to upwards of $60,000 for the top-of-the-line multi-user programs (for high-level project management). Generally speaking, for $350 to $500 you can own a solid software package to handle the majority of your projects.

ESSENTIALS

Look for clear information about all the features of the program and make sure it comes with whatever documentation you will need to learn how to use it. Also, check for a customer service phone number and see if it is a toll-free number. Save all packaging until you are sure everything works. Then save key information.

The capabilities of these and other programs are quite impressive. Customized Gantt charts, histograms, network diagrams, reports, and detailed tracking systems are among the commonly found features. You'll need to look more closely for other features that you feel will help you as the project manager. The goal is to let the program manage the "paperwork," provide a clear picture of the overall project at all times, use calculations and formulas to guide you, and provide early warning signs when necessary. In the end, you'll want to combine modern technology (software) with your own ingenuity, decision-making ability, management style, and people skills.

Discuss your potential selections with others who may have purchased similar software. Very often a recommendation is the best way to determine which are the better of several program possibilities. Keep in mind whether there are potential future uses for the software, particularly if you are buying something for a home or personal project. A program with flexibility will be beneficial to you when you embark on your next project.

High-End Users

While this book is designed primarily for people who manage an occasional project at work, at home, or in the community, there are products designed for high-end users. Project management pros often handle numerous projects at once for a major corporation. Software for intensive use needs to meet advanced demands, allocate resources (including labor from the talent pool), and track progress on a number of projects simultaneously. As one might expect, this level of software can run thousands of dollars. Cobra, Primavera Project Planner, and Micro Planner X-Pert are just three of these high-end software packages.

Technology and Communications

Voicemail, e-mail, and a variety of beepers, pagers, and other communication-based technology also enter into most project planning. The most effective communication allows you a two-way exchange of ideas and information with team members and others, regardless of the location. If you need an immediate response, use the phone; if you need a response soon, use your e-mail.

Communication systems need to be:

- Easy to set up, customize, and use
- Fast and reliable
- Cost-effective
- Able to interface with other systems (e.g., video conferencing is pointless if no one with whom you are working has the capabilities on the other end)

In a business environment, all team members should have their own e-mail and voicemail. While these may already be in place, you may want to customize e-mail for the project. For example, all team members can have a separate project folder for project-related e-mails, enabling them to save all project correspondence in one place.

Don't spend too much time recording and re-recording voicemail messages. People waste valuable time recording new messages every time they will be away from the phone for a day or two. Keep your recorded message brief, and use something generic unless you have information that *must* be conveyed.

Team members should be set up with an online address book with the names and e-mail addresses of fellow team members. The address book should also include outside contractors, vendors, and all key players with whom they may need to communicate. Set up a system so the list is easy to maintain on a regular and consistent basis

When using e-mail, it's a good idea to save the e-mails you send as well as the ones you receive. Your sent items record when you contacted a certain vendor, team member, stakeholder, etc. E-mail lets you save the messages you have previously sent and this can prove valuable. In fact, it may also be important for you to save key phone messages on your voicemail system for future validation.

When leaving voice-mail messages for others, follow these tips:

1. *Give your name and phone number first.* There may be a time limit on incoming messages, and your contact information is most important.
2. *Leave your question in the message.* When the person calls you back, he will already have an answer and information you need.
3. *Keep your message to the point.* Long, rambling messages that neither ask for nor provide information are torturous to listen to, especially for people who are checking in from remote locations.

A good team manager checks his or her messages often and calls people back in a reasonable amount of time. Prioritize your return calls based on the need for deliverables and maintaining your project schedule.

E-mail systems are all essentially similar in that you can get your message out quickly. If your project distribution list is set up properly, you will be able to easily send to one team member or to all the team members with the click of the mouse. If you can't access addresses that easily, you need to modify your e-mail's address book

As project manager, you will want to respond to e-mails in order of priority. However, you should get into the habit of answering all business-related e-mails. You should not be getting "spam" or junk e-mail unless you somehow let your e-mail address get onto unwanted mailing lists.

ESSENTIALS

For help in removing your name from unwanted mailing lists and reducing the amount of spam or junk e-mail you receive, check out a Web site such as *www.spambouncer.org* or *http://spam.abuse.net.*

It is very important that you remind all team members not to forward project e-mails to anyone but other team members or those involved in the project directly. Likewise, you need to remind vendors that you do not want to be on mass e-mailing lists. The last thing you need when racing to keep a project on schedule is to have to sift through junk e-mails. This also means you need to be very careful where you or your team members sign up on the Internet. Many sites will have newsletters, updates, and other information that you do not need sent to you.

Communications Awareness

Remind team members to check their voicemail and e-mail at least twice a day. It is not uncommon for someone to miss a meeting because he or she did not open their e-mail on that day. All team members need to be "communications-aware," meaning they need to periodically check to see who is trying to reach them or what details have been sent their way. Missed meetings and general lack of awareness regarding the rest of the project have no place on your team.

E-mail Etiquette

People have been accused of being sarcastic, accusatory, and otherwise inappropriate based on misinterpreted e-mails. Since there is no voice inflection or body language on the standard e-mail, your recipient does not always know the tone in which your message was intended. Therefore, it's to your benefit to be straightforward and send simple, rather than complicated (or subtle), e-mail messages. Be polite, to the point, and don't "shout" at people (using all caps is considered akin to shouting on the Internet). Use appropriate humor only with people whom you are certain will not misunderstand you. In other words, your first e-mail to a vendor should not open with a joke!

How many times have you sent the entire team a response intended only for your boss? "Reply" and "Reply All" are not one in the same. Take a moment to carefully respond to one or to all as needed.

Long e-mail discussions usually lose their focus and take more time than necessary. If you really want a solid exchange of ideas, brainstorm in person at a meeting or on a conference call, not by e-mail.

Memos and Other Means of Communication

In many offices, e-mail has replaced the infamous "memo." This is not to say that a memo cannot be an effective means of posting information or making sure everyone gets to read what you have to say. If you still use the old memo system, don't abuse it or people will turn it into wallpaper. One advantage of a memo is that if the computer system goes down or loses a file (or ten), the memo is a hard copy for your records. One disadvantage of the memo is that many people are so focused on their computers that they may misplace it before ever reading it. "If it's not in my e-mail or on my voicemail, I probably didn't see it" is a common response uttered in offices worldwide.

Communications are tricky in this world of the telephone and e-mail. Many people no longer want to be bothered with actually speaking to another human being so they hide behind their e-mails as a way of shielding themselves from potential confrontations (as well as positive interactions). It's a shame. It's also not the best way to manage most projects.

You need to use various means of communication to effectively handle the different aspects of your project. Use the right communication technology for the right purpose:

- *Short messages*—Ue e-mail, voicemail, or a handwritten, prominently placed note.
- *Longer messages*—Use an e-mail attachment or fax.
- *Two-way exchange of ideas*—Use the telephone or meet in person.
- *Multiple exchanges of ideas*—Conference calls are good for three- or four-way communications. Beyond four people a conference call often gets confusing. In-person meetings are still most effective.
- *Information or announcements to the team*—E-mail all or post a memo/notice in a central location.
- *Urgent message*—Call someone's cell phone, pager, or beeper. If he or she has none of the above, leave a concise phone message and an e-mail.
- *Personal matters*—Have face-to-face interaction, or by phone if the person is off-site.

Personal praise or a handwritten note can be a welcome break in this world of impersonal e-mails. Hearing someone's voice in a conversation can stress the urgency or significance of a situation, which may otherwise be lost with an e-mail. On the other hand, e-mails allow someone working on the computer to stay focused and not have to stop to deliver a message in person. E-mail is cost-effective for frequent long-distance communications and works well for getting messages to several recipients at once.

ESSENTIALS

If you're not sure what attachments the recipient will be able to open, send a text file. Otherwise, find out if they will be able to open an attachment before sending it.

You should also match the communications system to the type of project, the team involved, and the nature of the overall group or organization. There's no need to fax your son a note if he's working on a family project and he's upstairs in his room. On the other hand, you won't want to call the sponsor with every little question you may have—instead you may send one e-mail with a list of attached questions. A social organization might plan more face-to-face encounters or phone calls to handle a project since they are focused on the social aspect of their organization as well as the project at hand.

Remember, e-mail has not replaced the phone or the fax machine, nor have any of them combined to replace face-to-face communication. Use them all and use them wisely.

CHAPTER 9
Risk Management

The next two chapters will look beyond the scheduling, budgeting, and progress of the project and focus on what can go wrong. We will address two very different concerns that can befall any project: risk and conflict. There is much written about risk and how it is assessed, and controlled, throughout the course of a project. While risk is inherent in any project from the onset, conflict is not. In this chapter, learn how you can manage risks to your project.

The Nature of Risk

To begin looking at risk, we need a workable definition. From a broad-based perspective, "risk" is the exposure to uncertain, and potentially bad, consequences. In the scope of project management, risks are uncertainties that may negatively affect the project by challenging the project's constraints or parameters. Unforeseen consequences may result in loss of time, money, labor, or the project as a whole. This differs from the financial planning definition, in which greater risk is seen as potentially promising, with higher potential rewards. The financial planner looks at the risk/reward scenario, whereas the project management considers the completed project without negative risks to be its own reward. Positive outcomes of risk are generally not addressed in project management's definition. One of the reasons we continue to add in the positive aspect of risk-taking is that it is from taking a calculated risk that new discoveries and new methods of dealing with issues are founded. After all, if Christopher Columbus hadn't defied those who said the earth was flat and that the idea of sailing to discover the Indies was not feasible, he never would have discovered America.

People seeking excitement will often take greater risks. Hang gliding and other "extreme" sports are very much based on the excitement that accompanies great risk. Projects also take risks that result in positive outcomes, as there are risks inherent in any decision that you make. If you knew you could never be wrong, you would no longer be taking a risk. Even the simplest decision to order software package "A" over package "B" has some degree of risk involved. Package "A" might not work for your particular project. Of course, the other side of the equation is that if you take a chance on a package that you are not sure of, it could prove to be more beneficial than you had hoped and solve other problems for which you had not initially purchased it. Again, I remind you this is a different definition of "risk" then that usually associated with project management.

Any project is inherently a risk, because you are trying to accomplish a goal without the certainty that you will reach it. One might conclude (fairly) that project management is essentially a form of risk management in that from the initial plan you are uncertain as to the end result.

Furthermore, the initial plan contains variables such as time and cost that cannot be "set in stone," so to speak. Despite all the calculations, analysis, and research that you have done to create your initial project plan, the project will proceed without you, or anyone else, knowing exactly what course it will ultimately take.

FACTS

If projects didn't allow for some degree of risk, great discoveries and inventions would never have been made. The Wright Brothers and Charles Lindbergh took great risks to achieve their projected goals. Risk should be managed with precautions, but it should not stop you from proceeding with your project, unless you determine that the risk is too great or without reward.

Despite the common definition of project risk management, to seek out and avert potentially negative factors that will prevent the project from being completed in time and under budget, risk is actually inherent in many forms throughout the project, and is both positive as well as negative. For our purposes of understanding project risk management, consider risk a negative factor throughout the chapter. However, I will point out some positive aspects of risk taking from time to time.

Types of Project Risks

Risks associated with the project itself are termed internal project risks or technical risks. Risks associated with the impact of the project on the rest of the world are termed external risks, and may often include safety risks. Generally the project focus, at least in the corporate world, is on internal risk, or trying to prevent uncertainties from threatening the life or the direction of the project.

Obviously, the degree of risk, internal or external, will determine the attention such a risk merits. If a new Web site isn't launched on time, the world won't end. However, if a project goes awry that has an effect on the health or safety of individuals or the environment, such as a contaminating oil spill, there is greater concern because the effects of that risk are greater.

A project manager must look beyond the internal risks of time and budget of a project with a significant potential impact in order to see the "global picture." A project that might result in the next Three Mile Island disaster takes on a more significant risk than what's involved to bring your office project in under budget.

Assessing Risks

Assessing both internal and external risks means thinking through the probability of project success or failure and the subsequent results of any or all tasks involved in the project. How likely is it that task "A" will set you behind schedule? Will the need to add more resources to complete that task put you over budget? How likely is it that task "A" will be hazardous to the company or the neighborhood?

ALERT

Risk mitigation is a factor that needs to be included in your budget. Look at all possible repercussions before you make a move. If you find that you have too many areas in the project that call for advance action (or mitigation), you may want to rethink the feasibility of the project.

During the initial planning stage of the project, you are assessing risk each time you assign a completion date or a budget figure. If, for example, you plan to move the office but aren't sure whether to select June or July for the move, you will assess the possibilities of moving in either month and choose the one in which you have the greater likelihood of a successful, cost-efficient, and time-efficient move. From an internal or technical perspective, you need to determine in which month you will have the resources and the budget to complete the project successfully. From an external or safety perspective, you will determine in which month the move will be least likely to interfere with the overall workings of the company and its ability to conduct business. Assessing the risk as you plan your project will add up to this overall determination. Granted, most tasks on most projects have little external risk, but it's well worth keeping such risks in mind.

You may also face a quality risk. The project may be proceeding on schedule and within budgetary constraints, but the product may be inferior to what you were originally seeking. It may not be as easy to determine such risks to the quality of the final deliverables as it is to see what might set you behind schedule or cost more than your budget allows. Inexperienced personnel, poor equipment, dated software products, poor internal communications, and similar factors raise the level of risk that you may not produce the quality that you had hoped for.

For example, a popular freelance writers' Web site has writers bid against one another for writing assignments. The site does not set minimum bids, and ultimately some inexperienced young writer will end up winning a job that should pay $1,000 for a professional writer, because he or she is willing to do it for $100 to get his or her foot in the door. The company accepting an amateur for a job that should have a professional is taking a tremendous quality risk. Often they find themselves hiring a writer for $1,200 to do a rush job rewrite because the original work was substandard. Of course the flip side is that the young new writer could have fresh ideas and this could be his or her big break. The big question: Are you willing to take on this big a risk with your project's quality?

Dealing with Risks

Now that you know what the risks are, what can you do about them? First, you analyze each risk associated with the project. Take all the internal risks, anything that could stand in the way of successfully completing the project (on time and under budget), and prioritize them. Which risks need the most attention because they could shut down the project completely? Consider these your top priorities—risks that, if not addressed, will spell disaster. Next, look at risks that can be monitored closely, and managed with some adjustments. Finally, look at low-level risks that can easily be fixed, eliminated, or ignored with no impact on the overall project.

You will then need to respond in one of three manners, as discussed in the following sections.

Contingency Planning

Have plan "B," your backup or contingency plan, in place just in case. Contingency planning (discussed in detail in Chapter 12) is an important safeguard. It can range from a less favored, but perhaps more cost-effective, manner of handling a situation to a backup parachute, which can save the life of the project. The more critical a task or resource is to the outcome of the project, the more you need a backup plan.

If you are prepared with viable contingency plans you will have already minimized the level of risk. In fact, you may even be able to take greater positive risks. One project manager, knowing that for a yearlong project he had a backup plan that would still keep the project under budget, got management's permission and moved some surplus funding into a CD account. Thus the funding actually grew during the duration of the project. This was a calculated risk, since he was earning money that had not been earmarked for a specific task or resource. If anything had gone wrong he might have needed this surplus funding, but his plan "B" scenario did not utilize the extra funds.

ESSENTIALS
Establish a backup plan for your team members should they become ill or leave the project. Even the President of the United States has a backup, in the form of the Vice President! Cross-training your team will enable a current team member to fill in temporarily and keep the project moving.

No one is saying that you need to take such risks. Risk management does not necessarily mean that you have to make proactive decisions in favor of the project. Just be aware that being closed to innovative ideas may limit your opportunity for growth.

"The project is running great and I have a backup (contingency) plan in place just in case we run into trouble. Therefore, I say we should order some additional supplies," says a confident project manager, thinking positively. Good, well-thought-out contingency plans can give you some peace of mind.

Of course, there are also emergency contingency plans that are not simply another way of reaching your project's goal, but are a way of saving anything from a project to a life. Plans that you hope you'll never need must be in place for the safety of individuals first, and the project second. These types of plans aren't usually specific to the typical business or personal project, however. Often, such emergency procedures are already in place, in the form of smoke detectors or alarm systems. Unless you are working with chemicals or dangerous materials, such emergency situations are usually outside of the project scope. The larger safety plan of the environment in which you are working (i.e., the office building, school, community center, etc.) already has procedures for dealing with emergencies.

Risk Mitigation

When you act in advance—spend the time and money to implement methods of reducing or eliminating the risk ahead of time—you're mitigating risk. This approach requires you to make a judgment call based on the probability that a risk will interfere with the success of the project. Much of the feasibility study, used when you started the project, touches upon risk management or potential risk management. You don't want to start a project that isn't cost-effective, nor do you want to start one that is too high-risk, unless you have ways of managing that risk.

Sometimes a degree of risk mitigation is built into the plans by outside forces—such as registering your project with a particular governmental body, or taking safety precautions as mandated by government or policy makers. Risk mitigation that comes under your jurisdiction is similar, only you have to make the decisions. How prevalent is the risk? What would happen in the worst-case scenario? Loss of money? Loss of time? Loss of manpower? Before starting out on the project, perhaps you need to settle a labor dispute to avoid a slowdown or work stoppage. You might have to scale down an aspect of the project to mitigate a high-level risk. You will then need to address this mitigation to see the potential effect on various other aspects of the project, as well as on the project overall. Make sure that:

- Other tasks are not adversely affected by mitigating a risk in one area
- The project is still cost-effective
- The project will still produce the same quality results

If a potential risk is discovered after the project has already begun, you can still mitigate that risk. Once again, you will have to look at other areas of the project.

Risk Monitoring

To monitor risks effectively, you must have an adequate system of tracking the probability of a risk occurring based on re-evaluating that probability at various times throughout the project. A long lasting or complex project will obviously require more monitoring. If there is a delay in starting the project, this too will mean you will need to monitor the project more closely once it gets started. Often, project managers are forced to put a project on hold. They then start it later than expected, changing the due dates, but do not take into account all the added risks that may exist because of the change in starting date. From personnel no longer being able to meet the necessary time commitment to changes in policy or government regulations, risks have to be re-evaluated every time a project is delayed.

Monitoring also means knowing when you can accept a level of variance from your original plan. Remember, you should anticipate variance from the start, since very little, if anything, in your original plan is set in stone. Costs, labor hours, and numerous other factors will probably not be the same as what you anticipated in your original plan. As you monitor the project, ask yourself what level of variance is acceptable and what variance between the intended and the actual numbers shows high-risk for potential problems. You'll need to carefully make this determination and then act or not. If, for instance, you are looking at the date by which deliverables are due, you need to determine whether or not you can afford a delay from the standpoint of time and money. If you cannot afford such a delay, you may need to pay more money (rush charges) to get the deliverables in your hands on time. Monitoring will keep you abreast of this situation so you can best prepare. A poorly monitored project is in danger of undetected risks that may present you with many unwelcome surprises. (See Chapter 7 for much more on monitoring.)

ESSENTIALS

If we worried about every risk in life, we would probably never leave the house, and certainly not start a project. Risk is inherent in everything. Every time you take on a project, you risk failure. Therefore, it is important not to dwell on risk to the point of being immobilized. Remember, if the early bird dwelled too heavily on the risks, he'd never catch the worm!

If you had a dollar for every time someone managing a project said, "I don't even want to think about that," you'd be richer than Bill Gates. Most people don't want to face potentially negative risks. This is true in many aspects of life. We've all sidestepped a problem by pretending it wasn't there. But failure to address an issue regarding your project won't make it go away. You must be realistic about potential problems. Of course, on the other hand, if you focus on every little risk, you'll never start the project. You must be ready to take some risks to even begin the project. The bottom line is that you need to address all risks and weigh them—not ignore them—then decide what actions you'll take next.

Prioritizing Risks

You can label them in any manner you like, but it is important to prioritize potential risks. The following shows one way of prioritizing:

- Four-alarm risks (****) are those with a high degree of probability that will have a major impact on the project.
- Three-alarm risks (***) have a lower degree of probability but still pack a wallop and can have a major impact on the project.
- Two-alarm risks (**) are high in probability but are manageable or controllable with the right degree of attention.
- One-alarm risks (*) are low in probability and will not prove harmful, just perhaps a minor nuisance.

Each project is unique, so no boilerplate program can tell you what risk to put in any one category. Time and money will factor heavily into the issue, as will the nature of the project itself. Even the same risk in two scenarios can be quite different in scope. For example, a computer problem on a computer-based project is a four-alarm problem. Greater precaution needs to be taken to guard against the system going down, and a full-backup plan needs to be in place. The same crash of a computer that is storing information for a small dress shop's upcoming sale is a one-alarm problem because the information can be recreated and the sale can commence regardless of whether the computer is repaired. Perhaps just a hard copy of the discount structure would be a simple safeguard against the risk of being incapacitated.

Backing up all computer programs, files, and data is an easy and essential manner of risk mitigation that can save you hours of time, effort, and money in the event of a power failure or computer mishap. Make it a practice to back up your work regularly!

Similarly, a serious $3,000 financial risk to your small business project would be a drop in the bucket to a project at a major company like IBM.

As a project manager, you'll act quickly when you see a three- or four-alarmer, monitor a two-alarmer, and hopefully handle a one-alarmer quickly or perhaps delegate it to someone else.

Knowing how and where you could get your hands on another copy of a software program or having one installed in a laptop that is not plugged into the same electrical line as your computer system is a simple way to mitigate some technical problems. People rely too heavily on "the system" when too often the system is not up and functioning. Be able to work around it effectively.

Communicating Risks

So, do you want to ride through town on horseback yelling, "The British are coming, the British are coming," or do you only want to tell a select few, so as not to worry the others? The more global the risk, the more you will need to spread the word. However, you must be:

- Sure of what you are saying. (Rumors can pose a great risk to your project.)
- Ready with some plan of action. Even if your plan is to throw in the towel, you need to be ready to follow up your words with information so that people will know what to do next.

Carefully select the key people to whom you will relay either good or bad news regarding the project. If there are risks that could affect a specific department or a task being done by a team member, then that is whom you need to inform. Stakeholders who are privy to all information also need to be informed. Judge by the level of the risk. A defective product gets recalled because it can cause potential risk to the customers who have purchased it. Customers generally need not know about a strike by bottlers of a brand of soda since it won't affect them directly. However, investors, management, and others who stand to directly profit or lose money because of the impending strike need to know of the potential risk. You don't want to turn risk into panic situations. Make sure that you bring risk into the open, but don't just yell "Fire." Gather your information properly. Many projects have been halted prematurely that could have continued had someone not caused widespread fear of impending doom.

You can find yourself facing greater losses if you misjudge a risk, so it's important that you are correct in your assessment. If the time sheet is incorrect and you are bringing in additional manpower on a job where you really do not have to, you may be jeopardizing the project by spending extra money unnecessarily. Likewise, if a team member foresees disaster in his or her task before you consider the task risky to the entire project, delve further into how and why this team member has determined this risk. You need to not only find risks, but also make sure, before you assess and prioritize them, that they are indeed real, meaning they have potential consequences that could affect the project. Risks are sometimes based on improper estimates or improper methodology. Investigate the source and the assessment of the situation before simply acknowledging a risk.

Software programs can help you determine what the probability of a risk may be, provided the information was input correctly. The focus here is on negative risks and uncertainties. A computer program isn't going to say, "Hey, go for the touchdown, you're way out in front, take a chance!" Of course, you can't oversee every detail of every task, but you can monitor or have a way of checking as much as possible before you act on what could be inaccurate information. First, go back and look at the numbers and dates that were input before you take the word of the early warning system.

Monitoring Every Step of the Way

While not all risks are substantial enough to require constant monitoring, some level of risk monitoring is necessary throughout the project. The trick is to look ahead as you proceed through the project and see what you can find in advance. Twenty/twenty hindsight would only be valuable if we had a way to go back in time. It would certainly make the project manager's job that much easier.

ESSENTIALS   One way to assess risk is to study what went wrong in previous projects that were similar to yours. If you can determine why such errors occurred, you may be able to prevent them from reoccurring in your project.

If you find risks in your feasibility study and can address them even before starting the project, you will be that much farther ahead. If the risks are too great and the potential for disaster is greater than possible benefits, you won't bother starting—at least under the current circumstances. Only in the movies will you hear "We may all be killed, but we've got to try it anyway." In real life you won't embark on a project that risky!

Look Outside

The next place to look for risks is within your resources. Can you hit warp speed without blowing everyone to smithereens? Will the software program accommodate such a big project? If the wood you choose is mahogany, will the kite ever get off the ground?

Look for risks inherent in your resources, including your personnel. Are the people performing the tasks skilled at those tasks? Has she ever flown a plane before? Will he be able to spot an iceberg if you are sailing directly toward one? Giving responsibility to the wrong party can be risky. All resources, including people, need to be accurately assessed in advance, and monitored once selected. Careful monitoring of your resources is very important. A "loose cannon" on your team can spell disaster just as surely as faulty equipment.

You need to monitor externally as well as internally. Knowing the exact speed at which the ship is traveling at any given time still does not mean you are monitoring for icebergs. Monitor for all significant details. Usually this focuses around time, money, and quality in your project.

Monitor the Variables

Once the project proceeds, new risks can occur with every unknown cause and effect relationship. Many projects fail because the project team is not aware of the factors that lead to risks. When the risks become apparent, they are either not detected in time or they are not clearly identified and properly communicated to management or to those that can help avoid or eliminate the risk. Other projects fail because risks were actually detected and communicated, but the party on the receiving end did not fully understand the nature of the risk. If one party communicates a four-alarm risk and management perceives a two-alarm risk, it will not be properly resolved.

Risks can also be detected too far into the process to make adjustments. An error in phase two of programming may not be detected until phase five, at which point the project is doomed because it is too late to turn back because the time and cost limitations will not allow it. You must detect, assess, and monitor risk during every phase of the project, and testing needs to be implemented, especially for technical projects or new product development.

Risk Hunting

It's easy to say that you must look for risks that jeopardize your project's well being, but where exactly do you look? The risk is generally associated with the boundaries set forth by the project. If, for example, money were no object, then you could never be in risk of going over budget. If the project deadline were open-ended, you could never fall behind schedule.

ESSENTIALS

Sometimes assessing a risk factor and making a decision on how to handle it is a marvelous learning experience. As long as no one's safety is jeopardized, you may let some risks go so your team can learn from trial and error. Newcomers may also benefit from exposure to risks as long as neither they nor the project are in danger. Step back and see if he or she can find, and deal with, the potential risk that lies ahead.

The parameters that surround the project determine the need to monitor for specific internal risks. You have to assess what can make a project go over budget or fall behind schedule. Do you have proper funding? Are all expenses going through a set accounting system? How carefully have you researched and confirmed all costs? All estimates or quotes?

The biggest problems in budget management generally stem from:

1. Improper estimates of costs for resources (including manpower)
2. Unmonitored or uncontrolled spending
3. Not properly estimating the time or scope of the project and needing more money to cover additional time and labor
4. Not allocating proper funding for monitoring and testing.

Scheduling risks generally stem from:

1. Poorly estimating the duration of tasks and the overall project
2. Not accounting properly for dependency tasks to be completed before other tasks can begin.
3. Not allowing proper time in your schedule for monitoring and testing.

Other key internal risks include having the wrong person doing the task, poor communication between yourself and your team as well as among team members, and the always-prevalent technical glitches and failures.

Numerous other internal factors can present risk, which is why you should plan detail-by-detail and task-by-task, then monitor constantly. You must keep your hand on the wheel as you guide a project along its course.

Making an Educated Guess

External factors can be harder to gauge. The world serves up its own parameters, including the state of the economy, laws, and other external constraints. Depending on the project, you may need to keep tabs on the financial market, industry-specific news, buying trends, competition, legal issues, politics (office or government), and even the weather. External risk factors fall into two categories: those you can foresee, and those you can't.

Naturally you can take precautions against the former, but not the latter. In some cases, however, you can buy insurance to protect larger-scale projects from unforeseen risks.

Evaluating potential external risks will have you following the same logic investors use when they read up on trends, overseas economic conditions, and other factors that could affect their investment. You need to evaluate how external factors could impinge upon your project and take precautionary steps. Often, public relations is used as a risk management tool against possible negative publicity that could deter customers or clients. When the overall state of Web-based companies began to struggle from a glut of companies jumping on the Internet bandwagon, project managers working on Web sites saw the need to act quickly in order to not lose their funding. Those few that were able to catch this impending risk early (wherever possible) broadened their horizons and planned to expand into brick and mortar businesses so they were no longer solely dependent upon e-commerce.

FACTS

Managing against risk is all around us. We use many methods of risk avoidance daily, every time we buckle our seat belt in a car or wear a helmet while riding a motorcycle. Whatever the risk of an unplanned event, we take precautions. Other examples of risk management planning that you are familiar with include fire/emergency exits, rain dates for a scheduled event, sun block, anti-virus computer software, and safety goggles.

What if you know there are risks lurking in your project, but you haven't yet identified what they are? You could call in an expert or even someone who has managed a similar project at least once or twice before. You could also call in a consultant to find risks. Be forewarned, however, that there are many so-called consultants out there. Before hiring a consultant:

- Make sure you do not take a consultant at face value. Find out where they have consulted previously.
- Make sure they understand *exactly* what you need from them. Good communication is essential.
- Make sure the consultant is not using the old trick of telling you what he thinks you want to hear or spreading rhetoric around. If his guidance isn't supported by solid, documented research and findings, be skeptical.

Use Your Team

You need not fly solo when risk hunting. Team members, through meetings, questionnaires, and reports, can identify concerns and potential risks to the project that you may not have otherwise been aware of. Brainstorming can provide a marvelous forum for revealing flaws in the underlying plan or risks in the developing project. Effective brainstorming means allowing everyone present to have a chance to chime in. It also requires that you take good notes. After the brainstorming session, you should follow though on all ideas and see if they lead to a risk in the making. The flip side of this is that team members may identify a better course of action or cost-effective method that may be reason to take a "calculated" positive risk.

Worth Your While

Assessing and managing risk have additional benefits other than saving the project from impending doom. By monitoring and seeking potential pitfalls—or for that matter, areas of potential strength—you're encouraging forward thinking. Assessing risk and determining how you will get around it, work through it, tackle it, or succumb to it are all processes that encourage communication and analysis. Tasks are not simply being performed, team members are encouraged to look at the big picture. Strategies are emerging. Team members who look for risks as they proceed are thinking beyond their isolated roles. They are also looking at the potential impact of their work and the overall project. Evaluation and decision-making become part of the ongoing process and are therefore honed skills.

If the project centers on a product or service for the consumer, a positive step in gaining consumer confidence is to make the process of risk management known. Don't you feel more confident knowing a product was carefully pre-tested? In any project, there is a higher level confidence in the final product if you know that a lot of the "what if" questions were asked and answered during the development and production process.

Risk management also drives the development of a hands-on approach. A project manager cannot sit back and assume all is well. It necessitates monitoring and facilitates sound decision-making based on tracked and recorded results. The need for team–member accountability and accurate reporting of time and money status are elevated. People are responsible for the information they provide regarding their work.

From a financial perspective, risk management is a sound business practice. You pay little for using logic, analysis, brainstorming, and forward thinking to detect risks. You can pay much more if high-risk situations that could have been avoided suddenly occur late in the project. The majority of negative project risks can be avoided if they are detected soon enough. The more people appreciate and utilize risk management techniques, the less likely it is that risks will slip through the cracks.

ESSENTIALS

The fewer surprises that occur in a project, the more in control you will stay and the less variance you should have from your original critical path. This can be summed up in the equation: Greater degree of risk management = fewer surprises = less need for crisis management.

A discussion of the negative impact of risks would be incomplete without noting your stress level as project manager. If you are aware of potential risks as you proceed, you will have alternative strategies. You will have open lines of communication with your team members, who will be following your lead and also thinking ahead. Knowing all of this should reduce your stress level significantly. Having a sense of control and a firm grasp on where the project is at any given time will allow you to feel more comfortable.

Risk Interactions and Magnification

Have you ever been in a situation where one step in the process goes wrong, and that one disconnect leads to another and then to another, like a domino effect? A late deliverable at stage one of a project leads to a late deliverable at stage two. That leads to a delay in the meeting at stage three, which leads to delayed funding, and so on.

The project manager needs to research the capabilities of a technical team closely before hiring it. Be sure the team has done a project of this magnitude before.

Let's look at an example. One of the many dot-coms that did not survive the downsizing of the industry in early 2001 was a real estate Web site that hired content writers, a sales staff, and a technical team. The technical team, however, miscalculated how long it would take to set up the site. The project of building the site fell way behind schedule, causing the content writers to have to rewrite much of their material so that it would be timely, thus adding to the expense of the project (more hours necessary for the content writers). The sales team, meanwhile, had made co-branding deals that had to be delayed because the technical team was not finished with its end of the project. This cost the company a great deal of money as several of the co-branding deals fell through, which, in turn, cost the company more money and hurt its reputation since no one wanted to make a deal with the uncertainty surrounding the launch of the site. By the time the technical team finally completed their work on the site, the sales team had departed for greener pastures and the project had virtually run out of money to pay the content writers (or site designer, for that matter). Needless to say, the site is no longer around.

The project's phases should have been layered so the content and advertising sales teams did not start their tasks until the technical team was much closer to completion. That simple precaution—waiting to make sure the project was progressing as planned before becoming overcommitted—would have saved the company not only money, but their reputation. The technical aspect of the project should have been monitored more closely and tests should have been run to see what this site could and could not handle. With awareness and knowledge, a more realistic assessment could have been made to determine when this phase of the project would be nearing completion and what needed to be re-programmed in the first place.

Limit Your Exposure

The bottom line is that risks in one area can affect others. Schedule accordingly, and then monitor closely and take necessary precautions from the earliest stages.

A risk can also become more significant as the project increases. When writing a ten-chapter book, not having an anti-virus software program running during the writing of chapter one is risky. You could lose an entire chapter, or 10 percent of your book. Writing four more chapters without installing the anti-virus software or backing up your work means that 40 percent of the project is now in jeopardy. (As an author, I dare not even think beyond that!) Precautions early on save you greatly as your project grows. The longer you work without a safeguard in place, the more you risk losing should something jeopardize the project.

ESSENTIALS   Limit the degree of risk you may face by negotiating various escape clauses in contracts. If the other party does not meet its contractual obligations, you can get out of the contract without any repercussions. In other words, you are sharing the risk rather than taking on all of it yourself.

Here's another example. Let's say you are handling the money at a four-hour book drive (which raises a similar amount of funds every hour) and someone is scheduled to take the collected money to the bank every hour. The risk of that money being lost or stolen is only 25 percent, because that is the amount of money on hand at any given time. If, however, no one picks up the money for two hours, you may have 50 percent of the day's profits in the till, meaning there is more at stake should the money be taken. Risk increases as you fail to either monitor or take action.

Sample Risk Analysis

Even the simplest of plans has its tripwires. Ask (and answer) as many "what ifs" as possible before you begin, and remember that anything can disrupt your progress.

Location: A small business with twenty employees, occupying an old building.

Project: You have an area in your office space with plumbing and a sink that is now used for storage. The facility has windows and ventilation but very few electrical outlets. You would like to transform the space into a lunchroom facility for your employees. Your employees are willing to help.

Goal: Set up a lunchroom where employees can eat.

Below is a section of your risk management plan.
Risks that you need to consider:

What You Need to Assess	Risk Factors
Can the facility be used as a lunchroom	The electrical wiring and outlets won't support a refrigerator, microwave, etc.
Amount of time needed by team to complete the job	Taking people away from doing other work.
Resource costs	Cost factor will be excessive. High costs for electrician, contractor, etc. if needed.
What equipment and other items need to be purchased?	Lack of research Buying the wrong equipment Buying inferior products
Personal safety	Injury to anyone moving or lifting equipment.

Priority Risks:

1. Electrical wiring
2. Personal safety
3. Cost factor

4. Researching and pricing materials
5. Number of items to purchase
6. Time factor

Your preliminary plan of action:

1. Draw up a rough diagram of the new lunchroom facility. Consider how much space you have and how many people it will service. Determine that it is indeed feasible. (Your feasibility study may require you calling in an electrician to make sure the wiring will support a lunchroom facility. If it would take major rewiring, you might rethink whether or not this plan is feasible.)
2. Put together a team of people who will help you transform the space into a lunchroom and to discuss what you will need to purchase.
3. Determine who can best do each job and assign tasks.
4. Research the items that will need to be purchased. Have team meetings to discuss what to buy. Use brainstorming and then get a consensus as to what is needed.

5. Research the cost of any outside resources necessary, such as a carpenter, movers, etc. (This will be in conjunction with a need for expertise and to avoid personal injuries to team members.)
6. Draw up a budget.
7. Estimate a time frame for completing the lunchroom.
8. Meet with everyone again to determine what does and does not fit within the budget so you are sure you can afford to embark on this project.
9. Create/post your task breakdown.
10. Set up a preliminary schedule. Review with team before finalizing it.
11. Monitor your progress as you and your team create the new lunchroom space.
12. Look for risks to completing the project that may occur along the way.

Remember, the goal of this project is to transform an unused storage space into a comfortable lunch facility. Your team will determine exactly what needs to be purchased and help make the transformation. This will include cleaning out the space, cleaning and painting the area, and purchasing all the necessary items. You may note that the time frame is a low priority on this project since the facility has not had a lunchroom before and there is no one saying it must be ready by a specific date. Therefore, while you are picking a date by which you'd like to open up the lunchroom so that people can eat comfortably on the premises, it is not vital that it be completed in x amount of days, making the time aspect of the project less of a headache.

Monitor for conflict during projects where people may vary in their opinion of what is and is not necessary. Put people in charge of making certain decisions and have everyone agree to abide by that decision. The person responsible can elect to solicit outside opinions—or not—but ultimately, the decision is his.

And in the end—after much hard work, some conflict, and a few changes to the original plan and budget—a new lunchroom facility is born and the people can take pride in a job well done.

Common Project Problems

Risks are generally thought of as those things that can go wrong on the project. What about all those common things that are simply defined as "project problems?" Besides the risk of falling behind schedule, going off budget, or simply producing poor quality results, here are some of the common project problems:

- *Too many chefs spoil the project.* One person wants it done by Wednesday, one says "make it Tuesday"; another wants you to use Microsoft Project, while another hates that program. It's important to establish from the start who is in a position of authority and who is not—and figure out where you come in. If you have to answer to nine people, you'll have a project going in nine directions and none of them will be toward the goal.

- *Dust it off and try again.* Little do you know, but the project you have embarked on has already failed three times for numerous reasons. Sure, everyone is snickering, but you don't know why. Make sure you scout around and do a feasibility study—find out if this project can indeed be done, or if you are in a situation with too little funding, poor resources, and no clear-cut plan of action. If that's the case, run like hell. Old disasters under new names with new leaders do not work unless a key component has been changed. If, for example, an old project from twenty years ago will thrive thanks to new technology, then perhaps it's time to give it a go, but do extensive homework first.

- *Bad timing.* How many people saw ads for new start-up Internet companies at the time when so many were falling by the wayside? How many people wanted to jump onboard those projects? Just like selling those "Y2K" T-shirts was not a wise move in the summer of 2000, many projects fail because there is no market for them at a given time. Check economic factors, industry factors, competition, and other signs that may determine whether or not your project is a good idea at this time.

ALERT

Allow for the risk that comes with a learning curve. There is always a greater risk when you have no previous data available. If you've never done something before and you can't find anyone who has, then you'll have the added risk that your estimates will be off. The same holds true for team members performing new tasks, or technical equipment you haven't used before.

- *Oops, there goes another one!* Too many people dropping off the team means either the incentives are not keeping them onboard, they do not have a vested interest in the team, or they have no enthusiasm for the project. Losing a member or two along the way is not uncommon and shouldn't be a major problem, unless it's that one expert you really need. However, if you are losing people left and right, it's time to up the payoff, boost morale, or find out why so many are jumping ship.

- *We'll start tomorrow.* Some projects are constantly delayed. Something is always slowing them down, whether it's funding, permits, inspections, lack of resources, or simply low priority due to other, more demanding projects. This is not generally a good sign. Try to get a firm start date. The longer you delay the less likely the project will succeed.

- *Nobody speaks to one another.* Sure, there are plenty of documents, reports, and even e-mails, but poor or no communication between people is generally not a good sign. As far as we have progressed technologically, when projects that rely on people have no communication, they generally lose both enthusiasm and the element of creative thinking and planning that comes from such interaction among team members.

- *What a chummy group!* The opposite of no communication is a chummy, enthusiastic team that spends way too much time chatting, lunching, and socializing, but little time working. While camaraderie is great, you'll need to channel such enthusiasm into some productivity. Be tactful and make the work enjoyable, but coax people to get the job done.

- *What are we doing here again?* If there have been so many changes to the project in terms of resources, planning, and primary objectives that you're no longer sure what the goal of the project is, you're in big trouble. After all, how will you know when you've reached the goal if you don't know what it is? Make sure all of the changes, including those made to the schedule and budget, fit in with your primary plan and your initial project goal. Don't let changes occur faster than you can comfortably process them into the plan, or things can go spiraling out of control.

- *Naked Thursdays!* If the boss has odd requests, make sure to (tactfully) put them into perspective. You cannot do every offbeat scheme that upper management wants to "try." Be very selective and always explain that your decision is based on what's in the best interests of the project.

CHAPTER 10

Conflict Resolution and Handling Various Personalities

This chapter deals with conflict resolution, which, like risk management, is a method of problem solving within the scope of the overall project. Conflict may be considered by some theorists to be inherent in the course of human interaction. In essence, conflict is a type of risk, because, left unresolved, it could jeopardize the future of your project. Unfortunately, it is not a risk you can usually mitigate in advance since you do not usually know where such conflict will arise. However, if you're putting together a team, you can make an effort to include people who you know generally get along with one another.

Cooperative Resolution

The idea of cooperative conflict behavior suggests that parties work together to resolve their conflict. This, however, assumes that both parties are willing to enter into such a cooperative agreement. Getting two sides to sit down and cooperate is easier said than done. In any group situation there is also the potential for competitive conflicts, which perpetuate and lead to greater problems.

As a project manager you will need to address the need for cooperation while understanding that there may be a degree of competition involved at the root of a conflict.

Often conflict is also the result of attitudes, or a belief system embodied within the individual long before the project was ever initiated. Such prejudgments are often at the root of an impending conflict. There may also be self-doubt and lack of confidence in one's own abilities. Interacting with others, who may be more confident or highly skilled, can intensify these insecurities.

QUESTIONS?

What causes conflict?
Conflict is often the result of uncertainty or miscommunication. Frequently someone has simply neglected to include all of the details in their communications to another team member, or procedures or even intent was misunderstood.

To nip potential conflicts in the bud, a project manager needs to look for signs that team members:

- Are lacking in self-confidence or displaying uncertainty about tasks or procedures
- Are unsure of what their functions are, which is often the result of miscommunication
- Are predisposed to disregard authority, or have a prejudicial attitude toward others

- Are consumed by a competitive nature (although sometimes a healthy competition can be positive for a project)
- Are motivated by their own personal agendas at the expense of the project

Identifying Key Characters

Certain characteristics distinguish different types of individuals. You will likely discover some of these common types on your team:

- *Tigers* intimidate others by holding a degree of power over them. Often insecure about their own role, tigers will use any leverage they can, from a bully threatening to beat up a classmate to a manager who threatens to fire anyone who dares question his or her authority. Watch who you put in positions of authority, and make sure they have the necessary people skills.
- *Prima donnas* display inflated egos and a misguided sense of self-importance. These types can be condescending toward others and are often working with a personal agenda. Your best resource is to let them enjoy a false sense of importance as long as it does not impinge on the project.
- *Passive-aggressive types* operate in a quiet manner, yet communicate calculated or manipulated messages through judgmental comments, body language, well-placed guilt, playing the martyr, or displaying an attitude that often seems aloof or unconcerned. The more aggressive and obvious version of the passive-aggressive is the "brown-noser," who is always trying to appease the right person to score points and satisfy his or her own need for importance. Passively try to maintain control with the passive-aggressive and stay a few steps ahead of the "brown-noser."
- *People-pleasers* will do whatever is necessary for praise and a much-needed ego boost. They simply have a more basic need for approval than the brown-noser, who has an agenda. Let the people-pleaser know you are pleased with his or her efforts.

And finally, you'll encounter the legitimate team player, who is, at least as far as you're concerned, comfortable with himself or herself and content within the parameters of the project and the people with whom he or she is working. Yes, you'll have team members who will simply come to the project to work hard and interact socially (or not). If you're lucky this will be the majority of your team—or at least they will appear as such throughout the duration of project. After all, your primary concern is how they interact with you and the project team. A bully on the ball field or a manipulator at home is not your concern in the project environment.

Assessing the Conflict Situation

Okay, so you know the characters, what do you do when conflict rears its ugly head? First you will need to assess the nature of the conflict and who the featured players are. A conflict can manifest itself at various levels:

- Is it a conflict between two individuals on the project team?
- Is it a conflict between two groups of individuals?
- Is it a conflict between one individual and the rest of the team?
- If it a conflict between one individual and management, the sponsors, stakeholders, or even yourself?
- Is it a conflict of a moral or ethical nature, between one or more team members and their beliefs?
- If there a conflict between your team and an outside source?

Conflict is not always two team members not getting along. Several variations on the theme of conflict can arise within a project. There are also levels of disagreement, ranging from petty arguments to threats, actual legal action, or violence.

You, therefore, need to assess whom this conflict is between and its level of severity. You also need to assess where this conflict fits in the scheme of the project. Does it stem from something internal? Is the argument over the process that the project is following, or is the dispute about politics, parking spaces, or another issue that is external to the actual project but causing friction or tension that is affecting the success of the project?

Gathering the necessary facts is essential to successfully resolving a conflict. One side of the story, and sometimes both sides, will not provide the entire picture if the conflict is based on an occurrence or series of activities. Make sure you find out all the details before taking action.

Conflicts frequently arise during the initiation phase of the project based on scheduling, task assignments, work distribution, and clarity of the tasks to be performed. Often people disagree about how long a task should take, or because they are being given more of the workload and someone else is coasting along. As the project progresses, the team generally settles into a comfortable rhythm and adapts to each of the varying personalities, but at the beginning, team members can be resentful if they feel they are carrying more of the weight. This occurs most frequently in volunteer projects when there is nothing personal at stake. In these cases, the best you can do is remind the individual of the value of his own work and diminish the concern about what others are or aren't doing.

Before returning to how to deal with the various configurations of conflicts mentioned earlier, let's look at several ways to successfully manage them.

Methods of Conflict Resolution

Mediation is an attempt to find a peaceful settlement to resolve a dispute between individuals. The process uses a neutral party to mediate. As a project manager that often becomes your job.

Mediation

The underlying principle of mediation lies in the genuine willingness of all disputing parties to participate. As project manager, if the dispute is between team members and does not involve you, then you can act as intermediary (unless there is a clearly defined perception that you are aligned with one of the parties in the dispute). Depending on the nature of the dispute, mediation can present a short-term cure by bringing the project-related arguments from both sides to the forefront and trying to find a middle ground or compromise settlement.

QUESTIONS?

What is mediation?
Mediation is a method of resolving conflict in which a neutral third party intervenes to try to settle a dispute between two parties.

If, however, the conflict stems from underlying, non-project related issues, ranging from personal feelings to previous conflicts, the idea of finding a compromise and creating a true win-win situation is less likely. The best you can hope for is to find a temporary short-term solution through which everyone can work. If you are in the position of mediator, you need to hear both sides' arguments. Hopefully you can find a middle ground that allows each side to walk away satisfied with the outcome. If the situation is a clear-cut, win-lose argument, such as whether to use program "A" or "B," you need to make a clear decision and explain that it is based solely on the factors involved and not the individuals.

Conflict Transformation

A more complicated process called conflict transformation uses mediation, but focuses on the attitudes and perceptions of the parties and looks to alter these perceptions. On small-scale or short-term projects, the time frame won't allow this level of resolution to make radical changes in personalities. Long-term, large-scale projects with significant impact on a widespread population may require loftier resolution techniques in which the parties are encouraged to look beyond the project, to their feelings and attitudes. Conflict transformation is concerned primarily with changing the attitudes and perceptions of the parties to one another. In the long term, this can be very beneficial, as changed attitudes can result in less conflict moving forward. Television programs designed to teach youngsters how to properly accept and understand other people use the same techniques. Moralistic in nature, they work with adults too, but success is often harder to achieve since attitudes are more firmly embedded within adults.

To achieve such transformation you may need the help of outside professionals to get to the root of the conflict. Compromise is a key factor in conflict resolution. Once again, as in any mediation, both parties need to be amenable. Parties will need to sit down and negotiate a settlement that is satisfactory to both sides. In a situation that doesn't present a clear-cut, black or white, "A" or "B" decision, a compromise is often the result of mediation.

Compromise

When both sides have something tangible to bring to the table, compromise can be the fastest and easiest way to resolve difference. For example, if the dispute is over which person will do a specific task, the tangible factor is the task and it can be divided so that both parties will do various aspects of the task. A simple dispute over where to hold a retirement party could end with a third choice that has some of the best aspects of the two previous choices.

If various elements are involved, each party can gain something important to them while conceding something that isn't. Perhaps one individual wants up-tempo music with dancing for the company holiday party while another wants a more reserved, quiet, no dancing atmosphere. The compromise could be a quiet mealtime and a more up-tempo dance-oriented atmosphere after the meal, during dessert.

Even disputes between management and team members can offer an opportunity to compromise, show good faith on both sides, and bring different views together. Sometimes scheduling is at the root of the dispute and the schedule simply needs to be tweaked to meet the needs of both sides. When negotiating a compromise settlement, it is important to have a priority list from each side in advance to know which issues are more important and which can be sacrificed. Then it's a matter of trading off issues.

Compromise, however, won't work if someone is just plain angry that they are doing more work than someone else or that he or she is not being included in the decision-making process. Personal grudges and disenchantment lead to conflict of a less logical method that can't always be solved using tangibles that can be traded.

Shift Perspectives

Putting things into perspective is a most interesting method of conflict resolution. If, for example, Fred is furious that Maryanne is not pulling her weight on the project, you need to put the situation into perspective for that individual. Yes, you can talk to Maryanne and evaluate why she does not appear to be working as hard as Fred. If she is slacking off or just not trying, then Fred may have alerted you to a potential problem. However, maybe Maryanne is working just as hard as Fred. He may simply not be aware of what she is accomplishing or perhaps she is slower than he is at producing results. Either way, you need to remind Fred that he is a fast worker and not everyone can maintain his pace. Put into perspective that people work at a different speeds, and that as long as they are trying to fulfill their roles as best they can, that's all one can and should expect.

Before approaching Maryanne, you need to assess whether Fred has a valid claim. Maryanne may be doing an excellent job, but because they dated socially and it did not work out, Fred may have approached you for the wrong reasons. This goes back to conflict transformation, in which you need to address the root of the conflict between individuals, which is not always what it appears. The fact that he has ill feelings towards her and needs to address and work through them is an underlying issue—perhaps they were simply not suitable on a social level. Putting that into perspective and moving forward will help change Fred's attitude toward Maryanne's "work habits" and end potential conflict. For your purposes you need to find a manner in which they can work together and show each other respect.

Three other approaches to conflict resolution include a consensus approach, smoothing, and the dictatorial approach. A consensus approach means taking the issue to the people. If the conflict is between two groups with opposing viewpoints, you might—with their consent—bring the issue to a vote. Call a meeting and decide this issue once and for all. Exclude yourself from the voting. Try to find a time when everyone involved can attend the meeting and make sure that everyone understands that this is the final vote on this issue. Let both sides have the same amount of time to voice their issues before calling for the vote. Also, make sure everyone is eligible to vote. In organizations, unions, or associations, check the bylaws. On a project team, you may simply state up front that everyone involved in working on the project can vote. Make sure this is set up clearly before taking a vote.

ESSENTIALS

Put things into perspective for team members who may be arguing or complaining over issues that, in the grand scheme of things, are unimportant. Try, in a polite manner, to put these issues into proper perspective with the individual or individuals involved. Often people don't realize when conditions are actually pretty good.

In other settings, you may informally poll individuals and get a consensus of how they feel the situation should best be resolved. Once again, make it known in advance that you are going to ask all the team participants. You can even do your voting or polling with an anonymous survey. A consensus doesn't necessarily require an actual "vote." Informally get the opinions of everyone involved and make a decision based on the data you've collected. Make sure everyone understands that your decision is not arbitrary but is based on the information you've obtained.

Smoothing is essentially sticking with what you do agree on and glossing over or putting aside whatever causes conflict. "Let's table that discussion until the next meeting" is a means of smoothing over a situation for the time being. While this is actually buying time until the conflict situation comes up again, it may provide time to research acceptable solutions, find more money, or utilize better resources to help settle the conflict. If you're lucky, the conflict is not as heated when the issue comes up again, and in some cases the conflict has resolved itself. Smoothing is not an active way of dealing with problems and can only be used with less serious conflicts.

ALERT

You should have a zero tolerance policy toward any type of racist, sexist, or violent behavior. Make sure, however, that you are correct before acting or accusing anyone of any such behavior!

When the project is close to the finish line, or time is of the essence, you may be forced to take the dictatorial approach, which doesn't appease many, but keeps the project on course. If the team members have nothing to lose they could defect, but if they are on staff, receiving a salary or compensation, or hope to gain from their experience with the project, they may simply have to buckle down and follow your commands. If the project is seriously threatened and other manners of conflict resolution will take too much time, you may need to take control in this manner. Use this method only as a last resort.

To sum it up, follow these tips when trying to resolve a conflict:

- Carefully assess the nature and severity of the conflict. Do some research. Don't take things at face value.
- If you are not specifically approached to resolve the conflict, decide whether and when you should get involved.
- Make sure you know all the information before trying to mediate or reach any kind of agreement.
- Respect people's wishes whether to make a conflict known to others.
- Know when a conflict is minor and will either go away or resolve itself without your intervention.
- If you are involved in the conflict and feel that you cannot be objective, or perceived as such, have an outside party mediate or try to solve the conflict.
- If the conflict requires an expert to solve the problem, such as a technical expert who may have the best solution to a dispute over which software to use, seek one out.

- Look for compromise settlements and make sure each side walks away winning something in the negotiations.
- Work to solve problems within the context or the scope of the project. If, for example, you are working with someone who is clearly displaying anti-social behavior, don't expect you will change such behavior developed over twenty-five years. Just find a way in which you and the team can work with this individual. If, however, it is a two-year project, you may need to deal with deeper-rooted problems.
- Take a dictatorial approach only when absolutely necessary because of time or budget constraints, or because the quality of the product or service is poor.
- Mediate, negotiate, and seek solutions that are the by-product of collective ideas. Encourage positive alternatives to conflicts rather than rehashing and reiterating the conflict situation.
- Do follow-up monitoring to make sure a resolved conflict stays that way.
- Use a consensus or yield to a higher authority if necessary. Make sure all parties understand that that ruling will be the end result of the conflict and that they can then move on.
- Encourage people to use legal action *only* as a last resort.
- Always use tact, diplomacy, and take the high road.

Taking the Initiative

Knowing how and when to jump in to try to resolve a conflict takes practice and experience. It is not an easy call. Sometimes you may elect to stand back and let team members learn the hard way. People will learn from their mistakes. However, you cannot generally afford to do this if the project will suffer.

Most often it is up to you to recognize a conflict situation and monitor it closely. If it is brought to you by a team member, stakeholder, or dropped in your lap, you'll have no choice but to get involved. If you see conflict in the making, but it has not yet been brought to your attention, you have a few options. You can alter the schedule, task assignment, or other variables to ease the potential conflict without approaching either party directly. For example, if you have overheard hostile behavior between two parties or have gotten wind of it through your involvement in the project (or even casual walk-throughs), you might simply switch assignments so that these team members will have little or no contact with one another. Anyone planning a party will do this if they are putting together a seating plan and so-and-so should not sit next to so-and-so.

The opposite approach is to bring combative parties together and force the issue, while closely monitoring the situation. Making two children who don't get along partners on the class project may bring out their common concerns, likes, and dislikes, and the conflict may simply disappear when they get to know each other. The same may occur with adults.

The manner in which you approach the conflict depends on numerous variables. When an entire team is unhappy with one person, you need to address its concerns. Talk to the members individually and see if they all have a similar assessment of the situation. A valuable team member with a not-so-valuable attitude might be a pain to work with, but still gets the job done. Therefore, you might try to set up a situation in which the antagonistic party does not interact as often or as closely with other team members.

ALERT

Be wary of letting someone work off-site just because the person is difficult to work with. Telecommuting appeals to a lot of workers who would love to forego the morning commute, and it might appear to others that you are rewarding antisocial behavior by letting this person work from home.

Sometimes the team mentality becomes a mob mentality. A few people may have legitimate concerns, but others simply jumped onto the bandwagon and created a "monster" that doesn't really exist. People often direct their own tension and anger toward a scapegoat. A person may not be bothering anyone or causing any problems regarding the project, but the team perception is that the person is a problem.

For example, in an office setting, Mary was working at a slower pace on a project. Janice, a team member, who never liked Mary personally, kept spreading the word that Mary was so slow that she was holding up production. When the project eventually fell behind, based on numerous factors, of which Mary's role was of minimal consequence, the opinion of many team members was that the Mary was the cause of the project falling behind. They made her feel like she was to blame, when in reality the perception stemmed from one person's bias and was not a fair assessment of the situation. A simple story, but it illustrates two key points:

1. Groups of any type very often seek out a scapegoat when there is any deviation from "the plan."
2. Groups often make judgments based on hearsay. In this case, all anyone really knew was what Janice said about Mary's work.

Once again, people need to be presented with the overall picture, not just one little slice of the pie. In this case, the team members needed to understand that there were many factors that produced the delays in the project—it was not just the fault of one person. Internal conflicts within a project can be dealt with in a number of manners, depending upon the unique circumstances surrounding the project and the participants.

So how should you handle conflict?

- Do your best to handle conflicts early on.
- Take action that suits the particular project and situation.
- Don't act out of anger, panic, or any other emotion. Weigh the conflict before and make a decision based on facts.
- When you make a decision, stick to it.
- Make sure you listen to both arguments and address the issues on both sides before making your decision.

Other Factors to Keep in Mind

You will have to be respectful of the attitudes and beliefs of others when dealing with conflicts of an ethical or moral nature. For example, a magazine was putting out a special issue and members of the publication staff were being asked to work on the project. At the request of the publisher, however, the special issue was going to have a more erotic theme than the monthly magazine. A seasoned editor felt she could not work on this project because of the nature of the material. The project manager was obligated to carry out the publisher's wishes and could not compromise the content, but reassured her that leaving the project because of her personal views would have no repercussions on her status or position in the company. Ultimately, the editor did some work on another aspect of the project, but did not work on the rest of the material. Conflicts that arise because of beliefs, views, or personal values can only be resolved by respecting other people.

ESSENTIALS

If the conflict is project- or issue-oriented, work from the perspective of the project and keep personality issues in perspective. If the conflict is people-oriented, be careful to make no judgments and focus on what the individuals have in common. Start working from a people oriented perspective, then refocus everyone back to the project.

If external factors are involved, you may have to contact sources outside of the project to handle the conflict. This could be a conflict with a particular vendor, a government agency, or a competitor. In these cases you represent the good of the project team and the project. You want to stand behind your team members as often as possible. Make sure, however, that you have all the facts in such a situation.

If your team member is clearly at fault or if he or she acted in a manner unbefitting the team and the company or organization, you also need to be able to take the high road and apologize on behalf of the team. External conflicts brought about by others within the project team are your conflicts too. It is important that everyone involved in the project represent himself or herself in a manner that best exemplifies the organization or group.

Some good things can come from conflicts. Many new ideas come to the forefront because of an initial conflict. Sometimes, positive competition is the result of two parties not getting along initially. Conflicts can serve to present viewpoints that might not have been expressed otherwise, and such clearing of the air can serve as a catharsis of sorts. Finally, conflicts resolved by a project manager can serve to enhance the respect afforded to that manager. Once both sides sign a peace treaty, you'll feel very good. (Of course, you won't have much time to celebrate because you are in the middle of a project, remember?)

Handling Various Personalities

The beginning of this chapter identified some of the key personality types that are probably on your project team. Now you need to figure out how to handle them effectively. Being an effective project leader requires that you hone your people skills, which means being able to work comfortably with various types of personalities. Determine the degree of handholding, praise, or self-reliance each team member requires, and work with them accordingly. Many team members will work best if left alone to complete their tasks. Others will require constant affirmation or direction. In time, you'll learn which method produces the best results from the individuals. Be careful not to be misunderstood yourself. You don't want to appear to be favoring one individual over another.

As a leader, you may need to spend more time with a team member who simply requires closer attention because he or she has less confidence in his or her abilities. Someone else, who you believe works well on her own, may misread the attention you are giving to another team member and feel that you are showing favoritism. Just because someone works better without constant supervision doesn't mean there is no need to check in with this person as well. You may simply spend a few moments chatting, and mention that she works so well on her own, you don't want to crowd her. Remind her, however, that you're interested in her work and that you are as accessible to her as you are the rest of the team.

The scope of the project as well as the length and the setting will determine how much you will need to get to know the personalities involved. Naturally, if you are working on a weeklong project by telecommunications with someone 3,000 miles away, you probably won't get to know his or her personality very well. On the other hand, if you are one of three individuals spending day and night in a cramped office space for three weeks, you will most likely become quite familiar with the others in your group. The nature of the project and amount of work involved will also factor into how well you will need to know the personalities involved. There will be instances when you will work on a project for three days and can read someone like a book—his manner, gestures, and conversation will tell you all you need to know without even asking. Some people "light up a room," while others light it up like a keg of dynamite going off. On the flip side, there are people you can work with on a month-long project and who never reveal very much about themselves. As long as the work gets done and conflicts are minimal, it doesn't really matter how well your team members get to know each other. As a leader you cannot push people to divulge more of themselves than they choose, any more than you can tell someone who wears his or her emotions on their sleeve to just hold it all inside.

Other Characters

You'll find those who are competitive, those who are quiet or reclusive, and even the occasional slacker. You will also come across people who can't take criticism and others who think they are always right. There will be whiners and complainers as well as gossips. Jokers and crowd pleasers will also be on your payroll (or lack thereof, if dealing with a volunteer group or friends helping on a project). Keep in mind that the less your team has a personal stake in the project, the more you will have to be everyone's pal. After all, if Fred has nothing significant to gain by helping you move your furniture, there's no reason for Fred to stick around if he feels unwanted, uncomfortable, or unappreciated.

So how do you do it? How do you work with all these personality types? When working with competitive individuals, it's best to channel their competitive spirit into something that benefits the project. Can they sell the most widgets? Move the most office furniture? Write the most new programs? Let them compete, whether you or anyone else is actually competing with them. As long as the competition remains friendly and does not impact the project, let it be a motivating force—some people enjoy this type of work situation. You'll see how quickly your letter-mailing project gets completed when you make it a contest between your kids for an ice cream cone. (If you're dealing with young children, give the loser an ice cream cone too. Real competition can be a negative experience for young children.)

ESSENTIALS If repeated warnings and attempts to increase someone's work are not improving his performance, you may have to let the person go. Keeping someone who isn't doing his share is detrimental to the team and the project. It may be better to lose one person than to risk resentment and lowered morale among other team members.

The quiet, secretive, reclusive team members often simply come and go without any fanfare; often they want it to be that way. You should make an effort to determine whether the individual is comfortable with this arrangement. If he or she is quiet because he is intimidated or uncomfortable, you may need to modify the situation so the person can feel more a part of the team. However, if someone is quiet or introverted by choice, let him be who he is. One woman on a team project to produce a Web guide got the nickname "Elvis" because she just sort of appeared every day, then disappeared; she was very content with that arrangement and produced quality work.

Slackers need a proverbial kick in the butt. If someone will only do the minimum to get by, you'll have to make sure that the minimum is sufficient for the project's success. Someone who's not committed to moving the project forward should not be in a high-level role, and you may have to take corrective action to get the team member focussed and the project back on track. Within reason, find out what motivates your team—what you can wave at the finish line that will get them off their slacker routine.

If you're dealing with someone who doesn't take criticism well, start off with praise and highlight all that they do well before pointing out anything that is wrong. Acknowledge that everyone makes mistakes, and emphasize the importance of learning and applying new skills in the future. Avoid blame in any victimless situation, and keep your feedback constructive and positive.

If you are trying to work with someone who feels he or she is always right, let him or her be right in all the insignificant areas. On those where the individual just happen to be wrong, let him discover the right answer by laying out pieces of the puzzle in a manner so that he can find the right answer. This way, while he may be wrong, he will still save face by thinking he discovered the error of their ways. You are not out to say, "I told you so." Instead, you should skillfully, as the leader, point your team in the right direction for the sake of the project.

FACTS

When going into negotiations, the more you have to give, the greater strength and bargaining power you have. If you have nothing to give, then obviously you can't expect much in return. Determine what the other side needs the most—that is your bargaining chip. Prioritize your own needs, and you're ready to negotiate.

Whiners and complainers require a patient ear and an occasional reality check in which you point out some of the positives of the situation. As I mentioned earlier, often people don't realize that, comparatively speaking, conditions are not really so bad. Grin and bear some of the griping and complaining, but encourage anyone who is dissatisfied to make proposals or suggestions on how things could work better. In many cases, people complain because they don't believe they'll be heard any other way. Once you establish that you welcome contributions from all sources, use their negative energy to achieve positive results. If rabble-rousers are not willing to be constructive or positive, they will undermine the team and you do need to intercede.

Jokers can be listened to and may even be entertaining. If and when such clowning interferes with the flow of the team's work, or if they are insulting or offending others, you will have to gently but firmly explain that they need to tone it down.

A good project manager is a good people manager, which requires knowing and understanding all the players and what makes them tick. Obviously, on very large-scale projects with hundreds of team members, you won't get to know everyone involved. You will need to set up managers who are as skilled in managing people as they are the tasks you've delegated. Meet with your key managers to discuss ways of working with people. Make sure that they have the same understanding as you do.

As you assess the personalities of the people working with you, try to see their strengths, not their weaknesses. If, for example, someone is very outspoken and has an aggressive personality, see if that fits into a role in which you need someone outspoken and aggressive. Embrace the differences people have to offer, and never discuss one person's personality quirks with others.

The Art of Negotiating

Negotiating is a method of reaching a compromise settlement. As a project leader, you may find yourself in the middle, playing go-between in negotiations to end conflicts. Be fair, listen to each side, make sure both sides walk away with something of value—including their pride—and don't be hasty in making a judgment. But being the middle person is no fun. The art of negotiating goes a lot further than just that of arbitrator in a conflict.

Negotiating is a skill that will come into play at various stages of the project, and is useful in making numerous types of agreements with other parties. Many areas will require basic negotiating skills, some you may not even recognize. You may need to make special arrangements to have a key player join your team, or work out arrangements to have special speakers, hosts, or sponsors support your project. Then, of course, you have the standard negotiable issues: contracts, rates, and deadlines.

From the outset, you need to assess exactly what it is you want. If you are not clear in your ultimate objective, your negotiations may go off-course in the middle and you could end up with nothing. While working toward your objective, you will have a series of end results that you want, ranging from the ideal to the very least that would be acceptable. If you were negotiating with management for additional employees to put on your team, you might consider an ideal number to be ten employees. However, you know you could do the job with six or seven if you absolutely had to, and would keep this in mind as you negotiate.

ESSENTIALS
Start by making reasonable offers. You do not request everything, nor do you offer everything. Give something the other side wants in exchange for something you want, and build from there. Start with smaller points allows both parties to feel comfortable.

For example, a team member may want to have one day a week to telecommute. Whether this person telecommutes one day may be inconsequential to you, but you might take that opportunity to ask the potential team member if he or she could be available once a month on Thursdays to stay late for important meetings with the sponsors. This can be an even exchange: the person works one day a week at home, and in return is willing to stay late one Thursday a month. After this simple agreement sets the tone of reasonable cooperation, you can get down to the nitty-gritty: hours and compensation.

Look at the following tips for effective negotiating:

- Concede on points that are low on your list of priorities in exchange for points that are high on your list of wants.
- Save their top offer for your top priority. If a ball club trades away their best pitcher, it will become that much harder to acquire the other team's best hitter.
- Keep in mind that things need not be exchanged one for one. If you have two lesser items that are not as significant to your needs and they have one "biggie," consider trading two or three for one.
- Don't offer too much up front—give yourself room to build. Not unlike a game of poker, you don't want to throw in all your money on the first wager.

- If you win big, give back some concessions. It may be something of no great significance to you, but it's an act of good character and good business to say, "Listen, we really don't need this, why don't you keep it." Next time you negotiate, this gesture may be remembered.
- Do not be adversarial or put the other side on the defensive. When the other side talks, listen and work together in good faith to try to settle on something that makes both sides walk away from the table feeling good.
- If things are not working out and neither side is happy, stop talking and take a break. Try again later, possibly with a neutral third party to break the stalemate.
- Take time to think about offers before making a final decision. Let the other person know that you will get back to them promptly (in a day or two). Evaluate the offer and even get a second opinion or compare the offer to the rates of others. Then make and communicate your decision within the time frame that you set.

Effective negotiating will come up during crisis intervention and conflict management, but it will also come up throughout the entire project. In fact, negotiation is a good skill to have in life, and any combination of the above tactics will work for most situations. Give a little, get a little—that's what it's all about. Above all, have patience.

CHAPTER 11
Motivational Skills

To motivate is to stimulate to action by providing an incentive or a motive. Real motivation, however, is more than just action; it is based on an attitude. The drive to succeed, learn, grow, and attain a goal is motivation. Personal investment in a product, activity, or outcome will motivate individuals also. As a project manager, you need to keep your team motivated, focused on completing the project, and achieving the team goal. From wise words to cash rewards, motivation comes in many forms. You can use several techniques with your team, but the best two come from you: be creative, and be sincere.

What Motivates Us?

For people to feel vested in a project, they need to see the big picture and look at the project from a global perspective. This big-picture view needs to be established from the onset. Unlike a Woody Allen film, where most of the actors never get to see the complete script (just the scenes in which they appear), projects are not usually successful if the people involved are not aware of the ultimate goal. The more a person is attached to—or feels involved with—the overall project, the more motivated he or she will be to work harder.

Motivation is not something you use only when the project is going downhill or has fallen behind schedule. The need for proper motivation should be established from the start of the project. You want to put together a championship team from the beginning. To do this you need to:

- Seek out personalities that work well with others.
- Bring everyone together in an introductory meeting.
- Present the broad picture of the project and the impact it will have on other people.
- Establish a team identity.
- Let others know what this team plans to accomplish on the project. Spread the word—present the team and their mission to the larger group, be it the company, the whole organization, the school board, or the world.

Motivational Theories

Motivation takes on various forms. Internal motivation could be satisfaction of a job well done, an inner sense of fulfillment, or the sense of doing for others (which often provides an inner sense of fulfillment). External motivation includes material goods, awards, recognition, and of course, money. The nature of the project, the sponsor, and the setting of the project (corporate, family, charitable organization) will dictate which, if any, external motivating factors you can offer. On every project, you can try to inspire team members to seek internal rewards along with the external rewards.

To motivate others to perform, you need a basic understanding of human nature. Many people in leadership positions do not fully understand the basic elements of motivational thinking as it pertains to others. Motivation can be an individual factor. Although a desire for monetary rewards is somewhat common, one person may be motivated by a possible new title or promotion while another may simply want more time to spend at home with the family. Unfortunately, an enthusiastic leader often assumes that the motivating factors that propelled him to his level of success are the same for everyone else. It's as if they think, "I became a manager, so why shouldn't everyone else be trying to work their way up to the same lofty position?" This is not a broad-based view of what motivates others.

ESSENTIALS

A winning sports team believes from the outset that it is going to be the champion. The players tell everyone that they are intent upon winning the title. They have individual identities, as well as an awareness of what everyone is doing in the game. Loyalty, identity, and pride are great motivators.

Any team or group is made up of people who have different levels of self-motivation. Someone who grew up in a very wealthy family may not be as motivated to earn money as someone who grew up in poverty. However, the person from a wealthy background may never have experienced the satisfaction that comes from overcoming obstacles.

People at any level want to feel good about themselves and what they produce. It has long been debated whether or not people are born motivated, and if so, to what degree that may vary between individuals. Freud saw people as inherently lazy, not motivated, and wanting only security or gratification. Maslow embraced neither the behaviorist or psychoanalytical approaches popular at the time. He instead believed that man strives to reach his highest level of capabilities. He believed that people were born inherently good and that among the basic human needs were self-esteem and self-actualization, both of which can only be achieved with motivation. Maslow concluded that for human salvation, one must indulge in "hard work and total commitment to doing well the job that fate or personal destiny calls you to do, or any important job that calls for doing."

Maslow's hierarchical theory of needs begins with the most basic needs of survival and proceeds up levels of a pyramid to self-actualized needs. "Self-actualized" needs are considered those of people involved in "a cause outside their own skin." Maslow felt that self-actualizers are devoted people who work at something precious to them. Therefore, Maslow might see motivation as a person striving to reach a level of self-actualization, doing what they were "born to do," or finding their calling. Although an individual project will not usually take on that level of significance, the process of striving for self-actualization can be a strong motivating force.

Typically, studies in human behavior regarding motivation show us that proper nurturing or training can lead to self-fulfillment, which will in turn lead to self-motivation when the activity or reward can be replicated. Motivation will continue if the results are positive or positively reinforced. In other words, if a person feels gratified, they will seek out, or return, to the source of that gratification. Conversely, there is the motivation to avoid danger or situations that a person is fearful about. At any level of development, a person will be motivated to protect himself from impending harm. In society, avoiding negative consequences has been constructed in forms of discipline that might include staying out of jail, not getting fired, or avoiding any other type of punishment.

When it comes to committing to a project, rarely is someone involved for absolutely no discernable reason. In these cases, motivation comes from several factors, including:

- A need to be part of a team or group—to work with others
- A need to be recognized and acknowledged
- Awards or merit
- An innate desire to produce a worthy product or accomplish a task for self-gratification or self-fulfillment
- Desire to make a social or cultural change or contribution
- Monetary rewards or bonuses
- Potentially greater responsibilities, or a promotion in rank or stature

Most team workers will put forth a greater effort if there are tangible rewards such as money or a prize to be won. The trick is to get the team to work hard when the motivation is not as clear-cut as a shiny bicycle for the child who sells the most cookies. You need to tap into what motivates each individual. Unfortunately, the best you may have to work with in many corporate settings is the motivation to avoid getting in trouble, alienated, or fired.

Working only to avoid punishment does not lead to productive results, and this kind of motivation can produce discontentment and conflict. Negative motivational factors need to be counter-balanced with positive rewards in order for someone to give you her best effort.

Working for seven hours a day so as not to lose or fail is far less productive than working for seven hours a day to win and succeed. Same time frame, opposite motivation. Two classmates can do the same work and both will get a "C." The student who is motivated by simply passing will be quite happy with a "C," whereas the one who was trying to excel and earn an "A" will surely be disappointed. Because different things motivate the students, the next test may produce different results. The "passing" motivator knows he has done enough work to achieve his goal. The "excelling" motivator has not achieved his goal, and will therefore apply greater effort moving forward.

Lighting Their Fire

When it comes to motivating a team (just like rewarding or disciplining one), you need to reach both the individuals and the group as a whole. Your project plan may include incremental bonuses or incentives for the team. As a leader, you may have to take responsibility for the more personal motivation.

Here are some do's and don'ts for motivating your team:

- *Do* help the individual to identify what is in the project for them. Yes, it sounds like a selfish motivational factor, but no matter how team-oriented a person is there will be something that inherently drives that person to succeed. Find out what that is.
- *Do* provide praise, recognition, and approval. Some people are driven by that, and everyone deserves it.
- *Do* offer incentives, if possible.
- *Do* allow team members to feel empowered and invested in the outcome of the project.
- *Do* accentuate the positives and point out possible (less obvious) rewards than money or a pending raise, particularly if those don't factor into the equation.

- *Don't* assume that everyone has the same level of interest or initial commitment to the project.
- *Don't* offer rewards or incentive for some team members and not for others.
- *Don't* assume that the same things motivate everyone— people have different needs.
- *Don't* give people fluff when they need substance. Rah-rah doesn't work when the team is not happy and needs concrete motivational tools and training.
- *Don't* bring in preconceived attitudes or opinions about people. Try to start each project with a clean slate.

The last point is particularly significant. If John Doe has a reputation for not giving a 100 percent effort on previous projects, that simply tells you how he has acted in the past. You need to start off with the assumption that Mr. Doe will be as motivated as anyone else. If you see otherwise, you can respond by trying to find out what motivates him. The point is, start out assuming everyone is on the project and ready to go seeking a personal goal, as well as the project goal.

There will be instances when you will be able to motivate by competition. Certainly a sports franchise is motivated by the desire to win.

Rival companies, or even a friendly competition between schools, neighborhoods, families, small businesses, or any such groups can also provide a motivational force for participants. Sometimes the "Us versus Them" attitude is the impetus for motivating the team.

FACTS

A good leader acknowledges the contributions made by team members and even sets up situations for team members to offer new ideas. Encourage your team to find the answer, even if you already know it. A good leader can take a backseat to his or her team and still be a strong and effective leader. Good leaders can step away from the need for individual accolades and let others take the credit.

Friendly internal competition can sometimes be a motivator as well, provided the stakes do not make for a blood-sport event. Keep the stakes enticing but not worth serious battle. Internal competition should be based on a good-natured spirit and fun—anything beyond that can lead to trouble and conflict.

The best you can hope to do, once the project is under way, is continue to promote whatever it is that keeps your team members motivated. Whether it's looking forward to the upcoming rest and relaxation of a vacation or a trip to Las Vegas for the top sales rep (for a special sales project), it's up to you to keep the motivational forces intact. Remember, it's always much easier when money or material goods are at the end of the tunnel. Also, compensation in the form of vacation days, time-off, or a shorter workweek is high on the priority list of many employees. Offering "comp time" can benefit a company because it won't cost more in actual funds. If the team member who is putting in extra hours or traveling frequently knows that he or she will have three extra weeks off to spend with family, he or she can be motivated to work harder on the project. Always be creative in offering incentives, and solicit the opinion of your team—remember that people are motivated by different factors.

Motivational Seminars

Motivational seminars must fit the tone and nature of the group. Make sure the speaker is accustomed to talking to the type of group he or she is addressing. A corporate group needs a trained corporate motivational speaker. Sales teams need someone who can motivate people to be better salespersons. Artists need a speaker who is familiar with creative vision and whatever it is that motivates a painter to paint. A corporate executive and a fiction writer probably won't benefit from the same motivational speaker unless the speaker has a wide-ranging bag of tricks.

First, assess how your group would welcome an outside source, then search for one that can address the needs of the group and tailor their presentation accordingly. Some groups might respond to humor, others are dealing in areas where that might not be appropriate.

ESSENTIALS

People tend to meet high expectations. If you tell someone who is doing a fair job that he is doing a good job, he will do a good job. The opposite theory, practiced by many parents, suggests that you should never give too much praise, always saying "that's good, but you can do better." This has led to a generation of self-doubters who need constant encouragement as adults, since they believe that nothing they could ever do is good enough.

Look at the backgrounds and previous speaking engagements of several motivational speakers. Compare rates. If you choose to bring in a motivational speaker, make sure you've done your homework. You don't want to waste your team's valuable time or your company or organization's money. You can evaluate a speaker based on a video or audiotape, or, if possible, attend another seminar given by that speaker. Find out his or her credentials, what associations he or she belongs to, and whether or not he or she can provide an interactive presentation.

According to Rosita Hall (*www.rositahall.com*), a Canada-based motivational speaker whose upbeat speeches have wowed audiences in Canadian and U.S. companies, "One of the mistakes commonly made is that companies wait until they are at a critical juncture and then call someone in to save them. They believe that someone can come in like a messiah, and in one afternoon change everything that's taken place for the last six months or a year. It would be more beneficial for companies to work in such a speaker from the beginning, knowing that at some point people will need to be motivated. I can't think of anyone who doesn't need motivation at some point in their life."

ESSENTIALS

It's beneficial to all concerned that management be involved in any motivational speech or seminar. Don't make it just for "the team," or you are separating yourself from the group. This is like saying, "The team needs to be motivated but management is always motivated." Not true.

Motivational speakers are used (and needed) most significantly during periods of change. Hall, like many other speakers, focuses on making change less stressful. Instead of focusing on the change itself, she concentrates on providing people with an overall awareness of the self—encouraging people to feel comfortable with themselves before worrying about organizational change.

Consider the motivational needs you anticipate throughout the life of the project. The longer the project, the more likely it is that you will need to include a motivational speaker, especially if you expect changes to the project or the company.

It's the Little Things

Doing lots of little things can motivate your team to make big things happen. Set the tone, lead by example, and be a consistent and positive force. After all, if the leader doesn't believe the project will be a success, why should anyone else?

Don't pat yourself on the back or gloat about your own triumphs along the way. Lead with humility. It has been said that "upon reaching the summit, your first move should be to turn around and offer a hand to the person behind you." That philosophy holds true with your project team as well. If you are praised for the work done so far, turn around and pass that praise on to your team.

Little things that help motivate a team include a group lunch outing, a card and cake for a team member's birthday, an upbeat cartoon posted on the bulletin board, a funny story or tasteful joke, a saying—anything that gets people smiling or thinking positively. Some projects have even had slogans, like ball clubs who are on a mission to win (such as the '73 Mets, who coined "Ya Gotta Believe").

ESSENTIALS

The idea of motivating a team by making a project enjoyable goes back to what we try to teach children through learning games: If you enjoy what you are doing, you are more likely to do a better job.

Establish this "fun" principle early on. Roger Reece, a motivational consultant who runs Fuddwhacker Consulting, establishes a fun quotient from the outset of the project. Reece has worked in all aspects of project management and leadership for more than a decade. His consulting work ranges from one-on-one meetings to get to know the people on the project individually, to skits and games that present real situations in a new light. Reece believes that the stress level and intensity of a project will build as the project progresses, so it is very important to start out with the project and its goals in proper perspective.

"Motivation really is a function of attitude adjustment," says Reece, who strongly believes that you need to set the attitude on the right course from the start. "If you aren't encouraging positive attitudes, you'll have marginal results." He also introduces Buford Fuddwhacker (Reece's alter ego), a character to enlighten, entertain, and loosen up the often-tense team members.

Bridging the Gap

There is a fine line between conflict and motivation. If people are not happy with each other, or if they are unhappy with the overall structure of the corporation, organization, or management, they will not be motivated to work at their peak level of efficiency.

The popular cartoon character Dilbert illustrates the many foibles of life in the office, which are based on truths found in many office settings. The truisms apply to many types of groups and organizational settings. In business, in school, or in other situations in which there is a hierarchical structure, there is a tendency for people to regard upper management as the enemy. A team may feel helpless against the management, school board, local governing body, or other authority figure. You may hear responses like, "Oh, we've tried that before," or, "Management will never let us do that," from disgruntled team members. As the leader or project manager, you must break through that barrier that separates the "us" from the "them" and gain trust and respect from the team. If you can win points with management on their behalf, you can show the team that their efforts can make a difference. You need not make radical changes or stand on the table and rally the troops, but you can speak up on behalf of your team to get what they need to be successful. Winning even the smallest of battles shows that you can make things happen, and your team will respect you for it. Bridging the gap between your team and management, or authority, goes a long way toward motivation.

What Will It Take?

Besides money, some of the most important motivational elements expressed by people working on projects include:

- Time off, vacation, compensation, or personal time
- The option to work from home (telecommuting)
- Better working conditions, such as a larger office or an assistant
- Greater authority and decision-making capabilities (this can even be found on a home-based project, where children do such a fine job on a family project that they are given greater responsibilities and are allowed to make some of their own decisions)
- Acknowledgment that they are appreciated for their contributions

Beyond these wants, people expect to be treated with respect. Remember, the project is only as successful as the people behind it. Success is a by-product of self-confidence, and that comes from being treated well.

ALERT

Roger Reece points out that in companies, individuals often see dealing with management as an "us" against "them" situation. It's important, according to Reece, to set up circles of "we." Blending the hierarchy will create an overall company unity and a feeling that "we are all in this together."

You can't force positive motivation. If the well-intentioned company dinner to boost team spirit has a "must attend or else" tone about it, you're not helping matters. Likewise, if a consultant comes in and makes new demands that don't sit well with the team, the exercise will be ineffective.

Motivation comes about through respect, openness, good communication, and understanding of individual needs. Directives like, "You will all do this or else!!" don't inspire motivated performances. You cannot force inspiration, and you cannot force positive motivation.

Keeping Yourself Motivated

As project manager, you may need a kick in the proverbial butt on occasion to keep your own level of motivation high. It's easy to lose your drive and desire if all around you team motivation is crumbling. In that case, it's time to take one step back before taking three steps forward. Sometimes the best thing you can do as leader is take a day away from the project, physically and, more importantly, mentally. You cannot eat, sleep and drink the project, no matter how important it is. Remind yourself of your personal goal in this project. Look at your own vested interest in the project. Look at your goals and interests away from the project.

As you proceed through your career and work on various projects, you will be able to fairly assess what does and does not motivate you best. For some people competition provides the shot in the arm, perhaps knowing that another team is developing their software at a faster rate. For someone else it might be a setback. While some people see a setback as a time to throw in the towel, others see it as the impetus to buckle down and work harder. When you feel motivated to get out there and double your effort, remember what it was that got you off the couch and back to your desk. Know what motivates you and use that to get yourself going.

One project manager, who was feeling burned out after working ten-hour days to get the project finished, said he simply went home one night and watched his two young children sleep for about two hours. He reminded himself that when the project was through he would be getting an extra two weeks off to take them to Disney World. The time to spend with his family was his motivation to get the project finished on time. And his personal motivation is what kept him on track.

CHAPTER 12

Shifting Gears

If every possible solution to any risk, conflict, or problem comes up short, you will need to establish backup or contingency plans. Perhaps the most contingency planning ever took place in late 1999, when the Y2K "crisis" prompted a worldwide quest for backup plans. Entire projects were set up for the purpose of implementing backup plans in case computer programs failed to work. As we all know, with a few minor exceptions, nothing went wrong and the new year started without implementing any of the contingency plans. But what if the expected glitches *had* occurred and there had been no contingency plans in place to deal with them? It would have been a global crisis indeed.

Why Have a Contingency Plan?

Unlike altering the original plan, a contingency plan is designed to take on a life of its own, essentially moving into the place previously occupied by the initial plan. This doesn't mean driving faster to make up for lost time, it means taking a completely different route. If plan "A" is to serve Miller beer, then plan "B" isn't to switch to Budweiser, but to change the event to a non-alcoholic party instead.

QUESTIONS?

What is a contingency plan?
Your contingency plan, or alternative strategy, is a critical element of project management. Should one aspect of the project go awry, threatening the successful completion of the project, you will need to implement a pre-planned course of action. A contingency plan is one tool that will avoid or reduce your potential risk.

The need for contingency planning is an important aspect of project planning and management. Since contingency plans are designed to achieve the same desired result, usually the same time frame remains in place. You'll have to make the switch from plan "A" to plan "B" quickly, and the transition must be a smooth one. The Y2K crisis centered on having numerous plans in place and ready to go into effect immediately if all the hard work (on numerous projects) to avert technical disaster did not pay off. The time-critical nature of the situation required backup plans to enable quick reaction to all operational failures and any shutdown of power.

Contingency planning comes about through asking many "what if" questions such as the following:

- What if it rains on the day of the company picnic?
- What if the product doesn't work right?
- What if the community board opposes the plan?
- What if the main support beam isn't strong enough?
- What if too many people show up?
- What if the initial tests show the program doesn't work?

Ask all possible "what if" questions. Many will be answered by simple changes in basic elements of the project. Other answers will mean having a backup plan with details unique to the new plan itself.

Since you will never be able to foresee everything that could possibly go wrong, you should model contingency plans to be flexible and adaptable to various situations. You may have some overall backup plans for broad areas such as ordering resources (including human resources) from another vendor or moving to a different location. However, most of your plans will need to be adjusted to fit the specific project.

Contingency plans are like emergency exits: necessary, but hopefully unused. They provide you with comfort and some security, but also—like emergency exits—need to be tested regularly to make sure they will be operative if needed. For example, you should check that the backup vendor on your sheet is still in business.

Generally, a contingency plan is necessary when there is a breakdown along the critical path (the spine of your plan). These are plans that have a jumping off point from your main plan—a kind of safety net where you can roll into the new course of action. When the road is flooded and there is no way to get through the murky water, it's time for plan "B." Plan "B" is not necessarily an inferior plan, it may just be a different manner of approaching the same end results, one that is costlier or lengthier. It may, however, be the plan that will get you to the desired project results.

You may need to implement your contingency plan if your organization or team experiences the following:

- Program or technical failure
- Serious shortage of manpower
- Natural disasters such as severe weather, or physical disasters such as loss of materials, or damage to a site
- Breakdown in management, or new management implementing new business plans and strategies

- Serious breakdown in communications
- Resources delivered late or not at all
- Political or procedural changes
- Project falling behind schedule or heading over budget
- Quality or service levels not up to par

ESSENTIALS Wherever you see potential for serious risk, it's important to evaluate your original plan and establish contingency plans. It is always worth taking the time and making the effort to think about your backup strategy when your mind is on the big picture and you can allocate resources to keep in reserve. In the midst of a crisis, you may not be thinking clearly.

One of the most significant aspects of contingency planning is that your evaluation of the project and quest for potential problems will point out places where you can make adjustments to your current plan. Your goal isn't to have to move to the contingency plan, therefore if you can simply incorporate some of the ideas you come up with into your original plan, you may benefit from this level of in-depth scrutiny.

Establishing a Contingency Plan

How exactly does a contingency plan come about? After asking the "what if" questions, you need to establish practical answers that will lead to a second well-planned course of events. A new critical path will take over, much the way an emergency generator kicks in and keeps the lights on when the power fails. This will now become the main plan. You are not biding time until you return to plan "A," but rather moving forward with a new plan and hopefully reaching the same goal. Keep in mind, though, that contingency plans often mean more money will be spent in either resources or manpower hours. Rarely does a contingency plan come in at the same cost, or help you save money or time on the project. (If it saved time and money you would have done it that way from the start!)

Gathering Ideas

Brainstorming is one way to get a host of new ideas. Review all possible threats to the project and ask other team members for ideas of what to do just in case. You might also take some time to look back at previous projects and see how they might have been done differently. Sometimes the most efficient way of doing something five years ago may be the fall back plan today. You may have to figure out what to do if technology fails you completely.

Questionnaires are another good way of gathering ideas for "what if" scenarios. Try to include all team members to get a broad range of ideas and so that no one feels left out. You want everyone involved in creating and implementing your backup plan. No, you don't need to go through all of the details of a contingency plan with everyone unless it appears likely that you are going to make a switch, but people should know the basics of the plan just in case. There may be some degree of training needed (and that should be accounted for) to allow people to make a smooth transition.

ALERT

Often people will say, "I wish they'd told me they were changing the plan before I did all of this extra work." Notifying people of the switch to the new plan is one of the most crucial aspects of moving to a contingency plan.

Timing

Be prepared to shift to your contingency plan early on in the project if necessary. While you won't know until the last minute whether or not it will rain on the day of your wedding, you *will* know after some testing whether or not your new software package is going to be able to handle your inventory data. The sooner you can shift gears and make plan "B" your "A" plan, the less time and money you will lose. No matter when you switch to the new plan, at least some of the work from the old plan will probably need to be redone or the data entered into a new system.

Whose Call Is It, Anyway?

Can you make the call and signal for the contingency plan to go into effect or do you need upper management, the bride's family, the PTA, the board, the president, or some other person or governing body to make the decision?

It is vital that you know exactly what it takes, officially, to switch from plan "A" to plan "B" or "C." If someone else must make the decision, make sure you present the reasons why you believe such a switch needs to be made. Make sure you know what papers need to be signed, who has the keys to the backup facility, who can get the new permit, and so on. If it's your decision, make sure you consider all the variables, including:

- How the new plan will meet the intended goals
- The operational impacts of the new plan
- What it will take to make the transition
- How much time it will take to train or retrain team members
- How additional funding will need to be allocated
- How quickly you can implement the new plan
- How far back such a plan will set you in terms of your schedule
- How the plan will affect other processes in the organization or company
- How implementing the new plan will affect the product's quality

If you review all of the options and make the decision to move to a contingency plan, you must be decisive and immediately inform all those involved, including team members and stakeholders. Depending on the nature of the project, you may even want to inform outside sources.

You will need to put the same level of conviction into the new plan and motivate the troops again. Team members may lose motivation after abandoning plan "A." There may be a feeling that they have worked hard for nothing thus far. It is very important to make it known that many times the original game plan does not work as planned, but a new plan can jump-start the project to achieve the same end results. This is true with updating software packages, doing revision on a script, or changing your vacation plans from Aruba to Bermuda. Trial and error is a very frequent method by which we reach results in many aspects of business and life.

ESSENTIALS

Sometimes you can make a slight sacrifice to get the job done in time and under budget. However, if the new plan will drastically reduce the quality of the product, it may ultimately spell disaster for the project.

Place blame on no one and invite everyone to a brainstorming session to devise ways of making this new plan work. If you have already involved people in the building process of the contingency plan, they will already feel vested in this new game plan. It's a good idea to take some time and talk backup plans with team members early on in the process—you will ensure support of the new plan, and you'll be ready to roll as soon as plan A goes awry.

Once the contingency plan takes full effect, you need to monitor it just as you were monitoring your initial plan. Once again you will compare actual work and budget totals to those initially established for this new plan.

Emergency Plans

Contingency plans are often emergency plans. During the "Y2K Crisis," for example, many of the plans were designed to go into effect in the event of an emergency. Such plans must clearly define the emergency decision-making process, including who makes the decision(s) and when the decision must be made. When dealing with such emergency plans it's important that the decision-making hierarchy is clearly established. For example, in the event of an emergency, we switch to plan "B," which states that Jane Doe makes all determinations regarding evacuating the building, John Smith will handle all system recovery operations, and so on. Assigned tasks need to be in place for emergencies that can arise. If this framework is not clearly established, there is a serious risk of panic or chaos. Likewise, in any contingency plan (including non-emergency plans), all decision making must be clearly defined. Phil is in charge of A, Janet is in charge of B, and Fred is in charge of C. On smaller projects, all decision making might fall on your shoulders.

The Ripple Effect

Changing a plan can be like throwing a rock into a pool of water, and "ripples" need to be addressed. When you move to a new house, for example, along with the packing and the unpacking, there are other issues that need to be considered, such as changing your phone number, forwarding your mail, and so on. These are all interdependencies or resulting factors that come into play when you move. The same holds true when moving to a contingency plan on a project.

> **ALERT**
>
> Having a well-constructed contingency plan is vital when working with systems, programs, or new technology for the first time. Consider phasing in new technology one user group at a time, or having a taskforce help you transition. Any complications during a 100 percent rollover could paralyze your business.

If, for example, two weeks before the conference, your site suddenly becomes unavailable, you'll need to switch to plan "B," which could mean moving the conference to a backup location, or postponing it until later. Given the many processes involved in planning a large-scale conference, there will be many interdependent aspects of this project. Such contingency planning must recognize these interdependencies and not focus solely on individual tasks or activities independent of other tasks or activities.

Ensuring that you are prepared on all fronts requires you to:

* Look at a broad overview of the project to see such interdependencies
* Evaluate the dependencies of each task
* Communicate effectively to task leaders

In the conference site example, a contingency plan would present not only a new setting or a new date for the conference, but would also mean follow-up work on:

- **Materials.** Are you expecting items that will need to be rerouted or stored elsewhere, most likely at an additional cost?
- **Staff.** Check the availability of your staff. Will you have the same human resources available at the new location? On the new date? Will you need a new on-site staff? How much training will need to be done to familiarize everyone with the new facility?
- **Attendees.** Notices with change in time or location need to go to all attendees, including clients, vendors, and your staff.
- **Incidentals.** Who is responsible for reclaiming your deposit at the original site? What about printing new programs, or catalogs?
- **Additional charges.** Is there any recourse for the added expense of last minute changes? Who will track that in your project documentation?

Many details must be considered in the contingency plan. Like the original plan, each aspect of the conference will need to be thought through. Unlike the original plan, there also needs to be a detailed transitional phase that will be included in your contingency planning. Before you cut the cord and give life to plan "B" to operate on its own, you need to look at the interdependencies between all aspects of the new plan and those of the previous plan.

For example, let's say that in plan "A," food was to be served at a sit-down luncheon at noon. The food was to be ordered from Marsha's Catering and delivered to loading dock "J" at 7 A.M. Because of the change in time and facility of the conference, plan "B" has a buffet luncheon being set up at 2 P.M. The food is still being served by Marsha's Catering, but it will now be delivered to loading dock "N" at 8 A.M.

The two plans are similar in that they both include lunch and the same catering company. They will both require that someone be ready at the correct loading dock at the correct hour to receive the delivery.

Getting the food to the right floor to be prepared and served is therefore dependent on someone being ready to receive it at the new delivery area.

Contingency plans, while going their own route, often need to include the phase of gathering a trail of loose ends caused by the original plan. For example, if someone has reached the stage of the project when it's time to call Marsha's Catering and order the food, the step of calling Marsha's Catering and rerouting the food, or perhaps reordering it, will need to be addressed in the contingency plan. Similarly, if you have gone from waiter and waitress service to a buffet, someone will need to inform any servers who were already contacted.

It's rare that you can simply switch to a new plan with no transition necessary. In most cases the work of other people will be affected. Usually there are plenty of steps that have to be retraced because of interdependencies. When programmers switch to new software, there is a need for training and making sure that information already stored on the system finds its way to the new system.

FACTS

On rare occasions, a plan is changed so early in the process that the impact on other variables is minor, or the nature of the project allows for a completely independent plan to be enacted. These are the exceptions rather than the rule.

There may also be new parameters, often external, that affect the contingency plan. For example, the policy of the original conference facility may have required that you have your own AV crew set up according to your instructions. The contingency plan may have moved you to a facility that has its own equipment and can only be installed or set up by union members. Therefore, your new plans will not include your AV team members by virtue of the parameters dictated by the facility.

Rules and regulations need to be re-examined carefully. A movie shoot that is forced to switch to a new location will need to get new permits and may have to follow new state laws regarding unions, taxes, etc. Keep in mind, too, that contingency plans will generally have a shorter time span (less slack) than your original, unless you switch gears very early on. Most often you will have spent some of your allotted time on plan "A" before switching to plan "B." The shorter time frame will usually cost you more money since you'll have less time to shop around and make better deals. Make sure that you plan wisely and are certain that there is enough money in the budget and that plan B is cost-effective. If by spending more money you are eliminating your profit margin, the project may no longer be feasible.

You may establish a cutoff time as the last possible date by which you can implement a contingency plan effectively. After that date, it would not be feasible to switch to the contingency plan because it would be too costly. For example, you might state that if significant problems are found in the initial plan by the fifteenth of the month, then plan "B" will take effect. If, however, you discover problems after that point, you're stuck trying to work around them because plan "B" could not be completed within time or budget limitations, either.

Plans Within the Plan

An overall project may have many different sub-categories operating as sub-projects. For example, a new business might have various teams working on sub-projects to get the business off the ground. The overall project might be to prepare for opening the doors for business by June 1. Between November and the following June you may have teams working on designing the physical location, building the Web site, handling promotion and marketing, and so on. They may be working on these sub-projects in the same or at different locations.

Although there will be interdependency between some of these areas, others may not be affected by another team's changes. If you have to enact a contingency plan in one area, it's important to check that other areas are alerted to the change being made to plan "B" in a single area. This will enable other team members to confirm with you whether or not their area is affected by the sub-project contingency plan.

For example, if the Web site is supposed to carry a banner ad but the marketing department is now designing a different type of ad instead, they must alert the team building the Web site that it will no longer have a banner ad.

Returning to the conference scenario, the need to move the conference to a new location or reschedule it on a different date would require an overall project contingency plan. You might have other contingency plans in place for various aspects of the conference. You will therefore need to address the project with an overall contingency plan and sub-projects within the plan with smaller scale contingency plans. Remember to look over the entire list to see that a contingency plan in one area does not negatively affect another area.

Someone may be a great understudy for the lead role in a theatrical production, but you also have to consider that if he or she is already in the play, they too will need an understudy for their part. Likewise, if the system goes down and you have a manual backup plan for creating tickets to the show, you will need to alert the ticket sellers that tickets will be coming from a different source and look different from the originals. Every time you make a change you must think it all the way through the process. A contingency plan may be an overhaul of one aspect of the project, but its impact could be far reaching.

Contingency Planning List

When planning ahead, make a list and cover all the bases. The following contingency planning guide was established for a weekend special educational seminar. The project coordinator filled in all the details for each area so that the contingency plan was in place. (Obviously, many of these areas will require far more consideration than one line, but the idea is to list vital areas and to write out a backup strategy.)

Seminar Contingency Planning List (Sample)

Substitute plans for transportation and parking: ....

Reserve rooms and facilities for any potentially unusable rooms: ....

Substitute plans for speakers: ....

Substitute plans for staff: ....

Contingency plan for food services: ....

Emergency plans for evacuation: ....

Plans for equipment failure, including:

    Computers: ....

    A/V equipment: ....

    Phones and other communications systems: ....

    Other: ....

Services for the disabled, including:

    Evacuation: ....

    Wheelchair accessibility: ....

    Other needs: ....

    Health and medical emergency plans: ....

Non-violent crisis intervention, including:

    Staff for crisis intervention: ....

    Documentation method determined: ....

    Violence and unlawful activities: ....

Plan "A," the Original	Plan "B," Contingency
Outdoor wedding ceremony in garden adjacent to country club swimming pool	Indoor ceremony in enclosed ground floor patio
Folding chairs set up in garden	Have country club staff move folding chairs to enclosed patio
Outdoor breezes	Set up fans for cooling in patio area
Coat rack available in case someone has jacket/coat	In the event of bad weather (rain, snow, cold for for June) open up coat check room near country club entrance and call coat check person to work for that day. Add onto expenses.

Sample Original Plan and Contingency Plan

You may find it helpful to compose plans "A" and "B" together. In planning an outdoor wedding, for example, consider plan "A" your first choice. While it's on your mind, think of what the second best option might be. This way, you're hitting most of the details at the same time, rather than scrambling when clouds roll in, wondering what you may have forgotten.

This is just some of the thinking you'll need to do when formulating any type of contingency plan. Often, it's a lot of little things that need to be accounted for that help make up the big picture.

Contingency Planning Matrix

One way of evaluating which areas of the project need to be addressed first is to make a contingency planning matrix, such as the one that follows.

Vertically, you can list each potential problem that could occur in your project (those listed here are general). You can be as general or specific as you choose based on the size and potential for problems inherent in the particular project. Horizontally, list the severity of each problem, such as "Loss of Life" and "Severe Financial Loss." Then fill in the boxes to determine how necessary it is to have a contingency plan for that particular problem. Enter into each box the likelihood of each result: H for high, M for Medium, U for Unlikely, N/A for not applicable.

In other words, if there is a high likelihood that people could be killed, then you are looking at an "H" in the column "Loss of Life," which is the highest priority item and must be addressed immediately with a contingency plan in place. This might occur, if, for example, there are staff shortages in a medical facility. If, however, there are staff shortages on a sales project, then there might be a high loss of sales. An "H" in "Severe Financial Loss" might then be your highest priority item, provided no one's physical well-being is at stake. If, next to "Equipment Failure," the most significant result would be an "M" or even an "H" in "Loss of Public Perception," and all other columns have an "N/A," then this is the most serious problem you will have to deal with when seeking a contingency plan for equipment failure. Therefore, work accordingly. You can see the likely results for each potential problem, then determine which problems to seek contingency plans for first.

Potential Problem	Loss of Life	Severe Financial Loss	Loss of Resource or Services	Loss of Public Perception
Communications				
System failure				
Equipment failure				
Resources delayed				
Staff shortages				
Change in location/site				

Obviously, a high likelihood for loss of life will elicit the top priority for a contingency plan. Areas marked as medium risk should have a plan, while low risk areas may not need contingency plans.

Contingency Planning Outline

While a contingency plan matrix will help you list the potential problems in order of their impact, an outline will allow you to write down each problem and delve into ways to solve them.

1. Describe the problem: _____

2. Potential dangers: _____

3. Possible outcomes: _____
   _____

4. Can you manage the problem, or is it outside your control?_____
   _____
   _____

5. Describe contingency plan options (list in order of feasibility, and remember to consider the added expense): _____
   _____
   _____

6. List additional resources that are needed to implement plan(s): _____
   _____

7. Note time period needed to implement plan: _____
   _____

8. Name authority in charge of implementing plan: _____
   _____

9. List details of time and expenditures (e.g., if the electrical power fails, we will need to shut down for at least one day. It will take us x hours to test the computer system and x hours to do x, y, and z in preparation to return to normal operating procedures. Loss of one business day equals $\$n$ in lost revenue.): _____
   _____

10. List who will handle each aspect of the contingency plan:_____
    _____

11. List any effects the new plan will have on other areas of the company, your office, your home, or wherever this project takes place: _____

_____

12. Document your contingency plans for possible future use: _____

_____

_____

_____

FACTS

Your team members may have skills that can come in handy in your backup plans. Consider what team members can do and how you can use those skills. This strategy can come in handy when a labor shortage or strike is approaching and you need to determine which people on your team can fill in for striking workers. Discuss your plan with the team members first to make sure they can still (and will) do what you think they can.

Backing Up Your Backup Plan

Sometimes a third, fourth, or even fifth option is necessary. On simpler projects it is often easier to think of a variety of contingency plans. "Okay, we've lost our best actor to the flu and no one seems to be able to handle the part . . . new plan, let's do a different show!" Or perhaps you have another suggestion for a science project after your daughter's volcano erupted all over her new outfit.

The more complex and further along a project is, the less likely you will be able to switch more than once—and once is hard enough. In fact, the more complicated a project becomes (either by the nature of the project or by the amount of work that has been done or both), the less likely it is that you will be able to come up with very many viable contingency plans. There is much more to take into consideration as a project grows.

Like the evolution of the original plan, contingency plans are often forced to change too. What might have been a marvelous idea as a backup plan at one time may not be so marvelous any longer. One owner of a small import/export business was heading a project that had his team moving offices. Everyone would continue to work out of each office until the move was completed. That way, he did not have to shut his business down completely. His contingency plan was that in the event that the move was taking longer than expected, or the new office space wasn't ready in time, the office would be set up in his home until the new office was ready. He had extra room for all seven employees, but what he didn't anticipate was that his basement would be flooded by a winter storm, limiting the space he had available and changing his contingency plan. Now three people would have to telecommute from their own homes.

Some things are out of your control, and you may not be able to prepare a contingency plan for every possible problem. Be careful to address those areas that you can control, and prioritize which contingency plans will come first.

You will frequently need backup plans for your backup plans, or at least variations on a theme. As soon as you make the decision to switch to a contingency plan you should be thinking "what if" in case you have to move to plan "C." Particularly in cases where the project involves personal safety, it is imperative that you move as many contingency plans as you can think of in behind your new plan.

Monitoring Your Contingency Plan

Switching to a new plan of action doesn't eliminate your need to keep on receiving up-to-date, detailed progress reports. If the new plan requires a new process for monitoring the activities, clearly explain it at a meeting so that team members understand what is expected of them. For your business, you may still require that weekly reports be handed in on Friday afternoons. The nature of these reports may or may not be different depending on the new plan of action.

Contingency plans, like your original plan, must have a new game plan with an established baseline to use as a guide. You should compare the actual plan to the projected plan just as you did during plan "A." Too often people make the mistake of comparing plan "B" to the failed plan "A" instead of to an established baseline. Comparing the new plan to the original can be used to validate that your new plan is working in comparison to your old plan, but it won't tell you that your new plan is working in comparison to itself.

Let's say you decide to fly to your vacation destination instead of drive. The fact that you are flying instead of driving certainly means you will be getting there faster. That can be deduced by comparing plan "A" (driving) with plan "B" (flying). However, if your contingency plan says you will be there by 3 P.M., the only way you can determine whether or not you will get there on time is to monitor your progress thus far. If you're late getting to the airport or the flight is delayed, you'll be running behind on your new plan—that's the comparison you need to make (scheduled time versus elapsed time).

ESSENTIALS While monitoring a contingency plan, it's important to make sure people are not slipping into old habits. If the team has become familiar with doing something a certain way and that has changed, you may need to remind them that the new procedures work in a different manner.

Motivation, Round Two

Okay, so you've motivated the team to help you set up a marketing and promotional plan for your own small business venture. You found out, however, that the local radio and television stations on which you planned to run ads have been bought out by a large corporation, and advertising rates have increased significantly. Your team is discouraged because they now have to stop their work on "the big ad campaign" and work on a new direct marketing piece.

It can be hard to re-motivate a team that has seen the initial plan go belly-up. Many large companies need to find new ways to motivate team members to work on new projects after stopping old ones they can no longer finance, or for which they no longer see profitable results.

Just as you got everyone on board for plan "A," you'll need to sell plan "B" with the same or even more enthusiasm. Make sure everyone not only understands that you are trying to reach the same goal, but also why you made the decision to move to the contingency plan. Sometimes the reasons will be obvious, like when you see a tree lying across the road from the storm that knocked out the power.

Here are a few key points to remember while motivating the team to work on the contingency plan:

- *Don't point fingers.* You must make sure your team does not feel it was its fault that plan "A" did not work—even if it was. Unless someone absconded with the funds and left for Rio, don't point fingers and lay blame for previous activities that led to the first plan being halted.
- *Keep thinking ahead.* The team may have been working together for six days or six months. There may be a feeling of dismay from working so hard to achieve nothing. Remind everyone that they worked hard and because of unforeseen events, they'll need to forge on with a new game plan. Keep them focused on the new plan and moving forward, not looking back. Rehashing the pitfalls of plan "A" will only further delay plan "B."
- *Assign new roles.* If people are now assuming different responsibilities than they had originally, encourage the same attention to detail and dedication. Remind them of why they were selected for this new task.

CHAPTER 13

Finishing the Project and Evaluating the Results

S ome projects end with a bang and others a whimper. In this chapter we will address several methods of wrapping up a project, whether it is presenting the final product or transitioning it to its next phase. The end of a project will also impact the team, which may take pride in its success, be uncertain of what comes next, and have mixed emotions about breaking up as members move on to new jobs. Depending on their personal interest in the ensuing tasks that await them, this can be exciting, depressing, frightening, or a little of all three.

The End Is Near

While you may find it a bit presumptuous to start planning for the end of your project before you start (and some people focus too much attention on this), you should have some plans for a smooth closing that are in place from the outset. For example, do you have a file for each person who leaves the project? Invariably someone will leave along the way. You need to have information available should you need to contact this person when the project ends, for any reason from missing a report to sending a 1099 form. Make sure from day one that you have files on all vendors you use and anyone else who may only be involved with the project for a short time. You also need to make arrangements for:

- Returning items borrowed from other departments or from friends or neighbors
- Accounting for leased or rented equipment
- Cleanup after a conference, party, or banquet
- Presenting the final product or finished project to stakeholders

Final phase and "end" plans need to be in place from the start. There must also be a discussion of post-project evaluations (which I'll discuss a bit later in the chapter), so the team knows to expect them. Evaluations will provide a forum for team members to give and receive feedback on several aspects of the project, including its organization and leadership, as well as their own performance.

Beyond the End

If the project is one in which you are creating a product or service that will ultimately be sold or distributed to the public, you also need to set a time to start planning your post-project marketing strategy. One of the biggest mistakes a company can make is not looking beyond the actual project. For example, a project to make a Web guidebook was set to take three months. The project was completed and the books were printed and ready to go. However, no one took the time to put together a marketing plan. Thus, the project team was asked to scramble and try to start selling the book. They sold a few, but the results of this successful project were unsuccessful book sales. Why? Because the hand-off was not addressed during the project phase. Set the wheels in motion during the creation of a project so that the product or services have a life after the creation.

How many people have built something and never bothered to use it, or written something they meant to send to magazines or publishers but never did? There are many unfinished projects, but there are also many finished ones that never got beyond their creation.

Learn from the Past

Although you may not be doing this exact project again—after all, no two projects will be exactly the same—you may find yourself doing one that is similar in the future. You will want to learn from your experiences on the project. By the same token, another project team will be planning the organization's next annual conference. Make sure you are documenting what you do as you proceed for the sake of your own future projects and those of the group, company, or organization. Even in a family project, it's a good idea to save the plans of your trip to France just in case you decide to travel to Italy in a couple of years. Half of your research will be done, and you'll be able to learn from what you needed to do for your previous long-distance vacation.

ESSENTIALS Taking good notes for the duration of a project can benefit future projects. Documentation on research and initial planning is important, but don't forget the second half of the project. Information on what could (and did) go wrong (and your solutions) is critical in helping the next team create a better plan from the outset.

The Carrot

You might also consider doing some "motivational advance planning." If you're building a patio for the backyard and have a pretty good idea that you will be finished by June 23, why not plan a July 4 party to christen the new patio and show it off to all of your neighbors? Likewise, if you are moving to a new office space, plan a big "office warming party." Anything that you can imagine that will help encourage everyone to keep on plugging away is worth considering. Many filmmakers look forward to their big opening night even before the final editing. While a project-launch can be motivational, it is important not to think too long about the end results before you get down into the trenches and do the work. How many people have come up with a hundred things the new system can be used for before the project of setting up the new system has even begun?

If you're planning a conference, party, book sale, auction, picnic, or seminar, make sure you include the cleanup process. It's important to plan for cleanup, breakdown, or disassembly in the end. Put this in your initial plan along with other closing activities such as final evaluations and reporting.

Final Phase Responsibilities

Okay, so what *must* you do to properly end the project? The following list will get you on track for "closing the books."

1. *Make sure all unfinished project activities are completed.* Many project managers drop the ball at this point, assuming everything is done because most tasks are completed. Assume nothing—do a thorough review. Sometimes people cut corners to move on to their next project or on to operations. Don't let this happen to you. Set up a task list of final items and review it to ensure that everything is completed and the quality of the work is satisfactory.

2. *Have a team meeting to evaluate the project.* (You may do one meeting with your team to prepare a wrap-up presentation for stakeholders.) Determine how you got to where you are, and what you might do differently in the future. Review your documentation

to be sure it's complete for the next project team. Include a thorough review of the budget, your resources, and barriers. Share what you learned the hard way to save the next team time and money.

3. *Meet with stakeholders, sponsors, and anyone else who needs to approve or sign off on the project.* Make sure that everyone with final authority agrees that the project is concluded.

4. *Finish off all accounting procedures including paying final bills and fulfilling all contracts.* Make sure all bookkeeping is up-to-date and all information for team members is accessible, including personal information needed for 1099s or other tax-related documents. Your goal is to close the books on the project before shutting off the lights.

5. *Make sure all documentation lands in the hands of those who will need it in the future.* If you have created a new product or started a new service that the sales team will now be selling, make sure the sales force has all the information (such as product specifications, user tools, or plans for future development) they require.

6. *Meet with team members and thank them for their efforts.* Let them know that the stakeholder, sponsors, and others are pleased with the job they have done. Also thank vendors and others who were integral to the success of your project. Make sure everyone knows the project is indeed "officially" over, for better or worse.

7. *Reassign team members.* If you own your own business and the team was made up of employees, you will need to either assign them to a new project, move them into operations resulting from the project, or have them return to doing their original jobs. Let people know what they should do next.

8. *Return all tools, equipment, or anything you borrowed to its rightful owner.* If you purchased equipment for the project, decide what to do with it. Often when people leave a project a lot of "stuff" is left behind. You need to clean up the mess and determine what is necessary for project maintenance and standard operations, and what was part of the project phase only. Can this equipment be used on future projects? On occasion, tools and equipment have been known to "grow legs" as the project winds down—keep tabs on resources

and equipment. If you do have some dispensable goods, give them away to team members.

9. *If the project was a success, celebrate!* Sometimes even a failed project is cause for celebration, recognition, and appreciation.

ALERT

Be sure to get necessary information from temporary or contracted team members, including their computer passwords and file locations. If team members will no longer be around after the project ends, don't forget company badges, security cards, and office keys. If you don't have a formal exit interview process, arrange an informal meeting to give and receive feedback and (tactfully) collect company property.

Successful and unsuccessful projects need to shut down in a similar manner; however, on projects that have failed, there are a few additional considerations:

• You may have a hard time convincing stakeholders that the project is indeed over. Many "hopeless" projects linger on indefinitely because one or more of the stakeholders do not want to accept that the end has come.

• You will have less celebrating and more consoling to do, since team members may feel frustrated or disappointed. You need to encourage team members to focus on how much was accomplished, and what everyone learned. Do not rehash mistakes or lay blame; acknowledge that sometimes that's the way things worked out.

• It may take longer to close the books since there may be outstanding, or irreconcilable bills. Set up a time frame in which to try to close the books.

• Depending on the project and the attitude of the team members, you may need to pay special attention to security issues.

A project may fail for many reasons. It is important that at some point the project failure is realized and accepted, and there is an official "shutdown." This can take a long time if there are legal entanglements, but in most projects (particularly smaller ones) there is a need to acknowledge that at some point, it may indeed be over, even if you believe in your heart it shouldn't be.

And then there are projects that end while you're still going strong. All appears to be going well, but management, for whatever reason (a merger, change of direction for the company, cranky owner), decides to pull the plug. Team members are especially let down when a project ends abruptly, because it means the rug (and paycheck) is pulled out from under them. Sometimes there are warning signs, but not always. Businesses move quickly and changes are made in the course of a few days or even a few hours.

A sudden shutdown is never easy, and sometimes the only way to deal with it is to pick yourself up as soon as possible and move on. Console and comfort others who are likely as shocked and angered as you are. Even in this scenario, you are often expected to tidy up a bit. The team will be gone, but as a leader, you may have to straighten out loose ends. If you are no longer on the payroll, you are in a good position to negotiate a deal to do whatever is asked of you at this point, but be sure to get it in writing.

Post-project Evaluations

In your post-project evaluations (sometimes called post-mortems), you will want to document in writing which methods worked and why. You will be able to look at how tasks were completed, and determine whether the best methods were used. If the process was one that the team found to be effective, you will want to carefully review the process so that it can be duplicated in future projects. If a task was accomplished, but the method could have been improved upon, you will want to list exactly what aspects of this process should be analyzed and revamped for future projects. Determine why the revised method would be more effective and what the implications would be if you used it on the next project.

Circle Back

Naturally it's important to look at the big picture to determine how close the final result was to the original plan. A completed project is rarely identical to that original concept. Trial and feedback throughout, plus testing, tinkering, and confronting numerous obstacles along the way, will change the course and alter the outcome of any project—sometimes for better, and sometimes for worse.

How much better or how much worse? That is a question you will want to broach during the evaluation phase. You want to have preset levels of what is considered acceptable. Perhaps the new marketing campaign resulting from the project is effective, but the message is not exactly what you envisioned when you started the project. Now is the time to evaluate what is different and discuss whether you sacrificed aspects of the original idea to complete the project, or simply found an easier way to reach comparable results.

If a print ad was too difficult or too costly to run with a glossy finish, you might have settled for something else. You may now be hearing a response that indicates people like this look a lot better than glossy (bolder) promotional campaigns of the past. Quite often, the new approach works very well without all of the details of the original plan. It's not uncommon for plans to become overloaded with "extras" and "highlights" that may not be necessary. Sometimes the act of planning a project takes on a larger scope than necessary, and too many details are added simply because everyone wants to have some input. Simple solutions can sometimes be the most effective.

Revisit the Detours

You should also review the changes and decisions that were made along the way. Obviously, if the project came in below budget, some decisions were made that worked in your favor. Hold a team review meeting and invite everyone in attendance to participate and describe how they succeeded at their various tasks. The learning process is twofold: Not only will future project teams learn from your detailed accounts, but you will also improve your skills for your next assignment.

In the end you and your team can have a strong impact on future projects, but only if you carefully retrace the steps you took and the alterations (and decisions) you made along the way.

If you are asking team members for their evaluations in written form, make sure your questions are simple and to the point. Ask for direct feedback to specific aspects of the project. If you are holding a meeting to get final evaluations (and you should), ask the team whether or not they felt the project really met the intended goals. Find out if they felt problems were handled properly, and if they agreed with your approach to issues that arose throughout the project. Look for constructive criticism. Ask team members to point out what could have been done in a different way, then ask them for suggestions for an alternative approach. You know where the project ended up—for better or for worse—now review how it got there and how it might have gotten there in a better, more efficient manner.

QUESTIONS?

What is a PIR?

The Project Issues Review (PIR), is a document that includes survey results, often featuring graphs or charts, which helps the team determine what was done well and what could be improved upon in the future. Survey participants are asked to complete the review in a specified amount of time.

The Nitty-Gritty

Let the team know at the onset that when the project is deemed complete, there will be a post-project evaluation meeting. When you are ready for such a meeting, make sure all key personnel have advance notice. Request that they bring as much documentation as they have of their work on the project. Naturally, on large-scale projects you can't expect people to carry in files of reports, but key information that helps define what they did and how they did it will be useful.

You also need to have your own project records and documentation on hand. Include the original and final schedules, original budget and final expenditures, progress reports, updates, and correspondence, along with other key information that helps you recount the course of the project. Essentially you want to present a post-game summary, calling attention to the key plays. You want to look at how you scored a touchdown and try to figure out why you fumbled the ball when you did.

ESSENTIALS

To review your records effectively, consolidate all your materials down to the key information. Highlight specific documents as you proceed through the project, making a clear notation of when critical decisions were made, and what processes were enacted.

Many aspects are involved in a project's success or failure. The environment, the economic climate, the schedule, the budget, the resources, or the organizational structure could be at the source. You need to differentiate between factors that were within your control and those that were not. If the project failed because of flooding or a hurricane, it obviously was out of your hands. Try to pinpoint each source of success or failure within the project. Ask yourself and team members to think through the various elements that made up the overall project. Consider the following:

- Was the initial plan too complex or too simple to attain the desired results?
- Were the best resources used?
- Was the team missing certain expertise?
- Were there too many or too few people involved?
- Was the communication system effective?
- Was there conflict that went unresolved and slowed down the project?
- Were there risks that went undetected and caused large-scale problems?
- Were previous projects reviewed and evaluated properly?
- Were the outside experts or consultants effective?
- Did management change the rules, and subsequently the project goals, along the way?

- Did outside agencies, policies, or other political factors impinge on the project's progress?
- Were there external factors that could not be avoided? What were they?
- Should key decisions have been made sooner?
- Should the contingency plan have been implemented at some point?

You should look for ways to improve on the things that did not work toward the best execution of the project, and ways to optimize those aspects that did.

Where Did We Succeed?

Quite often people have an easier time finding fault with (and complaining about) something they were dissatisfied with than they do in noting positive accomplishments and achievements. Success is often hard for people to grasp, especially when they are busily testing, evaluating, retesting, and reporting on each phase of a project. At some point, however, the actual project ends and the resulting product, service, or ongoing activity goes forth into the world.

Naturally it is hard to judge the real success of a project until there has been some impact outside of the project environment. Does the ship actually sail on the ocean? Does the new system enhance service for real customers? Can people actually play in the reopened park? Are people able to apply what they learned at the seminar? These questions will take time to answer as the project results meet the world. For your purposes, you can look at what you did in accordance with the initial plan and goals set forth at the onset of the project. If the initiator of the project, the manager, or others involved have deemed the project completed, then somehow you have succeeded in reaching that step.

Here are seven of the most common evaluation errors:

1. Only evaluating the final results, not how they were achieved or how they differ from the original plans.
2. Not getting a broad view. If the project is going to affect thousands of people, three people's evaluations may not be enough.

3. Not taking good notes. If you don't document the results of feedback, what good is receiving it?
4. Evaluating the work but not the team, or evaluating the team but not the work. If the team worked on the project, then both should receive evaluations.
5. Working with evaluations that are too complicated. If you've ever been handed a ten-page form to evaluate a twenty-minute lecture, you'll understand the need to keep evaluations within the scope of the project.
6. Only looking at the errors and neglecting to review and leverage what went right on the project.
7. Taking too long a break between project and review. Don't expect everyone to remember all the important details if you don't get around to the post-project evaluation until three months have gone by.

What Could We Do Differently Next Time?

This isn't necessarily "where did we go wrong?" because sometimes even a successfully completed task could be the starting point for a new and improved method of doing a particular job. Trial and error often produce positive results. These results, however, are sometimes overlooked because everyone involved is preoccupied with looking for negative factors. Wally Bock, a consultant, speaker, and publisher, whose helpful ideas are found at *www.mondaymemo.net*, says that he prefers to call it "Trial and Feedback." Says Bock, "You don't just want to analyze that which doesn't work, but you want to look at what did work well so you can find a way to leverage it."

The end product can be, and often is, run through a series of tests and analyses (this is after testing is done throughout the project). Even once the product or service hits the market, there will be a great deal of evaluation and reviews. Today, a successful company is one that continually plans ahead. As soon as a new product is created, the next new one is in the planning stages, particularly in the technology field. Project feedback and evaluation will guide the company into improvements on existing products and services as well as guidelines or suggestions for handling future endeavors.

The team can provide initial feedback. Feedback will also come from stakeholders, customers, clients, the media, and other sources. If the team's initial reaction is similar to the external feedback, then the team was very well aware of how it could improve upon a successful product, and has made a good assessment of its work.

ESSENTIALS

Identify the positives, even on a project that failed. Look for constructive suggestions on how a task might evolve from the project and be used more effectively in the future. A company may fail with its initial e-commerce business plan, but still learn enough about the potential power of the Web to produce a successful strategy for its next venture. You can have very successful battles even while losing the war.

Let's say that a team was pulled together to research and produce a new soft drink. After much trial and error, and many taste tests, the team successfully produced a new drink that satisfied the management and sponsors. The team, however, still thought that if there was a chance to do it over, the drink could be less "dry." The product was a success and customers enjoyed it, however, the comment the company received most often was that the soda was "a little too dry." In this case, the team itself knew what would have improved the product.

Internal changes are easier to identify than external changes because they directly affect the project External changes, those that affect the stakeholders, customers, and others associated with the project, will require outside evaluation and feedback. Aspects of the final product—the taste, smell, or service provided—connect with the external world and need evaluation on several levels. When the project is to create something brand new, there is a risk that others won't be as satisfied with the product or service as the sponsors or management are. No matter how much test marketing is done (and new products and services require a lot of test marketing along the way), there is still the chance that the project champion's idea will not be embraced by the intended market. Focus groups are essential for gauging the possible success of a new product or service.

It is always in your best interest to get outside feedback at various stages of production. Unless it's a top-secret project, it is usually beneficial to get feedback from people who are familiar with the project but not involved with the day-to-day process. Sometimes, an outside contractor who has been involved with the project can also provide good feedback along the way. He or she can see it from a different perspective. One of the most common post-project determinations is that there was a need for more testing. "We should have tested the system much earlier on" is a common post-project phrase. Ongoing tests, reviews, and evaluations are critical.

What to Do with Those Evaluations

While evaluations are important, they need to be used effectively. At the end of a major adoption conference in New York City, with some 125 workshops, an event coordinator asked, "Who collected the speaker evaluation forms so we'll know who to invite back at future conferences?" Everyone looked at each other. Sure, forms had been distributed to evaluate speakers, but no one had bothered to collect them at the end of the day and the feedback was lost.

Therefore, you need to:

1. Save post-project evaluations
2. Discuss and document the findings, including which methods you want to maintain and which ones need to be changed in the future
3. Document suggested changes
4. Create a final report, book, or file as a means of saving the information for future use

The last item should be a review of the project that traces the steps taken (in a broad manner) from the original plan to the end product. Show how the project reached anticipated milestones or why it failed to do so. Point out changes made to the original plan and key decisions made by you or management that impacted the project. Note the testing that was done throughout the project and how such tests helped the decision-making process. List the key successes in the project, such as new or improved ways of completing certain tasks. Also list those things that can be improved in the future, using some suggestions from your post-evaluation meeting.

FACTS

Wally Bock explains, "Most projects only have guidelines and not recipes. Therefore, in the end they will come out differently than you envisioned in your original plan." The hope is that the goal is reached in one manner or another and that the project guidelines are followed. But, he adds, "If a project has a set recipe, you shouldn't have any problem following it to completion."

You want to take what you have gained from the post-evaluation meetings and put together a guide (or template) for the next team. Your report will also serve as a guide for the future of what came out of the project (whatever it is that you produced, planned, etc.). For example, if the project was to create a new automated filing system, besides providing instructions on how to create such a system, you will have information on how the automated filing system works. Having created and tested the system, you'll have the initial "user guide" ready for the people who will now be using this automated system on a regular basis.

The Hand-Off

While projects by definition are finite, their impact should continue after they have been completed. If not, one may question what the point of the project was in the first place. Many projects roll themselves into operations. The company should now be using the information or system that resulted from the project. A transitional period will often take team members directly from the project into their roles in the daily operations of the company. Now that the project is deemed complete, it's important to determine:

- Who will maintain it once it becomes operational?
- When will upgrades be made?
- Who will handle troubleshooting?

Setting up the system was the project; using the system is the operational process that follows. Often people from the core project team are the perfect fit for these positions. In fact, some may have been borrowed from similar positions to work on the project. If you used the services of an expert or outside consultant during the project, you may need to continue using that person on an ongoing basis after the project ends, at least until someone else has been trained to take over.

Regular corporate operations may also change because of the project. You have to look at how the project affects the manner in which business is run, including corporate communications, cultural implications, and so on. A successful project should have an impact, and when the project is drawing to a close, that potential impact needs to be addressed. For example, what will the flow of company information be now that lower-level managers have access to the same information as the top executives? The technical staff can often train upper management and senior VPs on processes and procedures for the system. As the knowledge base shifts, what new procedures will have to be addressed?

ESSENTIALS The transition that takes the project from completion to real-world activities will require reviewing reports and other data generated throughout the project to answer questions that arise. Therefore, it's important that you organize and store all key documentation.

It's worth noting that almost every project has a carryover effect. Rarely does a project end without any discernable trace. Even a small-scale school fundraising project will result in that money being spent on something—and that purchase will hopefully be educational or helpful for the children who attend the school.

The effects of a single project can also be widespread. Projects in small businesses or large corporations frequently result in new and efficient methods of assimilating and storing data or enhancing production, communication, or marketing efforts. Projects from a wide range of places, including laboratories, may result in the discoveries of new medications or create new and useful products.

From personal growth to expanding global technologies, projects differ in numerous respects and can impact one person or millions. Whether it is keeping the weight off after your two-week project to lose ten pounds or maintaining communication with the space station after your project was to supervise its building and launch, the steps necessary for making the transition from project into actual operations are vital. It is this transition that can ultimately make all of your hard work worthwhile. After all, if the project was to build the space station, it's worth your effort to make sure it is operational and that the team is trained how to use it efficiently.

The Sign-Off

While the sponsor, stakeholders or management will officially "sign off" on the completed project, you will also have to finish your tenure as project manager. Along with the need to see that all loose ends are neatly wrapped up, you will want to take time to review the decisions you made and the strategies that you implemented along the way. Which ones worked? Which ones did not work as you hoped they would? Was your style of leadership effective? You may not be able to determine all of the answers yourself. If you have a thick skin you may want team members to tell you what they liked and disliked about how you ran the project. Ask for honesty and be prepared to receive it.

As the project winds down, you will be faced with moving on to the next situation. In the corporate environment there may be another project waiting for you. Or you may be resuming business as usual. Having put so much effort into one specific project, you may feel let down when it comes to an end. Your daily routine may seem boring by comparison. On the other hand, working nine-to-five might feel like a vacation! Whatever you are feeling as the project winds down, don't allow yourself to give less than your usual commitment to the project. Just as you don't want team members to slack off as they see the finish line approaching, you must tell yourself that although the end is near, you will need to muster up one last burst of energy.

ESSENTIALS

During the course of the project, try to find a few moments to line up your next project. Don't wait until this one is in the final stages. However, you also don't want to divert your attention from the current project, so stay focused.

If the project is yours to sign off on, then you need to determine if everything has been completed to your liking, as you are "management," sponsor, and champion. Carefully monitoring the project along the way should have eliminated any major surprises at this point. Carefully evaluate what you were looking to achieve and compare it to the finished project that is now before you. Don't sign off on it if you feel that more work is needed. On the other hand, don't pursue perfection at the risk of never having a marketable product, or falling behind the competition. Maintain high, but realistic, expectations.

Disassembling the Team

How one disassembles a team depends on the nature of the project and the team. If the project was a one-time operation such as helping your buddy move, it's over. There's time for a parting beer, some handshakes, and "I'll see you soon." However, if the project is one that will require more work in the future, you need to determine who can do each job. Perhaps someone who set up the computer system wants to stick around and move into the operational side as systems manager. Others will learn new skills on the project with the express purpose of continuing to use them on a regular basis once the project moves to an operational phase.

Projects can promote learning, which can lead to greater talent on your workforce. Integrating people from the project into the regular flow of production is generally very effective, particularly with new companies or businesses that may need people to fill open positions. People who make the transition from the project team to the daily routine created by the project often have a more intimate knowledge of the inner workings of the new system or product since they were involved from the start.

When a project is terminated prior to completion, you need to make every effort to pull the team members together and be there for their needs. If management has no regard for the individuals who are now unemployed, the least you can do as project leader is let them know that you'll be happy to provide reference letters or help out in whatever way you can. As a leader and representative of the company, it's up to you to use your people skills. If you can go to bat for the team, by all means, do so. Keep in mind that a team member may be in a position to help you one day.

ESSENTIALS

Consider having the team members meet again in a few weeks or a month, after they have moved onto new things and have had some time to reflect and recover from the "end-of-project blues." Time and perspective will add a depth to their input that may not be evident in the original evaluations or debriefings.

There are also situations when a project is almost finished and most of the team can go onto other things. However, some small alterations need to be made, so a few team members need to stay on until the final one or two percent of the project is completed. It is not uncommon for one or two aspects of a project to need fixing, finishing, or a final touch. Again, be sure to continue monitoring and documenting the process until the very end.

Was It Good for You?

Now that the project is completed, do you feel a sense of relief? Do you feel a sense of accomplishment? Do you feel that you have achieved your project goals? Do you feel that, as the project manager, you have supported your team and fulfilled the stakeholders' expectations?

All the evaluations won't tell you how *you* feel about the project. People have worked on very successful projects and come away feeling empty. Sure, they made money, but they felt they did not learn or grow in any way. Some projects succeed despite unpleasant working conditions or unscrupulous methods that take a toll on team members. Other individuals will feel a strong sense of learning and growing from a project that went nowhere. Filmmakers will often recount early flops that taught them about how to do it right in the future. You might even recount a personal project that went no place, but from which you made a personal discovery, like a hidden talent or a new friend.

After the project phase is completed, sit down and assess what you personally got from the experience. Ask yourself:

• Did I learn from any or all aspects of the project?
• Did I grow?
• How will I continue my affiliation with the product, service, system, or function that resulted from the project?

At the end of the "official" project phase you can do a personal overview of your project management skills. Be honest. These are some of the questions you may ask yourself in your own self-evaluation of the project and your role in it:

1. Did I deal well with other team members?
2. How well did I communicate my ideas?
3. Did I keep management, stakeholders, and any other key parties informed of the project's progress?
4. Was I able to maintain the schedule I planned?
5. Was I flexible enough to make alterations in plans when needed?
6. Did I deal with conflict situations well?
7. Did I catch risks in time?
8. Did I take any unnecessary risks?

9. Did I monitor properly so that I felt I had a firm grasp of where the project was at any given time?
10. Did I reach the planned objectives of the project? If not, why not?
11. If not, could I have prevented the project from failing or was it out of my control?
12. Did I have proper contingency plans?
13. Did I make the right call to use—or not to use—contingency plans?
14. Did I learn any new skills regarding project management? Specifically?
15. Would I do it again? What would I change and what would I keep the same?

ESSENTIALS

Take a few moments to assess what type of leadership qualities you displayed. While working in a leadership capacity, it is often hard to step back and take a look at exactly how you are doing.

Assess your leadership skills by asking yourself these questions:

1. Do I usually take additional time to go back and review information before making decisions, or do I just make the decision and move forward?
2. If a team member asks me a question and I don't know the answer, do I seek outside help in finding the answer or try to research and solve it myself?
3. Do I allow for a learning curve, or learning while doing (trial and error), as I go?
4. Do team members consider my approach methodical or very direct?
5. Do I include gut feeling and intuition in making decisions or rely strictly on data and specific information?
6. Am I flexible in my methods or do I try hard to keep the same methods in place as much as possible?
7. Am I closer to believing that conflict situations can sometimes work themselves out or am I closer to the idea that immediate intervention is necessary?

Obviously there are no right or wrong answers to these questions. The situation, environment, and time frame will often dictate which answers are more suitable for a particular project. You can make a positive argument for either approach, and certain leaders will vary from one method to another depending up the team and the project. The ability to adapt is one characteristic of an effective project manager.

The first choice generally indicates a less aggressive approach, such as stepping back to re-evaluate or letting the conflict work itself out. In non-pressure projects, such as those over long periods of time, or those for which the outcomes are not highly consequential, you may use intuitive feelings, review rather than move forward, and so on. In projects where time is critical, you may not have the luxury to visit and revisit an issue; it may be necessary to act quickly and rely on data alone.

Along with the situational understanding of these questions, there is the "style" of leadership you display and how that affects your team. A high-energy team in a hard-working, fast-paced environment may expect someone who is more direct, stays with proven methods, and uses facts and figures for decision making. A smaller organization, a casual setting, or an artistic or creative project, however, may need a leader to be particularly flexible and adaptable to new ideas. The team may look to you as someone who will follow a gut feeling now and then, and not always go by the book.

While you cannot completely play the chameleon role and change your leadership style for each project, you can consider the following:

- What type of leader will get the best response and results from this particular team of individuals?
- What does this particular project call for in terms of flexibility or rigidity?
- Before I take on this project, can I be the right leader for these people and this job?

There's nothing wrong with determining that a particular project needs a specific type of leader, and you are simply not the person for the job.

Not every leader fits every role. Perhaps if more leaders evaluated the situation carefully and truthfully, they would know when they were not the right fit.

Down the Road

A project may be evaluated further down the road to determine whether sales indeed increased, customer service improved, the movie was a hit at the box office, or the patio you built held up all summer long or started leaning to the left by late July.

For a fair assessment of the impact of your efforts, look at the project results after three, six, or twelve months. You can learn a lot about your initial plans and all of your hard work when you examine the results from a distance.

FACTS

A card, note, or simple "thank you" to each team member means a lot. Let everyone who was involved on the project know that you appreciate the team's hard work. Hold a party or go out for dinner and make a toast, hand out small awards, or give gifts to say "thanks." Even if the project didn't meet final expectations, you should let everyone know you appreciate their efforts.

Ongoing evaluations will provide details for future projects. Teams can look at the fruits of your labor and see how the project results stood up over time. In the case of a new product, the data may tell you when a newer, updated version needs to be created. With technology, that may be ten minutes after you've signed off on the project.

Some projects are meant for short-term purposes and others are meant to have long lasting implications. Know the limitations and evaluate accordingly. If something was created to last for six months, you should have realistic expectations if you evaluate it after one year.

Appendix A

Anatomy of a Project

Not all projects are for your business, home, or personal needs. Often, groups or organizations sponsor conferences or special activities for their members or the general public. A local town fair, a community gathering, or a charity auction would fall into this category. Although many of the same processes listed throughout the book are included in the plans for similar projects, they may be done in a less formal manner. Variations on Gantt Charts may be simple graphs and timelines. Formal lists of tasks may be arranged and rearranged to meet the needs and skills of the membership base. Nevertheless, it's important that all of the basic elements are considered, including time and budget constraints. In many cases, the budget needs to be monitored closely because funding may be limited.

The Adoptive Parents Committee (APC) is a New York–based, nonprofit support group for the tri-state area. APC provides information and resources for individuals looking to adopt children domestically or internationally, as well families formed by adoption. The organization, established over forty-five years ago, is comprised of four chapters including New York City, Long Island, the Hudson Region, and New Jersey, plus a growing Connecticut faction of members. Combined membership is close to 3,000 families.

Annually, the all-volunteer organization presents one of the largest adoption conferences in the nation. The chapters take turns hosting and chairing the conference, which draws as many as 2,000 people including members and non-members who join the organization for one year when they sign up for the conference.

The APC conference serves as an excellent example of how a large-scale project for a nonprofit (charitable or community) group can be organized and run by the membership. The following details provide a basic overview of how this project is put together, not strictly by graphs and charts, but by committees working on activities for the good of a common goal. The time frame is important, as activities need to be scheduled well in advance, and the workload increases as the conference date approaches.

Preliminary Planning Meetings

Each chapter has a board of officers who will begin discussing the conference they will be hosting nearly two years in advance. The New York Chapter hosted the 2000 conference, held in November (November is National Adoption month), but as far back as 1998, meetings began broaching the subject of how the conference would be handled. Informal discussion centered on who would chair the conference or, unofficially, become the "project leader(s)." The committee decided to have co-chairpersons for several reasons.

1. Being a volunteer, any one individual may only have a limited amount of time to dedicate to the project
2. Different individuals have different skills, including those pertaining to leadership and organization.

    For example, one person may be more effective dealing with non-members or representing the organization to outside resources. Another individual might have a stronger rapport with the membership base, or knowledge in specific areas.
3. Co-project leaders can oversee different committees depending on their expertise, and present diverse viewpoints, which will bring more than one idea to the table.

It helps if co-project managers, or chairpersons in this case, have a similar standing in the organization so that neither will "outrank the other," and they will be able to make decisions unilaterally as well as together. If one person is a long-time member and one person is a newcomer to the group, then it's necessary to establish from the beginning that the senior member is helping to guide and train the junior member, if that is the case. Clearly defining relationships will prevent other committee members from second-guessing one of the leaders, or playing them against the other.

Since this particular conference has been run nearly twenty times before, the chapter does not have to reinvent the wheel. In the initial meetings and preplanning stages, there is discussion about obtaining the literature and information from the chapter that ran the previous conference. Likewise, any group running an event that has occurred before can look for templates based on previous events of its own, or presented by similar groups. Most conferences, fairs, auctions, and other such events have been run before in a manner similar to that which you are planning to present.

A template can provide a broad base into which you can put the specific details of your own event. How well your team or group organizes all of the details, plugs them into the template, and then produces results will determine success. All of this can be likened to a chef creating a recipe. The recipe is the template, and the chef needs to fill in the ingredients and use his or her own special skills to make a culinary masterpiece.

Hint: Good leadership involves knowing when to rely on old methods and when to look for something new.

Project Definition

The initial steps involved in running such a conference include both:

1. Defining what the conference will achieve—the goal of the project
2. Deciding on a name for the conference

Since the conference is an annual event, the groundwork for what the conference will include has been, for the most part, established. The conference goal is to present comprehensive information on all aspects of adoption in a nonpartisan manner. The size and scope of the conference can vary depending on the location and the available resources. In the twenty years of the conference, it has grown in size from a small informal gathering to a major, full-day conference with experts and professionals in the field speaking, and agencies from around the country setting up exhibits. The host chapter can add new definitions and include new elements once they are presented to the state board of the organization for approval. For example, the 2000 conference, hosted by the New York Chapter, added accreditation for professionals in the field of social work. Attendees would then receive graduate-level course credit for attending the full-day conference. Preparations for accreditation and administering the process would be added to the project plans.

The conference name was selected and voted upon by the chapter board members, and the plan phase then began.

Plan Phase

The chairpersons utilized a two-week time period to plan and prepare for the initial conference (project) kick-off meeting. During the two-week period, the chairpersons had to:

1. Spread the word to board members about the time and place of the meeting
2. Decide what the agenda would be for this meeting.
   Agenda items would include:
   - A review of the previous year's conference
   - A discussion of the necessary committees (and tasks that each committee would handle)
   - Listing suggested committee chairpersons based on a list of available chapter volunteers and their specific expertise and their individual personalities

Committees included:

Conference registration	Finance
Programming	Printing
Site coordination	Publicity
Bookstore	Fund raising
Exhibitors	Security
Volunteer coordination	Hospitality
Cleanup	

- Establishing a rough timeline for activities
  Timeline includes:
  Finding and securing the conference site
  Establishing committees and seeking out volunteers from the chapter
  Establishing the conference budget
  Establishing a time frame and rough guidelines for accepting workshop proposals from prospective speakers
  Sending letters to speakers regarding requests (approved/denied)
  Contacting speakers from previous years and from other sources
  Contacting and confirming a keynote speaker
  Creating the complete program of workshops
  Coordinating the opening session
  Making determinations regarding rooms to be used for workshops
  Making hotel and travel arrangements for a few key out-of-town speakers
  Making arrangements with site for food and hospitality services plus other needs including security and A/V crew
  Making arrangements for raffle prizes
  Preparing signage for day-of-conference site navigation
  Ordering supplies for pre-conference and day-of-conference activities

Contacting potential exhibitors for day-of-conference exhibit tables

Final date for confirming exhibitors

Preparing all printed materials including brochures, ads, and posters

Preparing conference program

Preparing all registration forms for both members and non-members

Proofreading and editing of all printed materials including raffles, posters, signage, etc.

Final dates for sending all materials to printer

Final date for receiving printed materials

Anticipated mailing dates for all printed materials

Ordering books/doing inventory of books in storage for sale at conference

Deadline for all promotional material and conference information to be sent to all media

Preliminary site walk-through

Preliminary set up

Day-of preparation

Day-of activities

Day-of cleanup and break down

Many of these areas will overlap and other determinations must be made. For example, where in the building will the collected money be counted and kept? How will the flow of traffic be directed to minimize overcrowding or congestion in the buildings so that attendees will be able to get to workshops and see the exhibit tables easily? What resources will be set up for people to find help navigating the site, which is usually at a university and may include several buildings? The location for the 2000 conference included several buildings that were not easy to navigate without adequate signage and hall monitors to direct traffic and answer questions.

The First Milestone

The kick-off meeting is the first milestone reached as the plan is set in motion. In addition to reinforcing the goal and generating excitement for the project, the meeting will cover the previously listed agenda items to clarify expectations and deliverables. At this time, it's also helpful to plan future meetings.

Subsequent meetings would follow to:

1. Develop the project infrastructure, in this case referring to who would report to whom and what committees would need to start meeting when. Also, it would establish which committees would be dependent on one another. The process for obtaining necessary funds from the conference treasurer and other guidelines for the project are outlined to define the infrastructure.

2. Risk assessment, including discussing the costs involved with the conference and ways in which they would be offset. Other risks include back-up plans, in the event that workshops are overcrowded or in the event that speakers do not attend.

Note: When working in a volunteer organization there is also the risk that volunteers might not complete a task, since they are not held accountable by monetary or other compensation. Therefore, contingency planning for finding and utilizing backup volunteers should be discussed in the event that someone may not be able to complete a task.

In this organization, volunteers who are still in the process of trying to adopt a child may have an adoption situation arise in which they need to fly somewhere to meet and bring home their new family member. This is always an understood (and welcome!) reason to step away from conference business and bow out of the project temporarily.

Action Plan

In this phase, each committee is responsible for working on specific tasks and reporting its progress to the conference chairpersons. Each activity will be listed succinctly under "Action Phase" on the project-planning chart. For example, Development of Program, which will include all of the workshops and speakers, will be listed as a rolled up item, indicating that there are other tasks rolled into the one posting. These tasks will be performed by the programming committee, then turned over to the printing committee.

Much like a business has marketing, sales, and administrative divisions responsible for certain functions, the committees are comprised of specialized project team members. The tasks are distributed on the basis of who has interest and expertise in a particular area. Because of the nature of such a group, no one individual is generally responsible for more than two or three tasks unless he or she requests otherwise.

Here is a brief analysis of the individual committee responsibilities.

The **Registration Committee** will determine the cost of the conference for members and non-members. One-year membership is included in the cost of the conference for non-member attendees.

Since this is a nonprofit organization, APC does not attempt to make money from the conference; they simply aim to cover expenses for the site. Speakers for the workshops are not paid. Therefore, the price for a full day of workshops and information presented by professionals and experts in the field of adoption is kept very low for members.

Registration forms are prepared using the forms from previous years as a guide. To accommodate a variety of needs, there will be forms for individuals registering in advance and for attendees registering at the door. Preregistration is encouraged by offering a discount rate, and is designed so that:

- Less money needs to be handled on the day of the conference.
- The registration process is speeded up, allowing preregistered attendees quicker, easier access.

Packages of information are prepared in advance for day-of distribution to each attendee, including the conference program, information on the organization, and evaluation forms for evaluating the speakers/workshops.

The process for receiving, verifying, and listing all preregistered attendees will be put in place, and cards will be sent notifying attendees that they are officially registered to attend the conference. They will be able to use these cards as passes for entry on the day of the conference.

The day-of planning will include determining where registration tables will be situated for easy accessibility as attendees enter the facility. Volunteers will be appointed to handle specific duties including any problems that arise.

The **Programming Committee** will evaluate all of the proposals for speakers to determine if they fit the tone and purpose of the conference. They will decide which speakers to include, based on the proposals, and invite speakers who have been well received in previous years. Panels are also set up to include APC members well versed in a particular area of adoption or willing to share their particular experiences with adoption.

The committee will send letters of confirmation to the many professional speakers (including licensed social workers and attorneys) who are attending. The committee is also responsible for sending thank-you letters to others whose workshops did not fit the scope of the conference or the current needs of the organization.

The programming committee will then use previous workshop attendance totals, popularity of the topic, and the popularity of certain speakers to determine which rooms will be used for which workshops.

A final grid will be made up to include workshops, speakers, and room numbers. This schedule will be included in the conference program. The programming committee will then prepare the conference program, designed according to guidelines from the printing committee to meet space requirements. All speakers' credentials will be double-checked and included, and succinct write-ups will be designed to best describe each workshop. Once again, the programs from previous conferences will serve as a template for writing up the new program.

In this type of organization, as in any group with specific goals and requirements, it is important that the program and, in particular, the speakers, are discussed with the organization's governing board members before final approval.

The programming committee also arranges for the printing and distribution of speaker packages, which provide each speaker with information about the organization and the conference.

Day-of-conference activities include meeting/greeting and registering speakers. Members of the committee are also responsible for implementing contingency plans for missing speakers or rooms with overflow attendance, should any problems arise.

The **Site Coordination Committee** interacts with several other committees, including programming, registration, exhibitors, security, hospitality, and bookstore. The site committee's tasks will be scheduled to start before most of the other committees', shortly after the kick-off meeting. The committee will first secure the site. Finding (and securing) an acceptable site includes drawing up a contract with the university (or host site), which includes the number of rooms necessary, all food service arrangements, and custodial services. Additional requirements will be discussed. The site committee then determines specific needs for various committees and makes recommendations of locations in the facility. For example, they must plan for:

- An area for registration near the entrances (only specific entrances are used)
- An area for collecting, counting, and securing the money taken in at registration
- A hospitality area for the speakers and volunteers
- A location for the bookstore
- A location for the exhibitors to set up tables

- An area (or areas) for selling raffles
- Classrooms to accommodate well over 100 workshops throughout the day
- A/V equipment and a sound system must be set up in conjunction with the school policy and crew since this conference, like others, has an opening session that takes place in one of the facility's auditoriums

The site committee will work in conjunction with the university personnel to make sure all of the needs and requirements of the conference are carried out as contracted. This includes set up of chairs and tables for speakers and exhibitors. Additional chairs and tables will be ordered from an outside source if necessary.

Just prior to the conference, the site committee will oversee the preparation and layout of the building, and will handle signage as necessary throughout the facility.

On the day of the conference, the site committee helps guide the attendees through the facility.

As the conference breaks down, the site committee's goal is to coordinate with the "Cleanup" committee and the custodial staff to ensure that the facility left in the same condition as it was found.

The **Bookstore Committee** will coordinate with the site committee to determine the best location (from a high-traffic flow perspective) for the bookstore.

The committee is also responsible for reviewing the chapter's current inventory of books for sale, and ordering titles that need to be replenished. Books are then priced accordingly.

Book lists are made up for day-of distribution and volunteers are recruited and listed for selling books and breaking down the "store" on the day of the conference.

A **Security Committee** will work in conjunction with the school. The committee will pre-arrange for day-of-conference walkie-talkies for communication between chairpersons, and will pay special attention to all areas of money transaction.

Since the conference is scheduled for a Sunday, the actual school usage by students is minimal. The school maintains its own weekend security staff, which may be beefed up for the high volume of people in the building on the day of the conference. The security committee will be obligated to notify the school security guards if there is a serious problem.

The **Exhibitor Committee** will determine (with the site committee) the best location in the university to accommodate both the exhibitor's tables and the attendees. The committee's goal is to avoid unnecessary crowding, and prevent any safety or fire hazard. They will further determine the criteria and parameters for exhibitors who are buying table space. This particular conference does not allow the selling of commercial goods unless a specific exception is made and the product is for the benefit of adopting families. In order to be considered, an exhibitor will:

- Be in the best interest of the adoption
- Be a licensed agency (if an agency) in New York State or New Jersey
- Have a good reputation in the adoption community, and as a business entity

The committee is also responsible for drafting and printing the paperwork necessary for exhibitor/conference agreements.

The exhibitor committee will determine how much table space can be sold in the area of the facility that is allotted for exhibitors. On the day of the conference, the chairperson and committee members will assist with set up and break down of exhibits, and will also be available to handle any problems that should arise.

The **Hospitality Committee** will work with the site committee to determine the best location for a hospitality suite for speakers and other guests for the conference. The committee will also meet the needs of any special guests, including politicians or the media.

Other tasks will include ordering food from the facility's on-premises catering service and having committee members on hand during the event to make sure the food supply is replenished and the catering staff maintains service in the hospitality area.

The **Finance Committee** usually consists of a conference treasurer and some day-of-conference assistants for collecting and counting money from registration, and bookstore and raffle sales. The treasurer prepares the initial budget, and will interact with committee chairpersons to determine their financial needs. The treasurer will monitor spending as the project progresses.

The **Printing Committee** interacts with several committees to establish due dates for drafts of printed materials for layout purposes, dates for revisions, and absolute final due dates for all materials including programs, registration forms, evaluation forms, exhibitor agreements, brochures and fliers, raffles, signage, book lists, and other needs. In this organization, the committee generally consists of one overworked volunteer member who is a professional printer.

Many of the deadlines established on the project work plan will be based on the lead time necessary to print materials and distribute them to members, the media, and elsewhere prior to the conference.

The **Publicity Committee** is responsible for the dissemination of marketing and promotional materials regarding the conference including postings in newspapers, public service announcements on local radio stations, and distribution of fliers and brochures. A publicity list of viable markets and media outlets is created early in the action phase, created, in part, from the previous year's listings.

The committee will work in conjunction with the printing committee. In some cases they will have materials run off independently to expedite the process of putting promotional literature in the hands of the media at least one to two months before the conference.

A **Fund Raising Committee** will be in charge of contacting merchants, vendors, and service providers to solicit and obtain prizes for the day-of-conference raffle drawing. The committee will also be in charge of having raffle books printed and sold in advance, as well as on the day of the event. The raffle drawing will be scheduled for late in the conference day. It is the committee's responsibility to make sure all prizes are distributed to the winners, including those who are not in attendance at the time of the drawing.

The **Volunteer Coordinator** works to create a list of volunteers, soliciting help during membership and board meetings, and various other organizational events. The coordinator will then work with the various committee chairpersons to determine their needs for volunteers, and try to meet the needs of each committee.

The **Cleanup Committee** is responsible for breaking down the conference set up and coordinating the cleanup of the facility (some of which is the responsibility of the custodial staff). Since this is a day-of activity, committee members are often recruited from other committees whose tasks were completed well before the conference. Since the breakdown and cleanup will start late in the day, the committee does not need to be at the conference from the start, but should be ready at the site as the first of the workshops ends.

Each of these tasks can be included in the action plan. In an overview, you might include "rolled up" information, with less detail about the smaller tasks.

A brief look would show:

Adoptive Parents Committee Conference Action Plan
(DURACTION OF OVERALL PLAN 425 DAYS)

Task	Duration	Start	Finish
1. Select site location	10 days	9/1/99	9/11/99
2. Define workshop requirements	120 days	12/1/99	4/1/00
3. Preliminary speaker list	60 days	1/15/00	3/15/00
4. Preliminary exhibitor mailing	20 days	3/1/00	3/20/00

and so on . . .

The action phase is carried out in two parts: pre-conference and day-of-conference (which includes the night before for setup).

Monitoring

The conference chairpersons hold periodic conference meetings with committee chairpersons to evaluate the progress made by each committee. They can then determine what additional resources are needed to complete the required committee tasks. E-mails and phone calls also keep the lines of communication open between chairpersons. Committees meet independently to plan and complete work. Minutes from most meetings are recorded. Chairpersons are responsible for following the timelines established for their individual committee activities, and the conference chairpersons monitor the overall work flow, using the initial project work plan as a guide.

Since most people involved in this project do not have project management or comparable software, charts and other written documents are made either on Excel programs, word processing programs, or even by hand. The level of technical tools utilized in a project of this nature has to closely match the level of familiarity with such products demonstrated by the group as a whole. In other words, team members who have greater familiarity with specific software packages need to either train others; handle the data entry and disseminate the information to others by disk, e-mail, or in hard copy form; or work on a more simplified program to best coordinate with other members of the group.

Often, volunteer organizations will consist of people with various levels of technical experience. If you intimidate people by using high-tech software systems, you run the risk of losing volunteers. Therefore, you need to find common ground when deciding on what technology to use.

Milestones

Key milestones in the planning and action phases of the conference project are set up in advance and highlighted when reached. Several such key milestones include:

- Securing and drawing up the rough contract with the site
- Completion of a preliminary speakers list to be approved by the state board of the organization
- Final contract with the site
- Completion of the workshop schedule including speakers and room assignments
- The printing of the initial conference brochures
- Completion of final exhibitor list
- The printing of the conference program
- Preregistration mailing to members

- Preconference setup
- Conference taking place
- Conference cleanup being completed

Contingency plans: Backup speakers, often from within the organization, are listed as possible fill-ins for certain workshops. Workshops for which specific expertise or professional accreditation is required can have an effective contingency plan if other speakers are willing do to additional workshops.

Additional classrooms should be set aside in the event that there is a problem with any specific room during the day, or there is such a great demand for a topic that an additional workshop needs to be added.

The volunteer coordinator, along with committee chairpersons, will also be prepared to move volunteers from one task to another as needed.

Review Phase

The final post-conference review meeting takes place several weeks after the conference. The review will consist of reports from each chairperson on how smoothly day-of activities ran.

Among the many questions that need to be answered are:

- Did we meet our conference goals?
- Were there as many attendees as anticipated?
- How easy was it for attendees to register?
- Were there problems with the traffic flow or navigation within the facility?
- Did all workshops go as planned?
- Which contingency plans, if any, were needed?
- Did all speakers attend? Did they encounter any problems?

- What other problems arose?
- What were some of the positive responses from attendees?

All phases of the conference are reviewed, and the group provides feedback on the various elements. It important that suggestions are made for the next conference/project—and more important that someone record them.

Note: It's common, when reviewing a project, to seek out the problem areas. Everyone wants to know what went wrong. However, it's also important to review and discuss what went right, especially with a volunteer organization that is not getting any pay for their efforts. Praise and a pat on the back for a job well done are very important. Therefore, look for the positives as well as the negatives when you review your project.

Also, evaluation forms are reviewed and filed for the next year's programming committee to assess the speakers' effectiveness.

Thank-You's

Following the review phase, the program chairpersons thank the committee chairpersons and all of the volunteers who made the conference a success.

The overall success of this project is hard to measure, because the goal is to impart knowledge and information. While the conference may "make money" for the organization, the true measure is how well the attendees use their accumulated knowledge to succeed at the adoption process. If children are adopted out of the foster care system or from international or domestic agencies, then the conference was a success.

APPENDIX B

Resources and Guidelines for Successful Project Management

Numerous Web sites, newsletters, and courses are available for those interested in learning more about project management. From basic information and answers to Certificate and Master's programs, you can find a great deal of additional information on all facets of project management. Following are some resources for expanding your project management skills and knowledge.

Web Sites of Interest

The Project Management Site (*www.projectmanagement.com*) provides listings and links to a variety of resources for project managers. The "Tools" section includes companion products for Microsoft Project, and the "News" section has the latest information from the companies making Project Management (PM) software. The "Online" section also provides useful questions and answers, but the font is a bit small.

The Project Management Center (*www.infogoal.com/pmc/pmchome.htm*) is a comprehensive portal site providing a wealth of resources and information. Seminars, software, organizations, links, news, articles, and even project manager jobs are part of this massive site. Numerous services are offered, including consulting and training, as well as listings of leading trainers and speakers in the field.

4PM.com (*www.4pm.com*) is home to a 5,400-page Web site that is a yearlong project unto itself to explore. From online distance learning courses to project management certifications to tools, software, and even a newsletter, plenty of information is available for the serious project manager. Courses are offered at all levels, and training seminars (in-person or on WEB CD) can also be found. And if you want to converse with, or hear from other project managers, there is a discussion board.

AllPM.com (*www.allpm.com*) is designed to provide IT project managers with all the resources and information they should need. Hardware and software are available in the Project Manager's Store, and resource links include articles, reports, services, training, products, and project managers for hire. There is a bulletin board for posting as well as several discussion forums and an ALLPM newsletter.

PM Forum (*www.pmforum.org*) is a global project management site that includes numerous resources. You can find a directory of regional and international professional PM organizations, a PM library, globally accepted practices, and a wide range of services including a virtual office and currency converter. You will also find *Project Manager World Today*, a comprehensive online magazine dedicated to news and events in the PM industry.

Gantthead.com (*www.gantthead.com*) is a user-friendly PM site with articles, expert advice, discussions, industry news, templates, tools, and books. Professionals in the field will also find an upcoming events schedule. The comprehensive site is straightforward and offers guidance for all levels.

Max's Project Management (*www.maxwideman.com*) site presents news, checklists, and the most comprehensive and extensive glossary of project management terms you could possibly imagine—if the term is not found here, it probably doesn't exist.

Project Management Associations and Organizations

The Project Management Institute (*www.pmi.org*) is a nonprofit, professional membership association with over 70,000 members worldwide. In existence since 1969, PMI offer seminars, symposiums, training, career services, and resources. The Institute offers certificate programs and awards for top achievers in the profession. The PMI guidebook is considered the industry standard. Contact Project Management Institute, Four Campus Blvd., Newtown Square, Pennsylvania, 19073-3299; 610-356-4600.

Newsletters

EIS Horizons Newsletter (*www.esi.intl.com*) provides monthly articles and updates (which you can view online) on project management issues. All aspects of project management are touched upon in the informative newsletter.

Project Management Insight (*www.ospreypmi.com*) is a newsletter published by Osprey PMI in England, which features PM themes and articles by experts on worldwide project management issues and information.

Courses/Distance Learning

The University of Washington Project Management Certificate Program (*www.outreach. washington.edu*) offers courses covering the basics of project management from work breakdown structure to closing the project.

Through the use of distance learning modules you can participate in courses with Internet access, a CD-Rom drive, or high-density disk drive and 28.8-speed modem. For fees, schedule, and registration information, call 1-800-543-2320.

IBM Learning Services (*www-3.ibm.com/services/ learning/spotlight/project.html*) offers a course called Principles of Project Management, which covers the project scope from initiating and project planning to managing a project within budget to closing. The five-day course is offered at various U.S. locations. For information go to their Web address and click on the course name.

ESI International (*www.esi-intl.com*) has a course called Managing Projects with Microsoft Project. The online lecture course is available twenty-four hours a day in text or Real Audio formats. Case studies, quizzes, and chats are available. Call ESI at 888-ESI-8884.

The University of Wisconsin-Platteville (*www. uwplatt.edu*) has established a three-course certificate distance-learning program. The program is designed to set a solid foundation for project managers. Call the Distance Learning Center at 1-800-362-5460 for information.

The American Graduate University (*www.agu.edu*) in Covina, California, offers accredited distance learning programs with an M.A. in Project Management. Individual courses (non-degree) can also be taken. Call 626-966-4576 for information.

Western Carolina University (*www.wcu.edu*) features a fully accredited distance learning project management program and Master's Degree program. Part of the Research and Graduate Studies program, the course information is available by calling 828-227-7398.

The International School of Information Management (*www.isimu.edu*) offers a certificate program in project management. The forty-year-old, Denver-based institution has a three course certificate curriculum. The Web site has an FAQ page with helpful answers about courses. Call 303-333-4224 or 800-441-ISIM for information.

Project Management Events

Project World Global (*www.projectworld.com*) offers worldwide events regarding project management. Details on worldwide PM events, along with industry news, can be found on their Web site. You can register online or call 1-888-827-6699 for more information on upcoming conferences and expositions near you.

APPENDIX C
Glossary

Budget: A detailed list of costs for the resources necessary to complete the project within the anticipated timeframe.

Contingency plan: An alternative strategy predeveloped to avoid or reduce a potential risk that could jeopardize the successful completion of the project.

Cost-benefit analysis: Many companies determine the overall value of the project using this "formal" method of analysis. The process factors in all aspects of the project, including finances, manpower, and time, to determine whether or not the benefits outweigh the costs.

Critical path: A full sequence of activities that span the distance of the project and would take the most time to complete.

Deliverables: The defined end products, results, or services produced during the project. A project goal can also be a deliverable.

Earned value analysis: The process in which you analyze the progress of the project, comparing the money budgeted with the money spent and the work achieved. You can then determine whether you are ahead or behind your projected budget.

Feasibility study: A study that takes into account all the variables of the project, including budget, resources, and time constraints, and determines the likelihood that it can or cannot be done.

Gantt chart: A chart that puts tasks on a series of horizontal time lines, allowing you to track a project.

Mediation: A method of resolving conflict in which a neutral third party intervenes to try and settle a dispute between two parties.

Milestone: Checkpoint that you can look at to see whether you are on schedule in a project.

Network diagram: A diagram that indicates the order and interrelationship of tasks in a logical sequence.

PIR (Project Issues Review): A document that includes survey results, often featuring graphs or charts, which helps the team determine what was done well and what could be improved upon in the future. Survey participants are asked to complete the review in a specified amount of time.

Project: A plan, proposal, or scheme that requires a concerted effort within a specified amount of time. It involves a task that is undertaken by a group of people, such as updating software and training employees in its use; or one person, such as learning a language.

Resource directory: An organized listing of resources, including names and numbers for ordering materials and contacting contractors, vendors, and all human resources for this and future projects.

Risk: The chance that some activity or event will occur to prevent or delay you in your efforts to complete your project in the projected time frame. Look to assess and minimize risk.

Skills roster: A roster of potential team members that illustrates their individual skills and knowledge in specific areas.

Stakeholders: People who have an interest (from a personal, monetary, or business standpoint) in the success of the project. A stakeholder list or matrix includes the names of these people.

Task schedule or assignment matrix: A listing of who will be doing which task or tasks on a particular project.

Team roster: A listing of who made the project team, plus contact information and possibly other data.

Work breakdown structure: An organized list, made early on, that includes all of the tasks that need to be accomplished for the project to be completed. This may be used to formulate a budget, a network diagram, build a team, acquire resources, and so on.

Index

We Have
EVERYTHING!

Everything® **After College Book**
$12.95, 1-55850-847-3

Everything® **American History Book**
$12.95, 1-58062-531-2

Everything® **Angels Book**
$12.95, 1-58062-398-0

Everything® **Anti-Aging Book**
$12.95, 1-58062-565-7

Everything® **Astrology Book**
$12.95, 1-58062-062-0

Everything® **Baby Names Book**
$12.95, 1-55850-655-1

Everything® **Baby Shower Book**
$12.95, 1-58062-305-0

Everything® **Baby's First Food Book**
$12.95, 1-58062-512-6

Everything® **Baby's First Year Book**
$12.95, 1-58062-581-9

Everything® **Barbeque Cookbook**
$12.95, 1-58062-316-6

Everything® **Bartender's Book**
$9.95, 1-55850-536-9

Everything® **Bedtime Story Book**
$12.95, 1-58062-147-3

Everything® **Bicycle Book**
$12.00, 1-55850-706-X

Everything® **Build Your Own Home Page**
$12.95, 1-58062-339-5

Everything® **Business Planning Book**
$12.95, 1-58062-491-X

Everything® **Casino Gambling Book**
$12.95, 1-55850-762-0

Everything® **Cat Book**
$12.95, 1-55850-710-8

Everything® **Chocolate Cookbook**
$12.95, 1-58062-405-7

Everything® **Christmas Book**
$15.00, 1-55850-697-7

Everything® **Civil War Book**
$12.95, 1-58062-366-2

Everything® **College Survival Book**
$12.95, 1-55850-720-5

Everything® **Computer Book**
$12.95, 1-58062-401-4

Everything® **Cookbook**
$14.95, 1-58062-400-6

Everything® **Cover Letter Book**
$12.95, 1-58062-312-3

Everything® **Crossword and Puzzle Book**
$12.95, 1-55850-764-7

Everything® **Dating Book**
$12.95, 1-58062-185-6

Everything® **Dessert Book**
$12.95, 1-55850-717-5

Everything® **Digital Photography Book**
$12.95, 1-58062-574-6

Everything® **Dog Book**
$12.95, 1-58062-144-9

Everything® **Dreams Book**
$12.95, 1-55850-806-6

Everything® **Etiquette Book**
$12.95, 1-55850-807-4

Everything® **Fairy Tales Book**
$12.95, 1-58062-546-0

Everything® **Family Tree Book**
$12.95, 1-55850-763-9

Everything® **Fly-Fishing Book**
$12.95, 1-58062-148-1

Everything® **Games Book**
$12.95, 1-55850-643-8

Everything® **Get-A-Job Book**
$12.95, 1-58062-223-2

Everything® **Get Published Book**
$12.95, 1-58062-315-8

Everything® **Get Ready for Baby Book**
$12.95, 1-55850-844-9

Everything® **Ghost Book**
$12.95, 1-58062-533-9

Everything® **Golf Book**
$12.95, 1-55850-814-7

Everything® **Grammar and Style Book**
$12.95, 1-58062-573-8

Everything® **Guide to Las Vegas**
$12.95, 1-58062-438-3

Everything® **Guide to New York City**
$12.95, 1-58062-314-X

Everything® **Guide to Walt Disney World®,
Universal Studios®, and
Greater Orlando, 2nd Edition**
$12.95, 1-58062-404-9

Everything® **Guide to Washington, D.C.**
$12.95, 1-58062-313-1

Everything® **Guitar Book**
$12.95, 1-58062-555-X

Everything® **Herbal Remedies Book**
$12.95, 1-58062-331-X

Everything® **Home-Based Business Book**
$12.95, 1-58062-364-6

Everything® **Homebuying Book**
$12.95, 1-58062-074-4

Everything® **Homeselling Book**
$12.95, 1-58062-304-2

For more information, or to order, call 800-872-5627 or visit everything.com
Adams Media Corporation, 57 Littlefield Street, Avon, MA 02322

Available wherever books are sold!
Visit us at everything.com

Everything® **Home Improvement Book**
$12.95, 1-55850-718-3

Everything® **Horse Book**
$12.95, 1-58062-564-9

Everything® **Hot Careers Book**
$12.95, 1-58062-486-3

Everything® **Internet Book**
$12.95, 1-58062-073-6

Everything® **Investing Book**
$12.95, 1-58062-149-X

Everything® **Jewish Wedding Book**
$12.95, 1-55850-801-5

Everything® **Job Interviews Book**
$12.95, 1-58062-493-6

Everything® **Lawn Care Book**
$12.95, 1-58062-487-1

Everything® **Leadership Book**
$12.95, 1-58062-513-4

Everything® **Learning Spanish Book**
$12.95, 1-58062-575-4

Everything® **Low-Fat High-Flavor Cookbook**
$12.95, 1-55850-802-3

Everything® **Magic Book**
$12.95, 1-58062-418-9

Everything® **Managing People Book**
$12.95, 1-58062-577-0

Everything® **Microsoft® Word 2000 Book**
$12.95, 1-58062-306-9

Everything® **Money Book**
$12.95, 1-58062-145-7

Everything® **Mother Goose Book**
$12.95, 1-58062-490-1

Everything® **Mutual Funds Book**
$12.95, 1-58062-419-7

Everything® **One-Pot Cookbook**
$12.95, 1-58062-186-4

Everything® **Online Business Book**
$12.95, 1-58062-320-4

Everything® **Online Genealogy Book**
$12.95, 1-58062-402-2

Everything® **Online Investing Book**
$12.95, 1-58062-338-7

Everything® **Online Job Search Book**
$12.95, 1-58062-365-4

Everything® **Pasta Book**
$12.95, 1-55850-719-1

Everything® **Pregnancy Book**
$12.95, 1-58062-146-5

Everything® **Pregnancy Organizer**
$15.00, 1-58062-336-0

Everything® **Project Management Book**
$12.95, 1-58062-583-5

Everything® **Puppy Book**
$12.95, 1-58062-576-2

Everything® **Quick Meals Cookbook**
$12.95, 1-58062-488-X

Everything® **Resume Book**
$12.95, 1-58062-311-5

Everything® **Romance Book**
$12.95, 1-58062-566-5

Everything® **Sailing Book**
$12.95, 1-58062-187-2

Everything® **Saints Book**
$12.95, 1-58062-534-7

Everything® **Selling Book**
$12.95, 1-58062-319-0

Everything® **Spells and Charms Book**
$12.95, 1-58062-532-0

Everything® **Stress Management Book**
$12.95, 1-58062-578-9

Everything® **Study Book**
$12.95, 1-55850-615-2

Everything® **Tall Tales, Legends, and Outrageous Lies Book**
$12.95, 1-58062-514-2

Everything® **Tarot Book**
$12.95, 1-58062-191-0

Everything® **Time Management Book**
$12.95, 1-58062-492-8

Everything® **Toasts Book**
$12.95, 1-58062-189-9

Everything® **Total Fitness Book**
$12.95, 1-58062-318-2

Everything® **Trivia Book**
$12.95, 1-58062-143-0

Everything® **Tropical Fish Book**
$12.95, 1-58062-343-3

Everything® **Vitamins, Minerals, and Nutritional Supplements Book**
$12.95, 1-58062-496-0

Everything® **Wedding Book, 2nd Edition**
$12.95, 1-58062-190-2

Everything® **Wedding Checklist**
$7.95, 1-58062-456-1

Everything® **Wedding Etiquette Book**
$7.95, 1-58062-454-5

Everything® **Wedding Organizer**
$15.00, 1-55850-828-7

Everything® **Wedding Shower Book**
$7.95, 1-58062-188-0

Everything® **Wedding Vows Book**
$7.95, 1-58062-455-3

Everything® **Wine Book**
$12.95, 1-55850-808-2

Everything® **World War II Book**
$12.95, 1-58062-572-X

Everything® is a registered trademark of Adams Media Corporation.

We Have
EVERYTHING®
KIDS'!

Everything® Kids' Baseball Book
$6.95, 1-58062-688-2

Everything® Kids' Joke Book
$6.95, 1-58062-686-6

Everything® Kids' Mazes Book
$6.95, 1-58062-558-4

Everything® Kids' Money Book
$6.95, 1-58062-685-8

Everything® Kids' Nature Book
$6.95, 1-58062-684-X

Everything® Kids' Online Book
$9.95, 1-58062-394-8

Everything® Kids' Puzzle Book
$6.95, 1-58062-687-4

Everything® Kids' Science Experiments Book
$6.95, 1-58062-557-6

Everything® Kids' Space Book
$9.95, 1-58062-395-6

Everything® Kids' Witches and Wizards Book
$9.95, 1-58062-396-4

Available wherever books are sold!

For more information, or to order,
call 800-872-5627 or visit everything.com

Adams Media Corporation, 57 Littlefield Street, Avon, MA 02322

Everything® is a registered trademark of Adams Media Corporation.